the (CAUSES) of
EXCLUSION

cedric
CULLINGFORD

the (CAUSES) of
EXCLUSION

HOME,
SCHOOL
AND THE
DEVELOPMENT OF YOUNG CRIMINALS

**KOGAN
PAGE**

for Jenny Morrison

First published in 1999

Kogan Page Limited
120 Pentonville Road
London N1 9JN

Stylus Publishing
22883 Quicksilver Drive
Sterling, VA 20166
USA

British Library Cataloguing in Publication Data

A CIP record for this book is available from the British Library.

ISBN 0 7494 3039 7

Typeset by Kogan Page
Printed and bound by Clays Ltd, St Ives plc

Contents

Preface

There are a large number of books about crime and rather fewer about criminality. The books about crime referred to are not thrillers, that most popular of genres which suggests a universal fascination with human pathology, but studies based on research. On the face of it, we should understand a great deal about crime and its causes, and yet it is a growing problem, not a diminishing one.

One reason for this seems to be the fascination with crime rather than its prevention. Another reason appears to be the concentration on the manifestations of crime and how to deal with them, rather than the underlying causes. For all the books on crime, there are relatively few, of an empirical nature, on exclusion from school or truancy, or other social difficulties in the young. There are many policy initiatives, of course, but this is not the same thing. They reflect the urgency of reacting immediately to a problem rather than trying to understand it.

In all the work on criminality there are certain factors, like the home and school and community, that keep emerging. There is a consensus about the important influences on the young, a consistency of evidence that explains the significant patterns of events. This book, however, attempts to go underneath the surface and find out why particular people find school difficult or impossible and end up in prison. It does not merely describe the life experiences of the young criminals that are at the heart of the evidence, but attempts to analyse and explain their significance. The empirical data is the kind on which policy should be based.

The distinction between crime and criminality is not just a philosophical one. It is also a sign of divisions in the academic disciplines that surround the study of the human experience. This research draws on several different ways of approaching the same subject. It combines criminology with education, and the quantitative as a support for the qualitative. There are many territorial arguments between different subjects, 'turf wars' which suit the protagonists better than the understanding of the subject. This book attempts to speak to 'sociologists' as well as 'psychologists', educators as well as criminologists.

This book, whilst based on a particular subgroup of young offenders, is about exclusion. This exclusion is from the formal systems of society as expressed in schools. Exclusion, as the evidence makes clear, affects everyone. There are different forms, mostly self-imposed. Psychological exclusion, the refusal to be engaged in activities like learning, is common. Truancy, again self-imposed, can take many different forms.

The themes of the book are not limited to criminality. They should concern all who are engaged in any form of education. Given the difficulties that young people encounter, it is imperative that we should try to understand them and ameliorate them. There are lessons to be learned about parenting and teaching, and not just about policing.

The evidence presented here is rich and consistent as well as sometimes disturbing. It says much for the honesty and forthrightness of the interviewees. Granted that they were a 'captive audience' and longing to talk, but they nevertheless provided clear insights into their own stories and their styles of thinking. Whilst not condoning their actions any more than they excuse them, one cannot help respecting the way they analysed their experiences.

The transcripts are verbatim, except for the removal of redundant 'er's, but they do not attempt to capture the tone of voice or the dialects used. It is what the witnesses say that counts. Nor is the book about what specific acts the young criminals did to be in prison; that is not the point. The respect for, and understanding of, the interviewees is joined by a strong sense of sadness at what has happened to them. Whilst this does not lead to any diminution of moral outrage at their actions, there is a strong realization that what they did could have been prevented. Their emerging experiences and the consequences give a strong sense of the inevitable. But what seems inevitable in hindsight is also in retrospect unnecessary.

The ability to carry out sensitive interviews has been demonstrated by several people whose work has enriched my own: Clare Webb, Iain Williamson, and in particular Jenny Morrison to whom this book is dedicated. I am also indebted to others who have shared their insights, in particular Professor Ken Pease, and their support, in particular Susan Smith.

Cedric Cullingford
June 1999

1

Patterns of crime; patterns of control

Introduction

This chapter takes as its starting point the explanations for criminality and for crime. But the real root of the problem lies in the experience of home and school. Crime is a manifestation of something having gone wrong earlier. It is the last outcome of feelings of exclusion and dysfunction. Using the perspective of the knowledge of crime gives us a clear brief for exploring the underlying causes. And yet there is an irony here.

The fascination with crime sometimes appears to deflect concern away from its causes. The attention of Home Secretaries is often devoted to the small percentage of hardened and violent offenders rather than the long-term goals of crime prevention. The resources of the police are taken up by detection and prosecution, and those of the Home Office in controlling an ever-expanding number of prisons. There is widespread anxiety about crime and the sense that it is becoming a growing threat, especially in the young, and yet the normal reaction to this anxiety is to demand more and heavier policing.

One of the main reasons for this particular approach to crime is the psychological assumption that crime is somehow inevitable, that it will always be with us, whatever the causes. Just as Hollywood and all its associated industries could not do without crime as its central theme, so it is as if the fear of crime is only matched by the acceptance of its existence. The irony is that there are two conflicting reasons for this sense of inevitability.

In all studies of the experience of being human there is a tension between theories of nurture and theories of nature. For some, criminality is a genetic fault. It is inherited. They argue that there will always be those who are naturally violent, psychologically distorted. For others, crime is linked directly to the environment, to poverty and to certain housing estates. Whilst there is a sense of inevitability in either approach, the linking of crime to circumstances does suggest at least the possibilities of prevention, even if it smacks of social control. What this book explores is the subtle tensions between the individual personality and the factors that make some and not others turn to criminality. It does not only describe the patterns of experience but seeks to explain them.

Despite the time devoted to punishment and law enforcement, there are a number of studies that reveal some consistent patterns of experience in the early life of criminals, although they rarely go on to explore *why* they should have the effects they do. Much of the work that reveals these patterns, as in the work done by and for the Home Office, and almost deliberately ignored, relies on statistical evidence. Large-scale surveys both in this country and in the United States reveal consistent findings about where crime takes place and which are the best ways to react to it. These general findings are consistent with, and support, the qualitative work reported here. One conclusion to all this work is to question the assumption of the inevitability of social exclusion and failure.

The 'criminal' mind is not essentially other or different from anyone else's. Reactions to crime themselves give an insight into the very causes of criminality. The seeking of revenge is not psychologically different from the sense of grievance and personal threat expressed by the criminal. The sense of inevitability, the conservative assumption that some people will inevitably turn to crime, that society is inherently violent, is not unlike the kind of excuses given for their actions by young offenders. When children's attitudes to society are explored, they are shown to have an essentially bleak, even cynical view of human nature and a sense of being disenfranchised in society.[1] They cite the need for more prisons, the inevitability of football hooliganism and even the violence of the police. They suggest that politicians, either local or national, would never listen to them, and would only pay attention to a few influential people close to them. A fear of crime and a sense of exclusion develop early.

Definitions of crime

Given some of the experiences that people have, and some of the demands of society, one can argue that the surprise is that so many people do so well.[2] This underlies the fascination that many criminologists have with defining crime. There is a suggestion that each society defines crime differently, that there is no fixed concept of what constitutes a criminal act. Whilst a terrorist will almost inevitably wish to redefine murder he is not alone in doing so. When it comes to more complex criminal acts like drug trafficking, the social reactions become more complex and confused. At the heart of criminology is the relationship between the sense of being 'alienated' from the norms of society and its expression in action. 'Alienation' is, of course, a lubricious term.[3] Can one really be an 'alien' in one's own society? The term derives from the religious possibility of being excluded from heaven but was much used by Marxist philosophers who questioned the values and structures of capitalist society.[4] But the term does have a useful psychological ring. That sense of being excluded from certain aspects of society is widespread. A criminal action is, in a sense, the final expression of that feeling. What we need to explore is the relationship between the two, how that sense of psychological exclusion grows so strong that an alternative way of being and behaving is sought out.

There are some established patterns that are consistent in the experience of young offenders, although these are more psychological than social in so far as the reaction to certain events and certain relationships is as significant as the actual circumstances in which they find themselves. There are particular conditions that are strongly influential in leading towards criminality. One of the main conclusions of Sherman and his colleagues' massive survey in the United States is that the majority of crimes are in 'areas of concentrated poverty'.[5] This does not in itself prove anything about the underlying causes – not all people react to the conditions in the same way – but it does suggest that particular social factors have a major part to play. It also reveals something about the nature of influence. If certain actions become a kind of norm in a community, it is difficult to avoid following suit. It also questions whether crime pays, if it is so absorbed into areas of deprivation. The important factor in understanding crime is to understand how and why individuals react to certain conditions. Not all criminals, after all, come from poverty stricken or poorly educated backgrounds.[6]

That there are some correlations between crime and poverty is clear, especially as there are strong links between crime and unemployment. In a sense there is bound to be such a correlation since criminal activity is almost an alternative form of employment. Whilst there is a correlation, however, the reasons given for this differ. Fagan summarizes four different approaches.[7] One is economic choice. Does crime pay? Does it give a better return than a routine job? Another is the idea of employment as social control in the sense that work provides positive social bonds so that the individual would not think of breaking out of an habitual system of living. A third approach centres on the sense of strain and frustration felt by the unemployed, a feeling of rejection and dissatisfaction. The fourth explanation is labelling theory, the idea that the unemployed are made to feel their 'anomie' through stigmatic labels. These approaches imply that unemployment can be an actual cause of crime, whether it is an excuse or a pressure. It is probably truer to conclude that the correlation is a natural one, given the circumstances. Farrington and his colleagues examined the timing of crime and unemployment over a three-year period, and made at least the correlation, if not the reason, clear.[8]

Trying to find the causes, and not just the manifestations of criminality, means having to take a long-term view, and exploring all the complex variables that make up the human experience. The problem is that criminologists, like sociologists, perhaps inevitably take a short-term view.[9] Simple short-term changes or causal relationships do not allow for all the long-term and unplanned trends that nevertheless have a structure of their own when one lets the evidence emerge. Similarly, it is all too easy to form political rather than educational theories about violence. Downes, in outlining the different theories of violence – the way that the working class express their attitudes to a dominant culture, or the inevitable class conflict, or that violence will break out if not controlled, or that violence is an image created by the media, or that there is an inevitable tension between ends and means and that industrial political democracies harness their entire population into striving after certain common ends – suggests that such theories are rarely based on empirical evidence and rarely explore the more complex individual circumstances.[10]

Such approaches to the fact of criminal violence also suggest a sense of inevitability; that in these macro conditions crime will always take place, even flourish. They suggest that the task of understanding criminality is so vast that there is comparatively little to be learned from the study of new empirical evidence. This is one of the reasons that there are many critics of crime research, who suggest that simple correlations and the sifting of quantitative data does not meet even the most elementary criteria of evaluative probity.[11] Nevertheless, for all the criticisms, for all the sense that qualitative data can give us fresh insights into the 'why' and not just the 'what' of criminality, a study of the evidence as collected in the larger surveys does suggest some consistent and significant findings.

Communities of crime and poverty

If we look at the settings for crime, we begin to see a certain pattern that ties in with the findings that follow. There are certain places where crime takes place most often. These include communities.[12] There is also the phenomenon of 'repeat crime', the fact that a place once targeted is far more likely to be targeted again.[13] But beyond the focus on the families we also note how there are certain locations as well as specific places, in which crime takes place. One is the home. Whilst much of what takes place is hidden, the actions have their effect on the family, and cause a break in normal relationships, and from the normal standards of social interaction. Another significant locus of crime is the school. Sherman even goes so far as to say that schools can prevent crime. It is, however, not only because of repeat crimes and poor neighbourhoods that particular places are significant settings for crime. Whilst the motivation of criminologists in targeting specific places – like public housing – is immediate and the subject of short-term crime prevention rather than longer-term understanding, the fact that there are certain places that are significant reveals the subtle influence of peer groups and of the familiar. Sherman concludes that certain places should be targeted by the police because displacement is weak; the criminals, if they are prevented from their actions in one neighbourhood, do not simply seek an alternative place to carry out their intentions.

Particular places, including schools, are important because of the subtle and important nature of group relationships. Even programmes focused on individual adolescents at risk can be unable to succeed because of the influence of the neighbourhood and the people in it.[14] We will see how important peer groups are. 'Places' are not just those that are the targets for criminal activity but influences, zones of familiarity and custom. 'Places', like 'spaces', are personal as well as physical. Knowing the way round a particular street or building is one kind of familiarity; its association with other people and actions is another. Places are not just variables but influences. If we understand the way the mind thinks we realize that we cannot simply focus on genetics and criminality or on the environmental imperative.[15] The mind is a constant battleground of choices, most of which are made instantly and superficially, relying on habit and memory rather than reason.[16] The more we understand the ways in which people think, the more undercut is the 'nature/nurture' divide, and the more significant is the as yet unexplored evidence that lies behind the raw statistical facts.

The broad statistical correlations are not so much an explanation in themselves as an invitation for further exploration. They give substance to, and verify, the kinds of findings that emerge from exploring the mind-sets and influences on the young offenders. That there is a strong link between social deprivation and crime is clear, as shown in the longitudinal data from the Infant Health and Development Programme.[17] But this is not a simple matter of assuming that need or want automatically leads to criminal activity. More powerful and significant relationships are to be found between family income and poverty status and the cognitive development and behaviour of children. It is significant, for instance, that the duration of poverty matters more than its timing. Certain habitual patterns of relationships are set up. It is the results of poverty rather than poverty *per se* that matter. Anyone who has seen what it is like to be truly poor, let alone experienced it, will understand all the related emotional pressures that result from it. Can strong relationships be made easily in such circumstances when they are in contrast to relative affluence?

Poverty matters not because it causes greed but because it deprives people of all kinds of other, more developed interactions. The National Longitudinal Survey of Youth found that improvements in family income had strong effects on the quality of the home environment of children.[18] Whilst economic circumstances are, not surprisingly, important, they are the framework in which other factors thrive. The quality of a home environment is not just a question of the physical conditions.

Clearly, the emotional interactions are equally significant, whilst we acknowledge the relationship of one to the other. Even more important, and hugely neglected, are the intellectual interactions of the home.[19] Warmth and concern are necessary but not adequate. The effects of poverty are even more marked on the relationships that are expressed in dialogue than on those delivered through affection. One might suppose that common suffering is an emotional bond, but it displaces and undermines concentration on other things, like the ability to strike up a normal relationship with those who do not have emotional ties, or the ability to negotiate and mitigate rationally and successfully.

The overall finding that poverty matters is at one level very important, but essentially this is so because it points out the importance of circumstances in a variety of different ways. As many argue, the elimination of poverty by itself might not reduce crime, but the elimination of some of the results of poverty would. The crucial link is the one between poverty and cognitive development, more important because of the side-effects of poverty, emotional and intellectual, than those purely circumstantial or genetic factors such as family structure or maternal schooling.[20] Poverty has consequences on attitudes to parents and to money. It can distract and cause tensions. It exacerbates difficulties. The same tensions could arrive in affluent households – they often do – but poverty allows for no mitigations. It is clear that it is the effect of poverty on adult behaviour that is the most significant variable.[21] This does not undervalue the seriousness of poverty, especially in comparative terms, but, as in the case of the significance of the neighbourhood, it throws clearer light on the really important factors that foster criminality. As Huston *et al* point out, poverty is a complex notion, and not simply isomorphic with social economic circumstances.[22]

The correlation between poverty and crime is acknowledged but it is not automatic and nor is it complete. The concept of social deprivation, whilst seeming to be either an inevitable or rational reason for crime, is at last being understood to be a symbol of, and a responsibility for, other significant factors. The very shift of emphasis from the social condition to the way in which people deal with it suggests that underlying causes are ultimately more significant. This is doubly so if we connect the exploration of variables by those concerned purely with criminology to findings of research that has a quite different agenda. The ability to communicate, to make intelligent connections and to understand and adapt to the rule frameworks of social interaction is clearly important. As far as intellectual and academic success is concerned, a great deal depends on the very early years, not in terms of economics but in terms of dialogue. Wells found that the greatest indicator of subsequent intellectual success was the dialogue that took place between adult and child.[23] Richman *et al* similarly found that the one variable that seemed to connect the ability to cope with academic work at school and early experiences was the quality of interaction between parents (or other adults) and their offspring.[24] This suggests, and there are many other studies that come to similar conclusions, that the relationships made in the early years have a strong bearing on subsequent behaviour, the ability to cope and to adapt.

Studies of criminality

Given the intellectual parameters set up by different academic disciplines, for too many reasons to explore here, it is no surprise that the insights afforded by both the study of early childhood and the broader findings of the means and circumstances of criminality have never really been connected. That they cohere only points to the validity of the findings. The broad statistical sweeps might not explain the reasons for the findings but they should not contradict them. On the contrary, the concern of the qualitative analysis is to explain the general findings rather than dismiss or replace them. The statistical evidence (rather than some simplistic theories) suggests that there are certain patterns and correlations.

In dealing with criminality we are always working at more than one level. There is the constant and daily concern with control, with immediate explanations and actions. But there are also the underlying explanations that give us an insight into the causes and what could be done in terms of prevention. One approach singles out those who are likely to cause offence. The other has a wider remit: to understand what circumstances give rise to criminality. Thus we have on the one hand the phenomenon of repeat crime.[25] Given that there is such a phenomenon the first reaction will naturally be to target particular places, setting up cameras and acting on the probabilities. But at another level we wish to pursue the reasons for repetition. Are they rational? Do they connect with earlier well-formed instincts? The idea of 'state dependency', of doing the same thing for the same reason in the same conditions, sounds like a behavioural trigger, as if every action were automatic. But it is not. The fact that crime is associated with particular places and particular circumstances suggests that there are many other factors at work. 'Repeat crime' takes place against the same victim, or the same type of victim, in the home, against partner or child, or outside it, in terms of racial attacks or car crime and burglary. These are at once manifestations of outcomes, not inevitable but seemingly inexorable. The temptation is to see crime in itself as a pattern, rather than pursue the causes of crime. The fact that a crime occurs in a high crime area and repeats itself in the same place soon after the first crime suggests more than the strategic positioning of surveillance.[26]

The association of crime with areas of concentrated poverty is a simple correlation of one problem with another. But even in large-scale quantitative surveys, such an explanation is neither adequate nor helpful. An international analysis of the rising levels of crime and psychosocial disorders reveals that rising crime is associated with rising prosperity.[27] Compared to the depression of the 1930s, our own time is prosperous enough. Yet at that time, compared to the present day, there was no increase in crime, suicide, drugs and drink abuse and all the other symptoms of personal malaise. Why? The reasons suggested, but not proved, are many and varied, but suggest the complexity of changes in the social environment. On a physical level the nature of adolescence has changed, with both earlier puberty and a far greater emphasis on an adolescent youth culture in which at least the awareness, if not encouragement, of sex goes hand in hand with the promotion of designer wear and the sexual attractions of pop stars. Longer education and the resulting postponement of independent status are balanced by far earlier sexual experience. Changes in family structures and functioning are a kind of euphemism for the instability of early family life – divorce, single parents and the growth of other agencies involved in child rearing due to the employment of females. And, perhaps coincidentally, there is the growth of the culture of individualism, a changing morality, and the huge development of the mass media. In every way the 1930s, with its poverty, looks like a different world. All the recorded changes play a part: the question remains what impact they have on the individual.

It is not difficult to detect all the cultural changes in society. At one level, the means of communication and the impact of technology, the rapidity of the changes are obvious. But it is more difficult to analyse their impact on the outlook, attitudes and behaviour of individuals. Similarly, we know the basic statistics of the rise of crime and the increased expenditure on its prevention, but little about the underlying causes. One barrier to understanding, already cited, is the fascination with the immediacy of crime, and its control. Another is the assumption that there must be either a simple explanation or one so complex that it is unfathomable.

Crime prevention, in fact, has two dimensions. One is the immediate efficacy of the best practice. How should the police be deployed and where? But the other is more subtle and consists of intervention at points in which individuals can most usefully be helped. The latter needs pursuing because policy should be based on empirical evidence, even if, given the political nature of human judgements, one finds oneself crying in the wilderness. But the two overlap. All the measures to prevent crime corroborate the evidence that follows in this book. Whatever the human fascination with punishment of one kind or another, and some of these raise some serious moral questions, the real potential lies in the underlying causes of behaviour, given the complex, individual and yet understandable influences that form certain kinds of behaviour.

Whatever the individual nature of genetic inheritance, there are some major environmental or circumstantial factors that have a major bearing on people's subsequent behaviour. The distinction must be clearly made between personality and behaviour. We are not arguing that individuals are merely the product of their environment, in terms of their inner selves, personal intelligence and temperament. But their patterns of thought and attitude and how they approach others are clearly marked by certain influences. At one level this is obvious. The language we speak is circumstantial. Each human being might have a similar capacity for language, and each will have an individual voice print and speech pattern, but each also grows up in a particular linguistic environment. Indeed, even young babies show a preference foı one language over another.[28] Language is the cultural imprint of the environment. It also helps to form the ways in which people think and the attitudes they possess.[29] The importance of the environment cannot be dismissed.

But the environment is not just a matter of socio-economic circumstances. It plays a far more subtle influence and can only be understood in richer, more complex terms. When Sherman concludes that certain urban neighbourhoods need to be targeted, since that is where youth crime in particular takes place, he is pointing out the evidence of the patterns of crime, but not the underlying reasons for them.[30] On one level the reasons for crime taking place in certain environments is obvious – peer group influence, familiarity with the victims and underlying shared motivation. But the actual circumstances that cause the actions of the individual are more subtle.

If we take language as an example we quickly realize that whilst all might share a language in common, the way they use it differs widely. This is not just a matter of dialect or accent. Nor is it a matter of vocabulary, however much that differs between people. It is to do with the uses to which language can be put. When Wells and his colleagues tried to trace the underlying early causes of failure in, and disaffection with, school they found that there was no single link with socio-economic status.[31] Instead they discovered a difference in the uses of language, between that used, as in school, for critical and explanatory dialogue and that used for expressions of emotion. Of course the two overlap, but in a number of studies the distinctions between the language of command and affection – 'Don't touch that! Keep your hands off!' – and the language of explanation – 'And what is that called? Do you know why?'– are made clear.[32]

Different uses of language make a difference to attitudes towards school. An American study of the different academic performances of the more successful and less successful in school similarly pointed out the distinctions between the uses of language.[33] In all the homes there was no lack of emotional warmth and plenty of interpersonal talk. But in some there was far less of the sharing of ideas about other things. What was needed was the language of negotiation, the language that can give such an explanation that conflict or confrontation can be avoided, and expression given to personal points of view. Yet another study found that the critical factor in early learning, and its impact on subsequent success, was the quality of the dialogue.[34] The ability to make a relationship with an adult, initiated by either the child or the adult, is seen as being a crucial factor.

When we talk about the quality of the environment, therefore, we are talking about relationships. The subtle and psychological factors of home life might be influenced by poverty or affluence but each person reacts to these differently.[35] The home is not a passive state but an active series of events and relationships. It is not just the 'neighbourhood' in the broadest sense that matters but what a neighbourhood consists of in terms of the people in it and how they relate to one another, especially in the home. Sherman's conclusion that crime prevention should be concentrated on certain areas is joined by his concern that there should be family-based crime prevention.

> ... how much a community benefits by having strong families that pro-
> vide their own mentoring, also known as parenting.[36] (p. 2–10)

And others, like Durkheim, conclude that shame or the lack of it is the crucial factor for communities and individuals. It is not just circumstances but the way individuals react to them.

Causes of criminality

Understanding the causes of criminality is important for all kinds of reasons. One is that although punishment is a part of crime prevention it is only a very small part. There is little evidence that putting people into prison for long periods, or the threat of doing so, reduces crime.[37] One can argue that the only way of preventing the activities of certain criminals is incarceration, but this has little to do with crime prevention. The threat of vastly increased prison sentences has no effect on crime. It is shame rather than fear that has an effect.[38]

Poverty has often been cited as a factor in criminality and causal links drawn. But definitions of poverty vary.[39] Whilst no one should deny the grinding effect of abject poverty, the crucial link between poverty and criminality is how people react to it. To that extent poverty is relative. Whilst individuals resent not having certain objects they desire, this has more to do with the comparison of themselves against others than the absolute state of their financial circumstances. It is how poverty is perceived that matters. A community consists not just of one equally shared level of income or possessions, for all the contemporary linkages of social status and postcodes. It is a place of comparisons and distinctions, of relative values and complex relationships. It is for this reason that one of the measures of preventing crime that does *not* work is community mobilization.[40] If poverty, like the neighbourhoods, were *itself* the central cause of criminality these community schemes would probably have some success.

Instead, what is successful in preventing crime is at a far different level, and is to do, as we have seen, with people and their relationships rather than purely external factors. As the large American study concludes:

> ... programs intended to improve parents' childrearing skills, children's academic skills, or children's mental health... have often resulted – almost coincidentally – in reduced crime.[41]

What is surprising about this is the fact that it is perceived a coincidence rather than a policy. The factors that we will explore in this book are all recognized as significant ones, but rarely acted upon. It is as if the research done on crime were not linked to any other discipline and the findings that have emerged about human development. The intervention programmes were not introduced directly as a means of reducing crime and yet the connection is clearly made. What we do know, in studying the patterns of crime prevention, is that there are certain places that have a strong bearing on criminality, and that some kind of intervention programme would work. But first we need to know why this is so.

We have noted that simple rises in police numbers, or threats of increased incarceration, make little difference to levels of crime. And yet this is where most of the attention lies. Perhaps this has to do with the 'macho' image of crime *and* its prevention, as well as an almost bland assumption about its inevitability. The very language used to describe 'fighting' crime suggests that it needs a robust response, that suppression and tough legislation will wipe it out, or at least keep it in check. But those who are concerned with studying crime prevention come to quite different conclusions. It might seem 'soft' to legislators and politicians, and yet certain factors like home visits work when police visits do not.

Patterns of intervention

Most studies of crime have concentrated on the external social factors at work and have sought out new methods to control it, often long after the criminals have moved on to something else.[42] What they have done far less is to look at the formation of the criminal mind. When work has taken place on theories of crime it has tended to concentrate on single different factors, like theories of aggression.[43] What we need to explore is the nature of the interaction between individuals and their environment. Social structures, after all, are not impersonal and constraining forces but consist of the individuals within them.[44] For a long time it has been recognized that a proper understanding of individual agency and action is more complex than the official structures, but this insight has rarely been properly acted on.[45] This is both partly understandable and a wasted opportunity. It is understandable in that the legislators, those who have responsibility, want to be seen to be taking action quickly rather than understanding the causes. It is a wasted opportunity because successful policy must be based on empirical evidence.

We live at a time that seems obsessed with intervention on the large scale. There are constantly new measures and policies and targets imposed and changed. This suggests concern with grand official schemes rather than with an attempt to understand, let alone measure, their success. This obsession with series of actions is a reaction to what are categorized as problems, like crime and education. But it is also a sign of action rather than thought, of the political trait of talking and never listening. Fear of crime is widespread; and some of the measures are designed to reduce this fear rather than prevent crime.[46] Whilst fear of crime is not a problem in itself, responses to it have become a greater priority than the reduction of real crime. It is also significant that the fear of crime is linked to authoritarian attitudes, and worries about society generally. That there is a lot of fear about is clear, but it is another reason that the underlying causes are not explored as much as they could be.

Sometimes the result of political intervention has the opposite effect to that intended.[47] Thus heavier policing, like 'zero tolerance', or the threat of 'short sharp shocks' or army-style 'boot camps', are all experimented with and never linked to successful results. This does not prevent further experiments but it does again reveal the nature of the approach to criminality. Exclusions from school, often the sign of incipient criminal behaviour, are rising rapidly from year to year.[48] But whilst there are measures drawn up to act on it and prevent it, there is little exploration of the causes of exclusions. Sherman notes the importance of schools as a proper locus of attention in crime prevention for reasons that we will explore, but many of the measures to improve educational standards, if not deliberately designed to exacerbate the problem, certainly succeed in doing so. Whilst the government recognizes the problem, it does not admit either that its policies might be the cause, or that anything long-term or fundamental needs to be done.[49]

Even when there are clear correlations, as in the overall patterning of criminality, some of the inferences are not taken up. The study of the number of exclusions from school not only shows the steady increase but also the relatively small number of schools that account for the majority of them.[50] There are clear distinctions between successful schools and failing schools, just as there are clearly some neighbourhoods that cause particular problems. It was always something of a scandal that some schools should perform so much better than others, that some should be so much better provided for. But the situation gets progressively worse, with ever-greater emphasis on league tables, targets and blame.

The desire to be seen to act, rather than to understand, is not just a political obsession, but a sign that people often think they know the answer to the problem, or if they don't, think they can find one. One example of this is the reaction to the Bulger case, when two young boys murdered a toddler they had abducted. The judge in the case mentioned a 'video-nasty'. To those who followed the case this was extremely puzzling.[51] But to others it was a clue that needed to be taken up, leading to yet another public enquiry into the effects of videos on those who watch them. Whilst there was a strong urge to find proof that watching such videos leads directly to violence, there was just sufficient intellectual rigour in the findings not to jump to such a simplistic conclusion. But this would not prevent people arguing the case that crime can be traced directly to what is seen on television. This subject has a huge if somewhat superficial history of causes and effects, but it does reveal the desire to find some simple explanations of criminality.[52] The problem is that over-simple explanations draw attention away from proper understanding. Perhaps in the end the explanation might seem simple, but it needs to be based on copious evidence.

That there are some patterns in the development of crime are clear. There are certain places and influences that matter. Both longitudinal surveys, like those of Farrington and West, and statistical analysis like those of Graham suggest that understanding of the underlying causes of criminality is possible.[53] There is a consistency in the evidence that links this study to that of others. Whilst what we are describing here is to do with the reasons that underlie the patterns, and explain them, the fact that there are strong correlations is important. But some of the explanations for this are more complex than might at first appear. The link between crime and poverty, for example, is clear, even if there are exceptions to this, and even if the term 'poverty' actually covers something more complex. An analysis of the relationship between wealth or poverty and crime suggests that there are no overall simple correlations. Wealth in society may represent both an incentive and disincentive to crime in so far as there is both more to steal and less need to steal.[54] The fact that there is more crime in times of relative plenty suggests there are other causes than economic ones.

What could be termed 'rational' causes of criminality, for example the need for, a greed for, money, are often undermined by far more complex, personal and interactive ones. At one level economic factors have an influence on trends in crime, both property and personal crime. The statistics suggest that growth in personal consumption is universally related to growth in recorded property crime, at least in the short term.[55] Yet personal crime, signs of aggression in one form or another, actually increases with overall wealth. The answers lie far deeper than simple correlations. The number of unemployed, for example, is independent of fluctuations in the number of offences in terms of property theft. And yet violence against a person is related to unemployment.

Changes in society and their influence

The more we study the statistics of crime, and the more we understand about the measures of control and the reasons for them, the more we need to acknowledge the fact that there are other underlying causes as yet relatively unexplored. Patterns of outbreak, of symptoms and results, are clear. But there is also a corresponding pattern of causes. The link between the two lies in the fact that the distinction between individual and community influences is unhelpful for the purposes of crime prevention.[56] It is possible to detect patterns but there is also a need to explore how individuals think of themselves in relation to each other and in relation to the communal statements of society, especially in its official manifestation, like schools. Individuals either think of themselves as part of a larger society, in all its forms, or as part of a smaller grouping as in the 'communities' of crime.

The pressures of 'belonging' to some group, larger or narrower, are not only strong but growing stronger. One of the ironic effects of the mass communication system is not only a growing sense of awareness and knowledge of other people in their communities but also a growing sense of distinction. In the past one could argue that each community was bound up in itself, occasionally intruded upon, but taking its own identity for granted. But now there are not fewer but more badges of distinction, some of which are parochial, like the place you were born or the football club you support, and some of which are international, like the label of the designer clothes you wear. There are tensions between traditional and modern forms of living.[57] Whilst on the one hand there appears to be more tolerance of different styles and opinions, there is more pressure to be defined as belonging to something in particular. The close and ambiguous relationship between the individual and the community was always there. The fact that there is also an international sphere, in terms of knowledge and awareness, only makes that tension between the two stronger rather than weaker. The sense of belonging cannot be taken for granted but needs to be defined.

The awareness of the whole system of social justice is rarely fostered. Even amongst those who are assumed to become reliable citizens, there is little effort made to promote sensitivity or knowledge towards laws, politics and the justification of a community and public social system. All are involved in a democratic system in which each individual has both freedom and responsibility. And yet little attention is paid to what this means. The ostensible surprise, if there is any, at those points at which the 'system' appears to break down, is unwarranted, since there is so little concern in inculcating understanding. Perhaps it suits those in power to neglect the very people for whom they are responsible, as opposed to those whose votes brought them to their positions of affluence. There is not only widespread ignorance of the constitution, and of government, but also of the role of the individual within 'official' society. In any survey of attitudes we find not just ignorance of the ways of politics but a sense that it is a different world, with little relationship to the individual.[58] The assumption that politicians do not listen to anyone, and have little time for the individual citizen, is widespread in children aged 8 to 11. There is therefore a deep-seated capacity for the sense of disenfranchisement. The tension between the official, distant State and the needs of the individual, even in a democracy, affects all and not just those who become 'excluded' from the system.

Part of the 'system' is criminal justice. Young people express several consistent attitudes.[59] An ignorance of how the law works is widespread. At the same time young people hold primitive attitudes. They see the legal system as one that needs to enforce its will through ever-increasing punishments on the recalcitrant wrong-doer. They see it as a clash of wills, almost symbolically through the images of the police in riot gear fighting the hooligan element. The police have a public relations problem, for despite visits to schools they are perceived as often violent and potentially corrupt. It is as if the attitudes to the police, formed by the images of news stories, made them distant and suspect. This is a far cry from the idea of the local policeman, part of the community, there to succour and support.

Feelings of distance and alienation, of the sense of psychological exclusion, affect all young people and not just the few who actually play truant from 'normal' society. There is a huge seed-bed and potential for crime. To this extent some might be surprised that a relatively small number offend. This suggests that so much more could be done, actively, if only the evidence were listened to. Those who offend have been neglected as if nothing *should* be done in the home or school to help them. Problems have grown because they are not being addressed. Negative views of society breed ignorance. They also inter-breed. If there are no other sources of knowledge than peer-groups, then the sense of being on the fringes of society grows stronger.

Relationships and communities

This is why the more subtle notion of the community is so important. It consists of a series of relationships within and outside the home. It is affected by the number of stable or unstable relationships within it. It reinforces those attitudes that have been learned at home through peer relations.[60] It is sometimes an alternative to the constraints, either the intimate impositions of a household or the more general rules of school. Young people form clear views of their societies and are aware of tensions between traditional and modern forms of living.[61] There are also inevit- able distinctions, once again, between classes. Not only are the types of language different but so are the potential of analysis and understanding. The middle classes tend to be more open-minded and tolerant than the working classes.[62] But this typology of class, like that of communities, should not be taken as simple labelling, or cause and effect. Beyond class distinctions lie relationships; and these can be fostered, learned and developed.[63]

We know the broad patterns that lead to criminality and we know some of the causes, even if not always in subtle detail. It is important to note the consistency of the findings, whether longitudinal or statistical. The Home Office Research and Statistics Department itself provides a clear picture of the general profile of offending – even if nothing is done with the results.[64] They found that involvement in offending and drug use is widespread even if just 3 per cent of offenders are responsible for a disproportionate amount of crime (about a quarter of all offences). They found that females aged 14 to 17 were nearly as likely as males to be involved in offending but as they get older this gets far less compared to males. And they found that the strongest influences on starting to offend are low parental supervision, persistent truancy and associating with their peers who are also involved in offending. All these are related to the quality of the relationships with parents. The question that remains to be addressed is how and why these factors are so significant and on that basis what could be done about it.

Many of the studies of criminality have locked onto a single hypothesis, isolating one possible factor, like genetics or unemployment. It can be tempting to proffer simple explanations or to pursue short-term solutions where the violence of the offender is reflected in the violence of the response. What is needed is the kind of exploration of the causes of offending that clearly demonstrates how a range of factors interact with each other. One of the crucial issues is the relationship between the definable circumstances, like poverty, and what is made of them, in terms of attitudes and relationships. It is the ways in which all these relate to each other that provide the clues that open up understanding.

One thing is clear in all accounts of the causes of criminality. The genesis of much of crime lies in the home. Whilst social deprivation is a factor, it does not by itself explain delinquency.[65] Whilst peer influence is important, its extent and nature depend largely on the early relationships forged in the home. It is with significant adults that children form the most important relationships through the ability to negotiate over time. Friends might come and go and are formed for pleasure rather than learning. But parents dominate. They teach, however inadvertently. They present attitudes and interests and are the first example to young children both of the importance of the point of view and how individual and idiosyncratic they can be.[66] Parents are also very important for the concomitant relationships with siblings.

There are a number of adverse factors that are associated with crime, like inadequate housing, a poor local environment and low income, but these do not in themselves become translated into delinquency. Instead they are stress factors that make it far more difficult to be an effective parent.[67] Social pressures affect the way that parents behave and that in turn affects their children. The association between social class and delinquency is related more to the parental and family problems associated with low social status rather than low social status *per se* .[68] The Cambridge Study in Delinquency also included parents and the home as one of the significant factors in predicting offending. The other factors, like family criminality, economic deprivation and school failure, all relate to this.[69] Parenting style is bound to have a strong, perhaps definitive, influence on children's development.[70]

At the heart of understanding the causes of criminality lies the home, not in isolation but in relation to other factors. In the complex interchanges that form the cultural milieu of the individual, the earliest influences are of vital importance. But their significance is not manifested until later. One can detect aggression in the very young but normally the first signs of real trouble, like truanting full time from school, appear around the age of 12/13. Year nine, the third year of secondary school, is particularly troublesome. Whilst there have been many studies of the various factors that can make home life difficult, there has been little research into the intimate details and experiences of the formative early years and their relationships to subsequent events.

The overall evidence based on statistics only takes us so far. From an analysis of 50 studies it is clear that the prevalence of delinquency in broken homes is 10 to 15 per cent higher than in intact homes.[71] But this comparatively minor variation does not explain the anger and tension of witnessing the scenes that lead up to it, and the guilt often felt as a consequence. Nor does it highlight the fact that children normally wish their parents to stay together, at all costs. We know that boys in families that had experienced divorce by the age of 10 display more behavioural problems than children in intact families.[72] But this does not explain the family discord, the longing for other relationships, the sense of low esteem and a feeling of discordance with the normal structures of society. Marital conflict can lead to behaviour and learning problems regardless of whether the parents remain together or divorce.[73] There is no evidence to support the assumption that two parents are automatically a better safeguard against delinquency than a parent raising a child alone, despite the general rage against single parents.[74]

Divorce is one of those factors which, taken in isolation, can be assumed to be a cause of delinquency in itself. But as the evidence demonstrates, the true factors are more subtle. There might be a correlation between the two but the real explanation is the deeper one. It is the facts of divorce rather than the effects of divorce that matter. These are not sudden or short-lived but felt deeply over a period of time.[75] The task of explaining the causes of criminality, as the research literature demonstrates, is to seek empirical evidence about all the factors that contribute to them. This includes clear patterns, and factors such as 'neighbourhoods', but whilst these support and corroborate the findings that emerge in this study, there is an attempt here to explain not just what the circumstances are but how the young react to them. At one level are the clear social circumstances, like the experience of the home or the personal events that happen at school. At another is the sense of self, defined through relationships with others. The whole is complex but consistent, with every element connecting with another. For the sake of coherence in the analysis there are divisions between layers of attitudes and events, but each chapter needs to be understood in relation to the others. In a sense the most important – since it is at the heart of the matter and relates most closely to the others – is left towards the end.

Nothing could point out more clearly the need to understand the experiences of home and school than the subsequent outcomes as expressed in the literature on criminality. There are layers and layers, all of which help explain each other.

References

1. Cullingford, C (1992) *Children and Society*, Cassell, London
2. Cullingford, C (1999) *The Human Experience: The early years*, Ashgate, Aldershot
3. Williamson, I and Cullingford, C (1997) The uses and misuses of 'alienation' in the social sciences and education, *British Journal of Educational Studies*, **45** (3), pp 263–75
4. eg Marcuse
5. Sherman, L, Gottfredson, D, Mackenzie, D, Eck, J, Renter, P and Buskway, S (1997) *Preventing crime: What works, what doesn't, what's promising*, A report to the United States Congress, prepared for the National Institute of Justice
6. Williamson, I (1999) The influence of estrangement in the lives of young criminals, Unpublished PhD
7. Fagan, J (1995) Legal work and illegal work: crime, work and unemployment, in *Dealing with Urban Crisis: Linking Research to Action*, eds B Weisbrod and J Worthy, North Western University Press, Illinois
8. Farrington, D and West, D (1990) *Kriminalität: The Cambridge Study in Delinquent Development*, Springer-Verlag, London
9. Elias, N (1997) Towards a theory of social processes: a translation, *British Journal of Sociology*, **48** (3), pp 355–83
10. Downes, D (1996) *The Delinquent Solution*, Routlege, London
11. Ekblom, P and Pease, K (1997) *Evaluating Crime Prevention*, HMSO, London
12. See Sherman *et al*, op cit
13. Pease, K (1993) Individual and community influence on victimization and their implications for crime prevention, in *Integrating Individual and Ecological Aspects of Crime*, eds D Farrington, R Sampson and P Wikström, BRA Report
14. Hagell, A and Newburn, T (1994) *Persistent Young Offenders*, Policy Studies Institute, London
15. Rutter, M (1996) Genetics of criminal and anti-social behaviour, in eds G Bock and J Goode, *Genetics of Criminal and Anti-social Behaviour*, J Wiley, Chichester
16. Pinker, S (1997) *How the Mind Works*, Allen Lane, London
17. In the United States. Duncan, G, Brooks-Dunn, J and Klebanov, P (1994) Economic deprivation and early childhood development, *Child Development,* **65** (2), pp 296–318
18. Garrett, P, Ng'andu, N and Ferron, J (1994) Poverty experiences of young children and the quality of their home environments, *Child Development,* **65** (2), pp 331–45
19. Cullingford, C, (1999), *The Human Experience: The early years*, Ashgate, Aldershot
20. See Duncan *et al,* op cit
21. See Garrett *et al*, op cit

22. Huston, A, McLoyd, V and Coll C (1994) Children and poverty: issues in contemporary research, *Child Development*, **65** (2), pp 275–82

23. Wells, G (1985) *Language Development in the Pre-School Years: Language at Home and School*, Cambridge University Press, Cambridge

24. Richman, N, Stevenson, J and Graham, PJ (1982) *Pre-School to School: A Behavioural Study*, Academic Press, London

25. Farrell, G, Phillips, C and Pease, K (1995) Like taking candy: why does repeat victimization occur?, *British Journal of Criminology*, **35** (3), pp 384–99

26. Farrell, G (1995) Predicting and preventing revictimization, in *Preventing Crime, Vol 19, Crime and Justice: A review of research*, eds M Tonky and D Farrington, pp 61–126

27. Rutter, M and Smith, D (eds) (1995) *Psychosocial Disorders in Young People: Time trends and their causes*, J Wiley, Chichester

28. Mehler, J, Jusczyk, P, Lambertz, G, Halstead, N, Bertoncini, J and Amcel-Tison, C (1988) A precursor to language acquisition in young infants, *Cognition*, **29**, pp 143–78

29. The literature on language and thought, eg from Piaget through Vygotsky to more philosophical texts is vast and multifarious, but with an underlying consistency.

30. Sherman, *et al*, op cit, p 11

31. Wells, A *et al* (1981) *Language Through Interaction*, Cambridge University Press, Cambridge

32. eg Tough, J (1973) *Listening to Children Talking*, Ward Lock, London

33. Heath, SB (1983) *Ways with Words: Language, Life and Work in Communities and Classrooms*, Cambridge University Press, Cambridge

34. Richman *et al*, op cit

35. Silverstone, R (1994) *Television and Everyday Life*, Routledge, London
Giddens, A (1990) *The Consequences of Modernity*, Polity Press, Cambridge

36. Sherman *et al*, op cit, p 210

37. Ibid, p 214

38. Hazlitt, W (1825) *The Spirit of the Age*

39. Townsend, P and Corrigan, P (1987) *Poverty and Labour in London*, Low Pay Unit, London

40. Sherman *et al*, op cit, p 334

41. Ibid, p 2

42. Pease, op cit

43. Skinner, BF (1970) *Aggression*, Rinehart, Holt, New York

44. Abraham, J (1994) Positivism, Structureationism and the Differentiation– Polarisation Theory: a reconsideration of Shilling's novelty and primary thesis, *British Journal of Sociology of Education*, **15** (2), pp 231–41

45. Halsey, AH (1972) *Trends in British Society since 1900: A guide to a changing social structure of Britain*, Macmillan, London

46. Dowds, L and Ahrendt, D (1995) Fear of crime, in *British Social Attitudes: The 12th*, eds R Jowell, J Curtue, A Park, L Brook and D Ahrendt, with K Thomson, pp 19–42, Dartmouth, Aldershot

47. Most civil servants would, in fact, say 'always'.

48. Imich, I (1994) Exclusions from school: current trends and issues, *Educational Research*, **36** (1), pp 3–12

49. This is symbolized by the way in which agencies are used to keeping a distance from evidence, eg Ofsted HMSO (1993) *Education for Disaffected Pupils*, HMSO, London (1/93/NS)

50. Imich, op cit
51. Smith, D (1994) *The Sleep of Reason*, Century, London
52. Cullingford, C (1984) *Children and Television*, Gower, Aldershot
53. Farrington, op cit
Graham, J and Bowling, B (1995) *Young People and Crime*, Home Office Research Study No 145, Home Office, London
54. Field, S (1990) *Trends in Crime and Their Interpretation: A study of recorded crime in post-war England and Wales*, HMSO, London
55. Ibid
56. Pease, op cit
57. Du-bois Reymond, J, Büchner, P and Krüger, H (1993) Modern Family as Everyday Negotiation: Continuities and discontinuities in parent–child relationships, *Childhood*, 1, pp 87–99
58. Cullingford, C (1992), op cit
59. Brown, I (1992) *The Criminal Justice System: Schoolchildren speak out*, Kirklees Criminal Justice Interagency Forum, Huddersfield
60. Kupersmidt, J, Griesher, P, DeRosier, M, Patterson, C and Davis, P (1995) Childhood aggression and peer relations in the context of family and neighbourhood factors, *Child Development*, **66** (2), pp 360–75
61. du Bois-Reymond, M, Dickstra, R, Hurrelmann, K and Peters, E (1995) *Childhood and Youth in Germany and The Netherlands: Transitions and Coping Strategies of Adolescents*, Walter de Gruyter, Berlin
62. Ibid
63. Ibid
64. Graham and Bowling, op cit
65. Utting, W, Bright, J and Henricson, C (1993) *Crime and the Family*, Family Policy Studies Centre, London
66. Cullingford, C, *The Human Experience*, op cit
67. Utting, *et al*, op cit, p 19
68. Rutter, M and Smith, D (eds)(1995) *Psychosocial Disorders in Young People: Time trends and their causes*, Wiley, Chichester
69. West, D and Farrington, D (1973) *Who Becomes Delinquents?*, Heinemann, London
West, D (1982) *Delinquency: Its roots, careers and prospects*, Heinemann, London
Farrington and West, op cit
70. Steinberg, L, Lamborn, S, Darling, N, Mounts, N and Dornbusch, S (1994) Over-time changes in adjustment and competence among adolescents from authoritative, authoritarian, indulgent and neglectful families, *Child Development*, **65** (3), pp 754–70
71. Wells, L and Rankin, J (1995) Juvenile Victimization: Convergence validation of alternative measurements, *Journal of Research in Crime and Delinquency*, **32** (3), pp 287–307
72. Capaldi, C, Nakagowa, N and Madden, C (1990) How Children understand sarcasm, *Child Development*, **61** (6), pp 1824–41
73. Furstenburg, F and Cherlin, A (1991) *Divided Families: What happens when parents part*, Harvard University Press, Cambridge, MA
74. Utting *et al*, op cit, p 20
75. Kiernan, K (1997) *The Legacy of Parental Divorce: Social, economic and demographic experiences in adulthood*, CASE Paper No 1, Shierd, London

2

The sources and the
styles of evidence

Introduction

There is an ancient, Socratic tradition in research. To use what seems like an old-fashioned term, it is to seek the 'truth'. Even in ancient times this was acknowledged to be problematic. What, in epistemological terms, is ultimate truth? What does such a term mean, given the fact of individual interpretation based on the idea that each wants to see 'truth' in precisely his or her own way, even in religion? But the ideal in research still remains. It might appear, on the face of it, rare but it remains.

There might seem the slenderest link between Socrates and the study of the causes of criminality. There are many problems in the research on crime which typify problems with all kinds of research. Research has become, after all, a major industry. It is funded, competed for and controlled. Those who are in control of funding know what they are looking for and the results that they anticipate. If the results of the objective pursuit of empirical enquiry are not what they hoped for, they are in the position to either ignore or disown them on the grounds of method-ological imperfection. This has put many pressures on researchers, so that those who ostensibly pursue the almost naive notion of what is 'true' seem to be in the minority. In fact they are not so, but the circumstances inhibit their impact. Valid and reliable evidence keeps being produced, but it is as often ignored. Results that have an impact are those of the more instant kind, the more superficial, the support for received opinion. The phrase 'research has shown', in conjunction with a per-sonal opinion, is the standard signal for the misuse of evidence.

Research evidence could be so helpful and yet is rarely used. One reason for this lies in the nature of the research itself. Now that it has become a method of employment, driven by competition for contracts or the means of promotion, there are all kinds of underlying motivations that affect it. In all research, whether to do with crime or not, there are two alternating forces. One is the necessity to show off, to demonstrate the cleverness of the researcher. This is not to blame the researcher but to explain the academic environment in which the arcane is more respected than the luminous. On the other hand is the pressure to produce results, to come up with whatever answer is required. Often the two go together, for they have a kind of symbiotic relationship. 'If you tell me what you want to know, I'll find a sufficiently obscure and complex way of proving it, so no one will know whether the result is valid or not.'

I signal the dangers of what happens to research, the way it is delivered and the way it is misused for two reasons. The first is that it is a great pity to waste so much human endeavour, absorbing so much energy and intelligence, for such little result. We could not only know much more about the causes of crime but do so much more about its prevention. It is, I suppose, a part of human pathology to obscure the very sources of information given to us. The second reason is ethical. Driven as crime research seems to be by the need for instant, almost experimental answers, the idea of the long-term search for what is empirical and sustainable seems to be obscured. Crime could be tackled far more effectively. But it is not. Why?

There are many reasons for this, and none have anything to do with a theory of complicity. Just as in the nature of criminality, there are certain circumstances, linked to human nature, that make such mistakes seem inevitable, even if they are unnecessary. There are, in a sense, 'good' reasons for the denial of evidence. One is, quite simply, modesty felt at the thought that there might be such a thing as valid and reliable evidence in a subject as complex as human nature. In the pure sciences it is possible to go on refining experiments and deductively proving them by repetition so that something verifiable emerges. It might not be worth the pursuit but at least one variable is supported or eliminated. This is not possible in the same way in the social sciences, however often tried. But it remains an attractive idea, attractive enough to have led to such a high reputation, for example, for Piaget's biological approach to the study of human development. This seemed carefully constructed, even if wrong. And, more crucially, it supported the popular, unexamined assumptions about the superiority of the mature over the young.

There is a dawning realization that the application of narrow scientific reasoning to a subject of huge complexity, containing what seems like an infinite number of variables, is not really tenable. This has led to an almost instinctive reaction against any positive findings. I used the term 'modesty' to describe the retreat from positive findings but it could be more a matter of embarrassment. Can one both take in all the empirical evidence and still make sense of it in a way that is rigorous and consistent? Can one uncover the truths that allow for the individuality of the particular person, the commonality of the human experience, and yet detect those cultural circumstances that are so significant?

The other reasons for shying away from drawing clear conclusions from evidence is the other 'modesty' of not wishing to intervene. That sense of inevitability, that people are always going to be as they are, is not just fostered by the fascination of what is gory and difficult but by a feeling not so much of helplessness (which underlines the fascination) as of not wishing to presume that anything can be done, as if action were interference. We see many reforms and many suggestions about how to deal with problems, how, in fact, to intervene. But these are almost never at the human level. They eschew the vital help that the individual might need. The policy decision to conduct a large experiment, affecting huge numbers of people, rarely appears to have empirical rigour behind it. Interventions have been extreme, as the dire history of the 20th century demonstrates. But the idea that we might help by understanding individuals, like ourselves, seems curiously remote. It is as if two conflicting beliefs came together: the belief that to cause change is impossible since there are so many factors at work, and the political will to make changes happen instantly. The holding of contradictory beliefs at the same time is common.[1]

Research and policy

Fear of intervention at the individual level is surprising given the many political reforms that are designed to affect the masses. And yet, as we have already noted, one cannot usefully separate the individual from society, the people and the criminalities they are part of.[2] The Socratic ideal of a community depends on individuals and the interchanges between them. It also rests on a respect for evidence, on gathering together the empirical facts and questioning them. The research reported here is based on the principle that one should not know beforehand what the evidence will produce. There was no attempt to seek out a pre-set hypothesis. In fact the search of the statistical and quantitative research came after the data had been gathered and the transcripts analysed. There were many surprises, especially in the consistency of the responses.

We live at a time when in reaction to scientific certainties we are surrounded by epistemological doubt. How can anything in the social sciences be 'true'? Whilst this is not the place to pursue this interesting argument, it should be reiterated that the validity and reliability of the evidence is of the utmost importance. We should no longer have to rely on the idea of telling a 'story'. We should not need to assert that the data gathered is not 'soft' but very carefully gathered and analysed.[3] The only way to gather information about what really happens inside individuals is through qualitative methods. Quantitative methods describe rather than explain.[4] Some social psychological approaches to sensitive data can be narrow, neglecting the complex processes of social interaction.[5] Qualitative data from systematic open-ended questions can reveal underlying social processes.[6]

The research reported here is derived from three different sources. One is the literature that describes, from an educational point of view rather than one of criminology, the ways in which people form attitudes and relate to each other. This literature is extensive but has rarely been applied to the understanding of crime. This is why Sherman points out that finding out that certain prevention programmes can work is almost accidental, and not deeply examined.[7] The literature has different traditions; one is the study of early childhood and the development of cognition and the awareness of central human social understanding as in seeing the distinction between truth and falsehood, found, for example, in the many studies reported in the journal *Child Development*.[8] Another is the literature on social psychology and psychiatry. But there are others, including the study of the effect of teachers and pedagogy, the analysis of the learning process, including motivation and response and the transmission of culture. And there is also the literature on peer groups and relationships from proxemics to friendship patterns. All these different approaches to the understanding of the human condition have a part to play in attempting to fathom the circumstances that create criminality, and help interpret and give meaning to the raw evidence. This is not to say that the evidence does not speak for itself. It does up to a point. But the evidence also has a wider, deeper social context and meaning. It is reinforced by not only its internal consistency but by its consistency with other research.

The second body of evidence derives from many studies based on semi-structured interviews with children aged between 6 and 16. Whilst the aims of the research were not concerned with criminality, but with views about society and their place within it, a lot of unexpected data that has a bearing on this subject did emerge, like clearly defined anti-social attitudes that could predict a tendency towards criminality in boys of eight. (One could be tempted in some cases to forecast a life of crime.) Whilst this evidence is not directly used here and is published elsewhere, it does inform our understanding of, and support, the main body of findings reported here.

All the quotations that are used here to illuminate the experiences of young offenders come from lengthy semi-structured interviews. The most focused cohort who provided the information was 25 aged between 16 and 21, 19 male and 6 female. But these are supported by evidence taken from another 40, half of them female. All were interviewed by themselves and welcomed the chance to talk; they were a 'captive audience'. The interviews were confidential and anonymous even if some prison governors might have been tempted to seek out the results. Access was granted despite pressures on the prison service, as governors and their colleagues realized the potential significance of the research. It soon became clear that the findings which emerged from individuals formed a consistency which meant that it was not necessary to go on repeating the same process – a consistency that included that of experience and outlook between males and females.

The dominant tradition in researching crime has been quantitative. The study of incidents, and correlations between different factors, indeed, the whole fascination with criminal behaviour and its control, has meant that qualitative research has been comparatively rare. This has meant that there have been few attempts to enter into the mind-set of the individual criminals in order to find out if there are certain events that they all have in common, and whether they react to them in particular ways. A general assumption that there are certain immutable factors that will inevitably cause criminality, whether personality factors or environmental circumstances, has drawn attention away from the empirical basis for understanding the individual mind. When there are attempts to explain there is a tendency to fall back on general theories of aggression, as if those would themselves explain the tendency to behave in a criminal fashion, whether the aggression is against the person directly or against property. There are several theories of aggression, some of which depend solely on the innate factors of human nature and others which explore the individual's interaction with and reaction to the environment. Biological explanations of aggression see it as an innate attack mechanism, resulting from an accumulation of aggressive impulses.[9] Aggression can also be depicted as a hostile reaction to perceived frustration.[10] Then again, aggression is described as a response to environmental stimuli and depends on reinforcement.[11] Others place their emphasis on the importance of modelling and reinforcement processes.[12] And aggression is also seen as a result of faulty information processing, in which children fail to go through all the necessary stages of learning social skills.[13]

The problem is that these theories do not in themselves help us gain insights into the way the individual young offender thinks and acts. They do not uncover the complex interaction between the individual and his or her circumstances, the 'cultural' factors that are so significant.[14] We have, then, psychological evidence on the one hand and clear patterns of behaviour on the other. Our purpose here is to draw them together.

Listening to experience: semi-structured interviews

There is only one way to do this, and that is through the insights afforded by the people themselves. It seems strange in this post-post-modernist time to have to point this out, and yet the richest source of information is often neglected. It is as if we have not learned to listen, or even recognized the importance of listening. This is partly because of a strong suspicion that people might not be telling the truth, and that they have no insights into their own lives. There is an ethical issue here that centres on the respect for the individual. The assumption that people do not tell the truth is based partly on the experience of interviews in which people defend themselves from critical scrutiny. Leaving the partiality of politicians aside, any manager or head teacher being probed about their job will give the best possible account of what they are doing. Interviews for jobs, or interviews about jobs, are a far cry from interviews with a counsellor, or any interview which is strictly confidential, where the individual remains anonymous.

Interviews are also mistrusted as they can be associated with 'Mori'-type surveys, which are not really interviews at all, but more like verbal questionnaires. Real interviews are lengthy and exploratory. Whilst the techniques differ, from just one opening question to clearly stated topics, they all seek to help the subject explore openly and in detail some area of his or her inner life that illuminates not just the individual but the human experience.[15] There is one factor, as in large-scale surveys, that is as important as the desire to deceive the interviewer – whether by putting the most positive gloss on oneself or deliberately misleading through persuasion – and that is the desire to *please* the interviewer. Just as children are brought up to try to guess what the teacher wants them to say, rather than to learn, so people have a tendency to give the interviewer what is required.[16]

Linguistic philosophers like Austin remind us that even when trying to lie, at least 90 per cent of what people utter is, strictly speaking, true.[17] When people have no motivation for saying anything but the truth as they see it, there is no reason to doubt them. The question is whether they actually *know* the 'truth'. There are many psychological theories, like that of the Anima and Animus, that are based on the premise that individuals are driven by deeper forces than they themselves understand.[18] But as the tradition of counselling constantly demonstrates, there are also many known elements and events in people's lives that are clearly capable of exploration and explanation. Some of the motivations might remain obscure but the significant life events and the sources of influence remain clear.

The interviews described here can be likened to counselling sessions in so far as the focus is purely on the individual. They describe certain important experiences and they also explore the way that the interviewees explain their own actions and the reasons for them. For all the quantitative surveys of behaviour there is only one way to gain an insight into the mind and that is through language. We wish to know what makes the 'neighbourhood' significant, and why some and not others turn to crime. The use of drugs, for example, is widespread and the most common form of deviancy or breaking the law, and yet not all find themselves driven, by the desire to find the money to satisfy their cravings, to more serious crime.[19] Why? What are the significant early influences that form certain habits and reactions?

As the quotations will demonstrate, the interviewees show honesty and a lot of self-insight. They do not make excuses. Nor do they suggest they will reform. They know their own limitations too well. They hide nothing. They are also consistent in that for all the individual differences, there are certain events, and reactions to those events, that they all have in common. This makes them significant. We are going beyond a series of case studies to trace what becomes a blueprint for a certain kind of human experience. We are not only offered detailed descriptions but clear explanations. Historiography centres on the crucial tension between primary evidence and its interpretation. The latter is a question of generalizability; what are the events that are significant beyond the individual experience?[20] Here both the empirical evidence and its interpretation are presented to us, up to a point, by the interviewees themselves. We celebrate the uniqueness of the individual, but are also presented with the shared culture of the human condition.

The interviews, both of the primary and secondary sources, were all semi-structured. This means that whilst the subjects were allowed to talk about whatever they wanted, there was a consistency of theme. They all covered home life, schooling and truancy. But the questions were all open-ended. Essentially, the young offenders were asked to describe their lives. It is as if they longed to do so. They did not defend their crimes or make excuses for them. Nor did they pretend to be virtuous. They accepted the strict confidentiality and the fact that no one would find out who they were. But this needed little assertion. They all had tales to tell and wanted the opportunity to do so – not to plead innocence or make excuses but for a chance to reflect on what had happened. Just as the questions were open, so were the answers.

It is important that the interviewer gives no hint of looking for certain types of material. The research question might be truancy, bullying or exclusion, but any terms of definition, like these, were avoided. This means a laconic style, like that of the teacher listening to the natural outpourings of a young child, accepting all that is said. The prompt questions were far more about times in the young people's lives rather than themes. The themes and definitions were all supplied by the interviewees. A sense of direction and honesty pervades these interviews, and should be clear in the examples. They provide, better than any quantitative approach, insights into the significant events and relationships in their lives and demonstrate the richness of data that can be provided by this method.

Creating the right tone and conditions for the interviews is important to ensure their reliability and validity. This means that they are lengthy, allowing time for anything that the interviewee says to be pursued in depth and allowing for that little prompt 'why'? What the interviewees said was not challenged or questioned beyond that, but the length of the interviews and the fact that certain topics were returned to several times ensured that any contradictions would be detected. The most important factor in the interviews, apart from the trust in confidentiality, was the sense of respect for what the interviewees said. There could be no guessing what kind of information the interviewer might be seeking.

Ensuring the validity of the interviews is important. So is ensuring the validity of the analysis. All the interviews were tape-recorded and transcribed. There were no signs of self-consciousness with the presence of a tape recorder, which was made as unobtrusive as possible, with no tape changes halfway through the interview. The transcripts were analysed and re-analysed over a long period, and double-checked. They were also subject to some quantitative analysis, mainly to check whether there were any differences according to factors such as age, gender and home circumstances. But this was merely another means of ascertaining the coherence and consistency of the findings. The fact that the transcripts were analysed several times and over a long period should have added to the validity of the interpretation where this is needed. To an extent the interpretation is provided by the interviews themselves; they 'speak for themselves'.

The presentation of the data

It is important to reiterate that the findings, including their consistency, were something of a surprise. There was no pre-set hypothesis that affected the interpretation. The original intention had been to explore the link between bullying and school, but what emerged was quite different and far more comprehensive. Analysis of the transcripts revealed certain themes, so that the quotations that illuminate them are symbolic of others as well as supporting each other. These themes emerged slowly and changed over time so that certain clues seemed to suggest more significance at one time rather than another.

The data presented here is rich and complex since all the separate strands interrelate. This means that careful judgements had to be made about the presentation, judgements about order and the avoidance of repetition whilst suggesting overlap. The research is presented in a series of layers, some to do with the circumstances, and others to do with certain types of behaviour. Some of the themes describe the facts. The experience and circumstances of the home is one, the conditions in which the young offenders lived and the structure of the family. Other themes centre on certain central experiences, like exclusion from school. Others explore relationships, with parents and peer groups and teachers. And others explore the way the young offenders think about themselves. The choice has been whether to explore the pattern of their lives over time, from home to school to prison, or to suggest the important central themes and their interconnection by looking at 'layers'.

It is probably more illuminating to try to enter into the mind-set of the young offenders layer by layer. This better illustrates the coherence of the whole, since the findings of one theme will add weight to another. It also demonstrates how one thing can lead to another and how their actions and the consequences of their actions can be traced back to earlier influences and experiences. It also constantly reminds us of the interrelationships between individual personality types and their circumstances. Thus we start by exploring the home, and go on to outline parents' attitudes towards authority, as symbolized by the school. We then go on to describe the young offenders' personal experience of school, both in academic and social terms, and analyse how they interact with them. We then centre on relationships with teachers and how this relates to truancy and exclusion, and on the way in which exclusion comes about. We then look at the influence of the peer group, not only in terms of behaviour or an alternative society but explaining *why* peers have such an influence in these circumstances.

This is followed by accounts of a life out of school and out of formal society when the young offenders are carrying out those crimes for which they have been arrested. After this comes a crucial chapter in which the young offenders describe and analyse their relationships with their parents. This analysis, which can be connected to their accounts of subsequent relationships, is followed by their reflections on their own personality and behaviour. They demonstrate a clear ability for self-analysis and insight – to the extent that they admit that they probably will not change, however much they would like to. Those young offenders who are parents (there are few exceptions) then describe how they mean to, and more particularly, how they actually do, relate to and behave to their own children, or how they did behave when they last saw them. It is as if we had come full circle, seeing the same patterns of behaviour perpetuated in the next generation.

All these themes form a coherent whole. Some of them add to the evidence that emerges from statistics: the prevalence of divorce or the example of criminality given by some parents. But the pattern is not as significant as the influence of certain events and why they have such an influence. Here we explore the 'why' and not just the 'what' or the 'how'. There might be little surprise, or a great deal of shock, at the prevalence of violence, including rape and child abuse. But they are the awful symptoms of something deeper. There is such consistency that one can be tempted to think that these young people's criminality is inevitable. So it might appear, with hindsight. But it is not inevitable. Insight into their experiences and their reactions to them reinforce the fact that their actions and the outcomes are unnecessary.

This suggests that something could be done. Crime prevention on a large scale is perfectly possible. As the stories demonstrate, these young people are redeemable. This is not to say that they will not reoffend, but to remind ourselves that interventions at certain points and greater sensitivity at others could have made a profound difference. Crime prevention, as Sherman demonstrates, needs to be targeted at certain spheres of influence: the home, the school, the neighbourhood.

This research demonstrates why. But it also demonstrates that it is possible to help. Prevention implies some kind of intervention and some would shy away at such a notion of society becoming concerned for and responsible for its own citizens, as if that were undue interference. But policing is itself intervention, only it takes place after the event rather than before it.

· One of the major ethical questions that surrounds any piece of research has to do with its aftermath. What do we do about it? Empirical evidence is all too easy to ignore if it gives a message that people do not wish to hear. It is then that, whatever the methodology employed, it is dismissed as invalid. But these young offenders give an insight into the causes of criminality which should be acted upon. This book is a 'story' of all the influences that accumulate in such a way that some gradually become disaffected and feel themselves excluded from formal society. It is not about a simple cause and effect but concerned with how many complex factors interconnect. The evidence is there. It needs to be listened to, and heard.

References

1. qv the books that try to understand the collective and complex schizophrenia of Germany before and during the Second World War; civilized yet producing the Holocaust, knowing and yet unknowing. Unfortunately this duality is part of everyday experience. Nature of Learning.
2. Pease, op cit, in previous chapter
3. Dunn, J (1988) *The Beginnings of Social Understanding*, Basil Blackwell, Oxford
4. Troyna, B and Hatcher, R (1992) *Racism in Children's Lives. A Study of Mainly White Primary Schools*, Routledge, London
5. eg Hammersley, M (1989) *Ethnographic Research Methods*, Open University Press, Milton Keynes
6. Sampson, R and Laub, J (1994) Urban poverty and the family context of delinquency: a new look at structure and process in a classic study, *Child*, **65** (2), pp 523–40
7. Sherman *et al*, op cit, in previous chapter
8. Published by the Society for Research in Child Development Inc.
9. Lorenz, K (1981) *The Foundations of Ethology*, Springer-Verlag, Vienna
10. Berkowitz, L (1962) *Aggression: A Social Psychological Analysis*, McGraw-Hill, New York
11. Skinner, op cit, in previous chapter
12. Bandura, A (1973) *Aggression: A Social Learning*, Prentice-Hall, New Jersey
Perry, D, Williard, J and Perry, L (1990) Peers' perceptions of the consequences that victimised children provide aggressors, *Child Development*, **61** (5), pp 1310–25
13. Dodge, K, Coie, J, Peltit, G and Price, J (1990) Peer status and aggression in boys' groups: developmental and contextual analyses, *Child Development*, **16** (5), pp 1289–309
14. Bourdieu, P (1984) *Distinction: A Social Critique of the Judgement or Tastes*, Routledge and Kegan Paul, London
15. Spradley, P (1979) *The Ethnographic Interview*, Holt, Rinehart and Winston, New York
16. Cullingford, C (1991) *The Inner World of the School*, Cassell, London

17. Austin, JL (1962) *How to Do Things with Words*, Oxford University Press, Newark
18. See the works of Jung.
19. Graham and Bowling, op cit, in previous chapter
20. cf Brecht's famous antagonism to the individually famous, as in Galileo.

3

The experience of home

Introduction

The large-scale analyses that seek out connections between crime and other factors concentrate on three: poverty, divorce and previous criminality in the family. All are factors of certain kinds of 'communities'. These correlations are important but they do not explain by themselves *how* they affect young minds. Not all poor people turn to crime, nor do the majority of young offenders have criminal parents. Those few studies that seek to go further than statistical correlations suggest that there are other intervening factors which are more important. This is not to say that the experience of poverty is not linked to higher incidents of crime, but that it is the effects of poverty on behaviour, in certain people, that matter. We have already noted that there are no simple correlations between overall crime and overall poverty or wealth. Suggesting that crime is simply due to need or to greed does not help.

The problem with overall correlations is not only that they do not explain the intimate actualities of people's lives, but that they divert attention from the real causes. They also imply that there is little that can be done about the problem; that there are no direct measures to make intervention or crime prevention possible. The distinction between the fact that there is a connection between poverty and crime and the fact that there are intervening variables can be quite tricky but it is important to attempt to make one. Otherwise we sit back and see the statistics rise and fall, as if we were helpless. Anyone who has experienced poverty, or, indeed, anyone who has experienced money problems, will know the deleterious effect they have on personal relationships. Money problems and the responsibility of looking after young children are a damaging correlation.[1] But it is not a simple matter of cause and effect.

There are, of course, many political temptations in finding simple explanations and then extending simple blame. Perhaps the most notorious of these is on single parents, and the 'breakdown of marriage'. There are several reasons for the citing of divorce as a significant part in the rise of crime. These include the fact that single parents, normally meaning single mothers, are expensive, a burden on the State. That there are correlations between divorce and crime is clear. A significant proportion of young criminals' parents divorced when they were young. But divorce itself is a symptom, a final outcome of what is already going wrong. There is little evidence that having a single parent is, in *itself*, a cause of criminality. We must distinguish between the untraditional household, including single parenting, and what it symbolizes. Some would wish to argue that poverty and a single parent is a potent combination in the causes of crime. And yet, whilst there are connections, these are far weaker than we might have thought. And they do not explain what really happens, or why.

Types of dysfunctional families

For the young offenders there is no doubt about the effects of dislocation in the family. They nearly all come from divorced parents – divorced often after they had turned to crime. But it is the kind of dislocation, the psychological disturbance of an unbalanced home that is significant. It is still a fine point to distinguish between the research evidence that suggests that divorce *itself* causes deviancy, and the research evidence that suggests that it is better for parents to stay together, whatever the arguments, than for them to break apart. Divorced parents often justify themselves by saying that it is better for the children that they part, since their children would otherwise witness strife. But the children of divorced parents wish their parents had stayed together, and feel deeply guilty for what their parents have done. As we will see, overhearing quarrels, or violent arguments, is a terrible experience. But the breaking down of a stable structure of relationships, however difficult they might be, is often worse. This is from the point of view of children, their own insights, and not the result of causal statistics.

The dysfunctioning of the home, from the experience of the young offenders, is a major factor in what happens to them, whether they are aware of it or not. All have experienced dislocations, either physical or mental. They have observed, with all their early natural insight into human relationships, the falling apart, the deceptions and the self-indulgences.

> When he was with me mum, like when we were only young, me and me brother, only young, he was always out, me dad was always out, with other women, but me mum didn't know, but when she found out, she always give him another chance and another chance.
>
> (male, 21)

Divorce, to which this leads, is just the final display of a breakdown in a relationship, whether fought against on one side or not. Even when he was 'only young' he had a sense that their dad was always out; but he also witnessed the attempts at reconciliation. That sense that his father was 'on the move all the time, can't settle down with one person' was with him from the start. Here there was no hint of actual, official, divorce. But of dislocation, of a sense of a lack of mutual connection, there can be no doubt. This, closely observed, is of great significance in itself. But the connection between this behaviour and divorce is also clear.

That there is a connection between crime and single-parent families is conceded even amongst those who have no wish to strike a moral stance.[2] But the connection is a far more subtle one. There are consequences of many kinds for children of divorced parents. Whilst one must have doubts about taking a small proportion of the longitudinal records of the large cohort of the National Child Development Study which was started in 1958 as a representative sample, certain statistical findings are no surprise.[3] The children of divorced parents are likely to have lower qualifications, are likely to have more difficult relationships, are more likely to become single parents and are more likely to suffer divorce themselves. But these results are to do with difficulties, with the psychological effects of divorce. They are not a simple conclusion that divorce leads to crime. Indeed, whilst the relative risk of emotional disorders in the aftermath of divorce is strong, the long-term negative impact is moderate.[4]

On the surface, divorce is a simple quantifiable variable. Under the surface what it represents, the breakdown of what was meant to be a stable and permanent relationship, is far more complex. Divorce can be 'amicable' or fought every inch. It can be agreed, or the sudden decision of one party. It can be the result of internal battles or the intervention of an outside agency. What divorce represents is more important than the statistical fact in itself. There are, from the children's points of view, so many different ways of coping, let alone the different ways in which their parents act.[5] The question, therefore, of what leads to most stress – divorce or parental fighting – is left hanging. In a sense this is rightly so, since the underlying, the prevailing and the consistent factors do not beg the question but bypass it. It is not just a matter of different types of observed behaviour but different kinds of internal reaction. What we witness, in exploring the mind-sets of those who have been palpably damaged by their experiences, are other consistencies that probe and analyse the phenomena of their lives at a completely different level.

The circumstances in which young people are brought up are a vital influence on what happens in the rest of their lives. This is a truism. But there are two kinds of influence. Circumstances can be interpreted, as in the literature of criminology, as general factors such as poverty, or divorce. But the real circumstances of upbringing lie below the surface. They consist of relationships, of observations, of forming an attitude to other people which is the result of reactions to experience.

Thus the effects of divorce can be profound and it is no surprise that there is a correlation between divorce and crime. The same is true of that other statistically recognized factor behind criminality, the example given by parents who break the law. It is no surprise that the young people should be affected by what their parents do, and that they find it far easier to emulate criminality than to react against it.

A minority of young offenders revealed, almost casually, that their fathers or brothers were in prison, either at the time or in the past. Like absent fathers, that was just a fact of life. They did not suggest that they wanted merely to follow in their mentors' criminal footsteps. On the contrary, there is both a strong sense that they despise those in prison – including themselves – and that the influences that led them to criminality were far deeper and more complex. And yet, as in the general concept of 'community' and peer pressure, their families had sometimes been disrupted by absences forced by prison sentences.

> Brother's just got out, just out of jail, and me two brothers, don't know
> what they're doing.
>
> (male, 16)

The important point is the ignorance of what exactly is going on. Clearly, from inside prison, it is impossible to know immediately and closely all the information about jobs and circumstances that fuel family conversations, but it is clear that spells in prison, never knowing exactly how long they will last, provide not only a disruption to routine, but ignorance about people. Prison disrupts normal life and any steady continuity. Those who mentioned that members of their family were in prison did so as if that were the significant fact in itself – not the crime or lifestyle that led up to it. About their own actions, which led to their sentence, they were quite open. But what mattered in their earlier lives was the absences, the dislocation.

The absence of a father, going to prison 'quite a lot', affects children, and affects them even when they are themselves in prison.

> Well, he's only just come out of jail. I think he's learned his lesson now. It
> does do me head in when I know he's in jail, and I can't really say much,
> but he says he's not going back inside again.
>
> (male, 17)

The problem is that he knows it is easy, from inside prison, to vow never to go inside again. As the young offenders all consistently declare, the intention not to re-offend is often overcome by the temptations and the influences of their peers and by their own acknowledged weakness. The hope nevertheless remains that 'he's learned his lesson now'; and this is for a man who has been in prison several times. The underlying desire is for him not to be in jail rather than not to offend. 'It does do me head in' summarizes the feelings that all the young offenders have about these enforced absences. The sad fact is that his dad is likely to return to his old ways, involving an insurance scam.

> He's not inside, that'll be alright, 'cos it's good money. It's not illegal what he does, but it's not legal if you know what I mean?
>
> > (ibid)

This possibility of continuing reoffending is recognized by the son. Vows have been made before so that they cannot be trusted.

> He keeps saying I won't come back, every time he get out he says, I promise I won't go back there and then the next thing he's back inside and so I don't know.
>
> > (ibid)

Spells in prison are just one form of dislocation and disruption. Instead of a nuclear family, with fixed relations, there are people coming and going, disappearing and returning. Relationships are often complex.

> Then there's me brother, he's just turned nineteen and there's me younger brother and he's seventeen, but he's a stepbrother as well, B, he's in prison as well.
>
> > (female, 20)

Whilst some of these young offenders are the only ones in their families to be sent to prison, others are accustomed to it almost as part of life. The crucial matter is that sense of impermanence, of disruption to normal relationships whether with parents or siblings.

> My dad's been to prison as well you see. And, like I can remember sometimes coming home, like he wasn't there, and like I wouldn't remember him for ages and ages and he'd just turn up.
>
> > (male, 20)

In this case, the constant absences and reappearances led ultimately to divorce, but by that time the son had been affected by not 'remembering' his dad. It was impossible for him to know where he was in relation to his parents. At one point on coming home the dad would simply 'not be there' without proper explanation and then he'd 'just turn up'.

The common factor in all the young offenders' early lives is the experience of dislocation. This can be both physical and mental. Of physical dislocation there are many signs: moving from house to house, into and out of foster homes, staying with aunts and uncles and seeing new people come and go, and entering into temporary relationships with the mother or father. These types of disruption are a form of deprivation. They inhibit the forming of strong relationships and they are also linked to poverty, the inability to have a steady income or to cope. Whilst the link between poverty and crime is not a complete or firm one, the link between family poverty and the cognitive development and behaviour of children is a powerful one.[6] This reinforces the notion that it is the effects of poverty on human behaviour and relationships that matter. Disrupted homes, constant moving and living in council homes are all signs of a lack of steady income. Poverty deprives children of educational resources but it also has a psychologically damaging effect on parents. It should be noted that child poverty is higher in the United States than it was two decades ago.[7]

Instability in the home

The absence of possessions is linked to the absence of permanence. The young offenders are all accustomed to a lack of stability in their lives. This lack of firm roots can be for all kinds of reasons, and does not necessarily entail moving from place to place, although for one reason or another many have done so. There are those who have been taken into care.

> 'cos I went to a children's home, then I went back home for a bit, to try to see if it worked, then I went back into the children's home voluntarily, my mum put me into care.
>
> (female, 21)

The need to be put into care speaks for itself but there is also a strong sense of the experimental. There is no sense of ontological security in the home. These young people remember witnessing and observing their parents' behaviour so that at a psychological as well as physical level there is no permanence.

> I had a lot of different step dads, 'cos I've been in and out of foster parents and children's homes…
>
> (female, 21)

There are few signs that these young offenders found any lasting place to stay, whether with foster parents or in children's homes. Everything remained temporary, even their own homes.

One effect of divorce is having to choose with whom to live. Often the children find themselves going from one to another parent on an almost experimental basis.

> She didn't put us in foster homes at first, we stayed with her all the way through, and then when me dad got out, she left and then we lived with me dad… and then we all got put in foster homes 'cos she couldn't cope with us and me dad was in jail. So I didn't know where me mum was, I knew me dad was in jail but I didn't know where and then me foster, I mean me step mum couldn't handle it no more through me stress.
>
> (male, 17)

The impermanence of every experience, the sense of rejection because people 'couldn't handle it' or 'couldn't cope with us' gives the strong impression of constant rejection, even if not intended. The whole family experiences a kind of diaspora. One home is forcibly interrupted by a prison sentence. And he did not even know where either of his parents were. Insecurity abounds.

The fact that parents or foster parents cannot cope with them is a result of young people having become difficult to cope with, itself a result of earlier upbringing. When normal relationships, in home or school, break down it affects all involved. The sense of being rejected is reflected in the desire to reject. Being 'chucked out' and choosing to go are closely related.

> I went to live with me aunty first. I was there for about a year, till I was about 11, and I was with me mum then till I was about 13, 14, and, er, obviously me dad, 'cos I was getting into trouble with the police and me mum had enough of the police coming round, searching the house and that, she didn't like that and, er, she didn't kick me out, I went of me own accord, just said, Oh I'll go and live with me dad, 'cos I could see she was pretty stressed out.
>
> (male, 19)

The temporary nature of different homes gives the young people a sense that they can live anywhere, that they can go where they please. The rejection of social discipline is strongly nurtured by such experiences. If he had not chosen to go would he have been 'kicked out'? A peripatetic style of living has already been formed, long before it is joined by yet another form of temporary residence, the prison.

There are also those who after the experience of moving from place to place are actually 'chucked out' for one reason or another.

> Her boyfriend didn't want me to stay there so she chucked me out. Well, she didn't chuck me out, I had to go back home and live with my mum. We've moved into six houses, moving from house to house. Got me mum chucked out of the last one, 'cos me mates kept climbing up the balcony and knocking on me window and that… I'd stay on the run for about two weeks or summat…
>
> (female, 16)

Being 'chucked out', thrown onto the streets, is a final, physical, rejection. But being 'on the run' is essentially an extension of the sense of the temporary where she does not really know where she is supposed to be located. There is not even a clarity of who is responsible, with her boyfriend's parents matching the volatility of relationships of her own. Those who are 'chucked out' normally find an alternative place to stay, but there are exceptions of enforced homelessness.[8]

> 'cos I was my Daddy's little girl and he left to go with someone four years older than me and I was only 12 at the time. She was 16 and I couldn't handle that... and then I beat her up really badly and me dad told me he didn't want anything to do with me. She was saying, oh you don't need your mum no more I'm your new mum and that just made me head go and I couldn't stop hitting her. I really just wanted to get her out of all our lives so me mum and dad could get back together, and when me dad come back and he seen the state of her, he just like chucked me out... I mean I was only 12, I was in the middle of Derby, didn't know where I was, and he told me to get out and he says he don't want nothing else to do with me.
>
> (female, 19)

This is a case of a violent reaction against the parents splitting up. She sees her mother crying herself to sleep, not eating and making herself ill. She believes that she can intervene, can put things right. Having her own mother's place questioned by a girl not much older than her is the final straw. But despite being 'Daddy's little girl', she has also in the past witnessed his physical assaults on her mother and has hit him in her defence. This final explosion is not sudden but arises out of a context of violent gestures. Being 'chucked out' is the final culmination. But in the background is the pervasive sense of insecurity, of the father going off with other women, being made redundant, spending money on girl-friends, and only coming home on a short-term basis. She is not just made home-less but has to adapt to that as a way of life, which in her case is finding people to stay with where she can.

The effects of isolation

The sense of displacement and the strong feeling that there is no real permanent and solid home as a centre does not consist only in moving from place to place. Even what should be the focal point of family life can appear like a temporary residence, a place that people use almost like a guest house.

> Me mum used to be at work, me dad, me brothers, sisters, they all used to
> be at work, so there was just me, and that was it.
>
> (male, 18)

This is the first hint of the absence of relationships, a theme to which we will be returning later, but it indicates the emptiness of the home, the sense of isolation and loneliness. The place where they live can become nothing more than a meeting place, less a focal point of familiarity and community than a convenient place that is secondary to what is perceived as their main interest. From this perspective the whole family's focus is work. 'Just me' has not just the ring of physical isolation. It is from that kind of emptiness that young people 'run away'. At one level being alone in the house has its temporary advantage. There is the questionable freedom of being able to do as one likes. For truants the empty house is an indulgent refuge.

> Me mum was at work as well sometimes in the day so me mates would
> come to my house.
>
> (male, 19)

But this too is the first hint of a greater sense of dislocation: laissez-faire.

The young offenders who are reporting their early experiences give clear indications of feeling both beleaguered by events and insecure. It is as if they felt that they were in a kind of war zone, with a mixture of separation and violence, sudden movements from one place to another and a sense of impermanence and threat.[9] At one level such a sense of dislocation and disequilibrium stems from obvious environmental facts, like poverty. At another it derives from more complex and more personal problems like quarrelling in the family. When an early study of delinquents and non-delinquents was re-analysed it was found that the connection between poverty and the likelihood of juvenile delinquency was mediated by the way in which the family processes of social control and order were inhibited.[10] The physical circumstances, as such, have psychological consequences, and poverty tends to lead to erratic discipline, at times over-harsh and at other times without *any* discipline *at all*. Movement from one place to another, the lack of a sense of home, are symptoms of something deeper. They are exacerbations and extensions of more internal wrongs.

What stays in the minds of children are not just physical but mental dislocations. The sense of impermanence is not only a matter of place but of people. Relationships tend to be complex in their lives, with stepfathers and stepmothers, boyfriends and girlfriends, but there are also hidden secrets, at last revealed, which can make what seems like permanence shattered.

> The night after me mum phoned up to see where he was, he wasn't in, and
> he phoned her the night after, on the Monday, told her he was goin' with

someone else, so me mum was crying her eyes out, she told me he wasn't me proper dad, so I had that on me mind as well. After all the years growing up with him and that, what was it, 11 years, I'd grown up with him for 11 years and just found out and she was angry so she had to tell me. It would come out someday, but I'm glad it came out then, when I was younger. I tell you now… Erm, found out he wasn't me proper dad, I'd never seen me dad at all, them things running through me mind…

(male, 21)

This is not just one shock, of seeing a parent abandoned for someone else, but the deeper one that throws everything into doubt, about personal identity, relationships and self-knowledge. The mother 'cries her eyes out' but reveals that things have not been what they seemed. He sees it is her anger that pushes her to the revelation rather than concern for him. Truth is the result of hatred rather than love. He realizes that such a changed view of relationships will affect him the more deeply: 'them things running through me mind'. Trying to concentrate on school at the same time proves to be an impossibility. Again, the disturbances of the home have a direct impact on performance in school: not socio–economic circumstance as such, but the inner realities of relationships at home.[11]

These young people find it impossible to be uninvolved. When we look at the bare statistics of the correlations we can easily forget the individual emotional traumas involved. The movement from place to place is not just a physical dismemberment but a personal one. Changes, movements, uncertainties can take place within what appears from the outside to be a secure place. What is witnessed and experienced runs deep and then affects the relationships with others. When these people are 'chucked out' it is because they have become difficult to cope with. This is not surprising given the anger that has been building up inside them. The problem is that the anger can be manipulated, used by one parent against another. The trauma is there and in certain circumstances, out of control. All families have difficulties, and all children internalize what they see is happening. But there is a distinction to be made between those 'happy' families who try to rationalize what is happening and who try to communicate and those who follow the road towards internal isolation and resentment. It is in these circumstances that we find both that sense of generalized anger, and a deep-seated rejection of parents, not the rejection of adolescence which appears almost universal, but a more profound sense of dislocation.

Me dad he's a psycho anyway, so, like?

(male, 20)

The dislocation of place is matched by the dislocation of relationships. Discovery of earlier relationships by the parents seems almost routine. There is little stability in the various relationships that have been struck up, both in the past and in the present. It is as if the whole field of relationships were seen as a battleground in which anything could happen, or a war in which there could be dire outcomes. They observe their past in all its tenuousness and temporarity.

> Bets all the time, gambles, but he's got a nice house and that... He's got two kids of his own, he's married. That's not by the wife that he's married to now, that's by another one. See, my dad had an affair with my mum... and, er, he was married at the time, but he had an affair with my mum, and me and [sister] was the result.
>
> (female, 21)

In some circumstances it is hard to keep up with what is happening but here, at least, it is clear, even if she ends up in a foster home. But she knows where her father is. The crucial factor is that sense of insecurity at home. Socio-economic status is not significant, in itself. Problems at home are. They directly relate to achievement at school.[12] Those who survive the public system and achieve success are not the result of class, money and inheritance, but that stability that implies no emotional, or physical, dislocations, journeys from one place or understanding to another.

Closely observed parents

Children are close observers of their worlds. They scrutinize the behaviour and the attitudes of those around them.[13] Sometimes what they witness is a clear demonstration of a lapse into some kind of escape or self-indulgence. Their parents can reveal what it is like to be out of tune with the normal reality of social expectations. One clear dislocation in home life is watching their parent or parents unable to cope. In one case this comes from a particular depression.

> Worse for me mum... she's addicted to tablets and that. When me dad left her it got worse. She was only taking them to sleep and that... just getting wrecked and that... she went to this hospital and she come out looking young and you know what I mean she was fresh and that, but then she went... soon as me dad left her she went on 'em again.
>
> (male, 16)

Personal difficulties are paralleled by addiction, rather than one thing simply leading to another. The son has observed his mother closely enough to detect obvious physical change, which demonstrates not only the length of time his mother must have been rehabilitating in hospital but the possibilities of what she could have been, as opposed to what she actually became. Generally she was 'just getting wrecked', the dismissive tone of which shows how little such behaviour, or habit, is respected.

If one mother is addicted to tablets, another is addicted to alcohol.

> She used to like drink a lot, but, she used to drink in the day and that and when I used to go to school… my mum used to just be on the sofa and that, drunk, watching telly or something.
>
> (female, 21)

This habit of drinking was copied by the daughter although she 'doesn't drink that much'. Again there is an example of obvious neglect through the incapacity to play a normal role, including that traditional one of 'cooking the food'. She and her sister had to look after themselves. Such behaviour presents a clear example of dislocation.

The observation, the misery, the self-pity and the self-indulgence of parents leads the children to make objective judgements, to find behaviour despicable or 'weird'.

> My mum had a nervous breakdown when I was about 10… I mean she used to drink a lot… I mean when my mum started first having a nervous breakdown, I mean she didn't used to do nothing. She just used to stay in bed all day and she used to act really weird and that and she used to come up into my bedroom and ask me weird questions and stuff… my mum smokes it as well. She used to smoke it in front of me when I was a kid.
>
> (female, 18)

Children not only are left to their own devices, having to take on the responsibility of looking after themselves, but are given a demonstration of deviant behaviour. The example of drink and drugs is joined by the example of someone 'dropping out'. The model they witness is something to be despised rather than sympathized with; it is 'doing nothing' or acting 'really weird'.

The general example of disturbed and disturbing home life is one of a physical or metaphysical mess. It is not only their own home life that is observed but that of their friends.

> 'cos there were nine in the family, girls and boys and they were all scruffy… she used to be able to buy ale and fags and that, and the home were just a mess. I did try cleaning it once… She used to sit on her ass all the time. Father used to be a taxi driver but I wouldn't get in his taxi 'cos he smelled as bad, smelled right bad of b.o., him.
>
> (female, 20)

Families can demonstrate clearly that vicious circle of not wishing to, and not being able to, cope. It is a sign of carelessness as well as circumstance. The social norms with which households are usually associated, or are expected to consist of, are ignored. Just as the school is a demonstration of a society that functions by a set of agreed behaviours and rules, so, in microcosm, is the home. Cooking, washing, tidying, keeping clean are all part of the function of the home. The 'mess' which is observed is as much metaphorical as physical.

The distinction between the physical manifestations of states of mind and the attitudes that bring them about is a fine one. It is as fine as the distinction between verbal arguing, shouting and physical gestures and actual violence. If home life is for these people marked by neglect, it is also characterized by violence, on a variety of levels. Sometimes it seems that the young offenders almost casually mention what they have seen take place between their parents, and what they have themselves suffered. But the laconic tone covers up the depths of feeling that they have been through. They have seen the ultimate in dislocation of relationships. This explains the correlation between marital conflict and developmental problems.[14] Children witness the extremes of anger and hatred and the inability to communicate. They are also neglected, since the all-consuming passions focus the attention of the parents entirely on each other. The hostility that parents demonstrate towards each other also spills over into hostility towards their children, who feel at once guilty and neglected. They learn to look on their parents' quarrels with a mixture of alarm and distance. The question for them is the extent to which they can alienate themselves from the quarrels, and how they can avoid being caught up in them. They are also learning to break out of a normal relationship. Even if the child is not hit, he or she feels pushed to one side, unimportant and mistreated.

> They was always fighting and stuff, arguing every time I come back, 'cos probably me dad's been out for a drink. He ain't doing nothing, me mum's been in the house all day working and that, me dad just goes out gets drunk, comes back shouting and that, he wants his dinner. It were funny and it weren't. It were funny in a way, they used to fight, 'cos I'd guarantee it wouldn't be me dad who'd win anyway, 'cos me mum always hit him with something, or does something, breaks his nose. My dad just stands there and laughs...
>
> (male, 16)

What is supposedly 'funny' about this to the observer is the fact that it does not follow all the 'norms', which include the man assaulting the woman. Other 'standard' items, if one can use such a term to indicate the shared, all too common traumas of these people's childhoods, are there. There are drink, shouting, instant demands and the almost inevitable outcome in violence. There is also a sense that such behaviour is not just observed but analysed: 'he *just* goes out gets drunk'. Drink is often a trigger for arguments.

They used to always argue anyway, especially at weekends and that. Drink yeah. Both of them I think 'cos they used to go out with each other, used to come back and they'd be arguing over something, some silly things, every weekend.

(male, 19)

This is, to the son, a demonstration of weakness as well as anger. They are led on by drink and argue about 'silly' things.

Violence and its effects

Whilst the young people's observation is acute, it cannot be wholly neutral, even if they wish it were. They are eventually caught up, and often physically caught up, in their parents' arguments.

Dad used to get up and start arguing with me mum and then they'd start fighting in front of me and I'd sort of get brought into it and then Dad used to hit me and then me mum would start and oh god…

(female, 20)

The cause in the daughter's case was the fact that the mum had a boyfriend she used to bring back to the house. So the fighting spreads. On a significant number of occasions the arguments are described as being mutual and fierce. But when it comes to violence it is often the use of superior physical strength of one against the other. It is at this stage that domestic arguing and general emotional violence spills into domestic crime. This violence, the deliberate physical abuse of one person hurting another, nurtures children's general psychopathology.[15] They witness what is not just a criminal act but the most clear demonstration of human beings out of control, unrestrained.

He used to batter my mum and that, and try to strangle my mum and that, he tried to strangle my mum. It's in all my court reports and stuff.

(female, 21)

The laconic addition of the evidence is both a realization of how shocking it was and a shorthand for saying that so much more could be described.

It is possible to detect, beneath the neutral tone, that sense of trauma and its effects in what has been seen. We are still describing what young offenders have *witnessed* before analysing what happened more directly to them.

> I started running away, didn't like it at all. It was just me dad and do you
> know what I mean, just like arguments between me mum, beating me
> mum up, you know what I mean. And 'cos I couldn't take it, I thought,
> don't want to be here… just used to run away… It was, mainly 'cos of me
> dad, beating her up and things…
>
> (male, 20)

On this occasion emotional alienation is accompanied by action. The son 'couldn't
take it'; a sentiment that is echoed by many others, and a feeling that leads to some
kind of outburst. It links to the ways in which the young offenders subsequently
react. What they all witness is the link between disagreements and violence.
Arguing gradually leads to uncontrolled rage.

> Like my mum and dad didn't get on, for ages, just pure fights and argu-
> ments and all that kind of thing and then I just, me and all me sisters and
> that just didn't speak to my dad in the end… because like, it was my mum
> that used to get beat up by my dad. My mum didn't used to beat my dad
> up. And, even when me dad was living with us, he was never there, he was
> always at work…
>
> (male, 20)

Absence, the breaking down of relationships by refusing to talk or ignoring someone, is one side of dislocation. And the other is the far too widespread tendency to
'beat up'.

These young people have been brought up in what can be likened to a
war-zone. They might be the 'innocent' bystanders but in war all people are
involved. The consequences of being brought up in danger, chaos and deprivation
can be severe.[16] It is bad enough witnessing physical abuse, but they are emotionally caught up in it. They are no longer safe or secure. They are dealing with feelings that go beyond the rational, beyond control. But they are often not only
emotionally involved, but also physically. It is difficult for them not to be 'caught
up' in the fighting. But they also become the targets themselves.

> When I was really really young me dad used to batter me and that… I
> mean I can remember back from when I was about four or five, but he just
> used to hit my sister… he used to hit my mum and he tried to strangle my
> mum once and he used to just hit us and that, shove us out of the way and
> he threw me across the room once.
>
> (female, 18)

> Me dad who I thought was me dad, he threw me down the stairs as well…
> He used to beat up me mum and that. That's the way it was.
>
> (male, 21)

Violence is uncontrolled and spreads from one person to the other. If the mother is 'beat up' it is quite likely that the children are also physically attacked. They see anger and loss of control directed against them. They see the distinction and the connection between 'battering' and attempts to strangle the woman to death, just as they see them between quarrelling and violence. 'That's the way it was.'

The signs of deep disturbance and anger are still there as a result of such violence. And there are some who have been even more severely abused.

> 'Cos he sexually abused me and battered me. He beat me up once, chucked me you know against the fire, right, and like I broke one of me arms, both me legs, you know like all the side of me ribs were black, do you know what I mean... he got in trouble for that... she were there when that happened. She couldn't do nowt. He were mad.
>
> 'Cos me step dad used to beat me up, I used to wet me pants, and like when me boyfriend started beating me up, I used to wee, and 'cos in here I've been so worried, I wet the bed the other day. I've never weed in bed for ages.
>
> (female, 21)

Such experiences leave more than physical marks. They present a clear mental picture of the world as a place where some people are out of control, and where normal restraint no longer applies. The place that should be most secure is a place of threat and anger. And this 'battering' is considered to be part of everyday life. The 'mad' stepfather has to do something quite extreme in order to get 'into trouble'. Otherwise the threat of being 'beat up' is constant. All this leads to greater fear and greater anxiety. Children who are abused are even more deeply affected by their parents' quarrelling so that even manifestations of verbal arguments or inter-parental disputes are taken personally.[17]

The question being raised is not just how all these events affect young offenders emotionally, but how they affect the way the young people subsequently react. They have seen dialogue replaced by raw emotion, reason and communication by violence. This is bound to give a raw edge to their outlook on life, and a sense of dislocation and disequilibrium. The home is then a place of profound insecurity. The way that the young offenders have all reacted has included violence in one form or another, as if the acts of one generation were emulated by another. This is not a matter of conscious modelling but a lack of awareness about alternative means of reacting. The strain of emotions can sometimes seem almost unbearable.

> I think the main thing that was really bad when I was younger was that when me dad used to hit me mum, and when like that used to happen I used to tell my uncle and my uncle used to go down and sort it out.

> And then he came round one day and asked her for five hundred I think
> it was and me mum says, I ain't got it and he started really hitting her and
> I just picked up a frying pan that was on the cooker with some oil in it
> and I hit him over the head with that and I got a carving knife to him and
> I told him if he didn't get out and stop coming near us that I was gonna
> kill him.
>
> (female, 19)

The daughter clearly means it. The frustration and the anger have been building
up. When the tension of watching and witnessing at last snaps she becomes the
perpetuator of violence herself. It might be deliberate intervention but it is also
something more. As she goes on to say herself:

> Like if I'd had erm, say me mum had been up all night crying and that and
> I was getting angrier and angrier with me dad and I couldn't see him to
> take it out on him I'd take it out on the first person.
>
> (ibid)

What seems like a matter of stepping in or helping a domestic dispute is a sign of
something deeper. The anger and frustration becomes generalized into other relationships. The behaviour is not just a matter of a particular circumstance but one
that can manifest itself in all kinds of places when the same feelings are triggered.

Confronted by violent emotions it is hard to remain calm or neutral. The volatile emotions of teenage daughters are often the result of abuse by parents. It is the
result of the pain of personal feelings, of taking things personally. The young people feel guilty. They feel that all violence is somehow directed against them and
that the only way to cope is to run away or fight back. Violence breeds violence.
Once there is a beginning, there seems no end of it. Violence is erratic and affects
many more than those against whom it is intended. What is absorbed at one age
manifests itself at another. All the tensions and anger displayed in other people, let
alone relations, are taken personally. If adults suffer from post-traumatic distress
syndrome, then children do so the more. And it takes much less of an extreme to
trigger this off. The distinction between a level of violence that gets someone 'into
trouble' and the daily 'battering' might be an important one from the point of view
of the law, but it is all part of the same seam of discontent, dislocation and insecurity felt by those who have to undergo the experience of pathologically
misfunctioning human beings.

These young offenders have certain experiences in common, even on the surface. The pattern that binds them together goes far deeper, but even in terms of
particular characteristics there is a consistency and even repetitiveness to their
experience that coincides with the statistics of crime. Some kind of dislocation and
disruption in the reliability of a steady life in the home, whether through divorce or

violent argument, has taken place. This disequilibrium is expressed either in physical terms, moving from place to place, or mental ones, with successions of step-parents or 'friends'. There are patterns of criminality and there are various forms of addiction to other things than people, until the responsible parent or the home no longer works as a safe haven. The most powerful manifestation of the juxtaposition of individual traumas and the structures of a more solid and permanent society is violence. A society at peace and in harmony has many levels. A society at war is full of the sense of threat. Violence of a general kind can invite or provide a sense of unity in small groups. But here we see a kind of 'implosion'; the general violence concentrated in the nucleus of the home. The question then is how these dysfunctional adults not only cope with their own children but with that world to which their children are still joined – the social organization of the school.

References

1. Quillam, S (1998) *Stop Arguing, Start Talking*, Relate, London
2. Dennis, N (1993) *Rising Crime and the Dismembered Family*, IEA Health and Welfare Unit, London
3. Kiernan, K (1997) Becoming a young parent: a longitudinal study of associated factors, *British Journal of Sociology*, **48** (3), pp 406–28
4. Chase-Lansdale, L, Cherlin, A and Kiernan, K (1995) The long-term effects of parental divorce on the mental health of young adults: a developmental perspective, *Child Development*, **66** (6), pp 1614–34
5. Sandler, I, Tein, J-Y and West, S (1994) Coping, stress and the psychological systems of children of divorce: a cross-sectional and longitudinal study, *Child Development*, **65** (6), pp 1744–63
6. Duncan, G, Brooks-Dunn, J and Klebanov, P (1994) Economic deprivation and early childhood development, *Child Development*, **65** (2), pp 296–318
7. Ibid
8. Research carried out for Kirklees MBC.
9. cf Macksond, M and Aber, J (1996) The war experiences and psychosocial development of children in Lebanon, *Child Development*, **67** (1), pp 70–88
10. Sampson, R and Laub, J (1994) Urban poverty and the family context of delinquency: a new look at structure and process in a classic study, *Child Development*, **65** (2), pp 523–40
11. Ibid
12. de Jong, P (1993) The relationship between students' behaviour at home and attention and achievement in elementary school, *British Journal of Educational Psychology*, **63** (2), pp 201–13
13. Dunn, J (1988) *The Beginnings of Social Understanding*, Basil Blackwell, Oxford
14. Harold, G and Conger, R (1997) Marital conflict and adolescent distress: the role of adolescent awareness, *Child Development*, **68** (2), pp 333–50
15. McCloskey, L, Figueredo, A and Koss, M (1995) The effects of systemic family violence on children's mental health, *Child Development*, **66** (5), pp 1239–61

16. Ladd, G and Cairns, E (1996) Children: ethnic and political violence, *Child Development*, **67** (1), pp 14–18, introducing studies on the effects of ethnic and political violence
17. Hennessy, K, Rabideau, G, Cicchetti, D and Cummings, E (1994) Responses of physically abused and non-abused children to different forms of inter-adult anger, *Child Development*, **65** (3), pp 815–28

4

Separate neighbourhoods: parents' attitudes to schools

Introduction

Parents' attitudes towards schools is strongly influenced by their memories of their own experience, and in all parents a certain amount of awe or suspicion remains. There have been many attempts since the 1970s to involve parents more closely in schools, sometimes as partners and sometimes as 'policemen', dictating through governing boards and formal accountability meetings what schools should do.[1] Parents have been welcomed in, to help with tasks such as the teaching of cooking, listening to reading or to talk to the teachers. They have also been encouraged through Education Acts to use their formal powers more heavily. Despite this, despite the good intentions of Home–School coordinator systems or Parent Advice centres, comparatively little progress has been made in schools' relationships with parents.[2] There is still a pervasive uneasiness in the relationships between parents and schools. Indeed, this sense of unease grows with every increase in formality. There is an irony here. The more that the government legislates for more parental power, the less parents feel involved in school.[3] The previous informality and welcome are in marked contrast to those meetings where the governors are formally brought to account, meetings which very few parents attend.[4] Teachers appear to be too busy to have time to talk to parents and the school reports, made more standardized and formal, no longer give the information that parents seek.

If the research on parents' attitudes towards schools and the education system generally reveals a sense of suspicion, of not being closely involved, despite the good intentions of teachers, then it is no surprise that the parents of pupils who play truant, or who exhibit behaviour problems and who are difficult to deal with, will demonstrate suspicion in abundance. Whilst a school acts *in loco parentis* and is assumed to teach social and moral awareness as well as academic knowledge and skills, it also looks to parents for support. When things go wrong the parents are easily blamed.

The school represents for many pupils and parents their first real relationship with the formalities of the state system. Parents who come from economically deprived backgrounds are found to have the greatest sense of awe at, and alienation from, schools. Whilst individual teachers are praised and their professionalism admired, there is still a widespread sense of insecurity with the school as a *system*. Whilst the obvious barriers to parents have to be taken away, like notices that say 'No parents beyond this point', both physical barriers and mental barriers remain. Since the Dunblane massacre schools lock their doors. Schools appear formal. The moment there are difficulties with pupils this sense of formality is strengthened.

The relationship between problem behaviour at home and achievement in schools is a close one, and much more significant than socio-economic status.[5] It is often assumed that it is the working-class parents, lacking confidence and not giving their children the necessary academic starting points that they need, who are the 'culprits'. Whilst there is some correlation, it is, as has been observed before, not as significant as the types of behaviour and language employed. A positive and secure home background is found to have a substantial positive relationship with attention at school. Some children are clearly more focused on their work than others, see or accept the purpose of schooling and strive both to please the teachers and to do their best. Disturbance at home has an effect on the work in school. Parents' positive attitudes to school and work also help. With the vast majority of parents this is the case.[6] They wish to support what goes on and view the education of their children as very important.

Attitudes to school

There are, however, exceptions. Whether it comes about from the memories of their own days in school, or disillusion with their own lack of academic success, or whether it comes from a sense of confrontation with authority, there are some parents who are openly hostile to schools. These attitudes are quickly and easily picked up by their children:

> Dad... he's just mad. He didn't want me to go to school in the first place. Said it was a waste of time. He'd teach me anything I didn't know. Taught me how to fight. That's about it. And like me Mum's easy going, she just like, she didn't mind me staying off.
> ... In another way he was wrong wasn't he? Think it was just 'cos he like didn't like school and that. Just rubbed it off on me.
>
> (male, 20)

With hindsight, of course, the absurdity of the father's point of view is clear. As happens so often, what appears to be attractive at the time is seen later in a more realistic light. Being taught how to fight is hardly a substitute for education. But the young man is dismissive of both parents, not just the 'mad' father. The mother is, in a sense, seen as equally culpable if not as obviously so, since she is so 'easy going' as not even to mind whether her son went to school or not. But whatever the subsequent analysis of their views, there is no doubt that they 'rubbed off' on the son.

Any parental equivocation about school, whatever the reason, affects their children. A dislike of school and a suspicion about its relevance create an oblique view of society and its organizations. If the State is not to be taken too seriously, and if the community has no clear part to play in the official way in which society operates, then all kinds of authority, both collective and personal, will be questioned. Whether it derives from memories or from more recent antagonism, that rift between the close, unstructured, informal and complex neighbourhood, and the relationships with peers, siblings and parents is set up against the more formal mechanisms of social organization which give access to the wider world of opportunity. There are all kinds of reasons for disliking school, including a suspicion of the particular one to which a child is sent.

> 'Cos I had time off school. Me dad gave me some money, I went up town shopping. They didn't want me to go to that school. Me mum went to see the Headmaster but me mum didn't know sort of what to do, do you know what I mean? She was sort of confused but she says if it keeps on our M's not coming to this school again.
>
> (female, 21)

Problems of bullying and tale-telling – a problem with this school – need to be addressed and if the parents perceive what is happening, and if they ascertain that the school is not dealing with the problems, then it is to be assumed that they have a right to communicate their concerns to the school authorities. But here we have a typical difficulty. There is an implicit acceptance that the child will be off school – she is given money and no doubt a sense of understanding that she has good cause not to be at school – and therefore a confusion about how to approach the matter. The school is to be blamed but is the parent in the position to do so? For some parents, particularly those who have no confidence in their own intellectual abilities, schools are not just awe-inspiring but positively off-putting. This is the case even when a school makes a conscious and concerted effort to be welcoming. When there is trouble at the heart of the dialogue there could well be both a subconscious suspicion on the one side and a sense of deep-seated alienation on the other. What is clear is that the mother feels 'confused', out of touch with the way in which she should approach the matter. That this is so is clear to her daughter.

Children are acute observers of people and pick up attitudes and points of view, very fast.[7] Soon they can take some over as if they were their own.

> It's amazing what you can learn without going to school. I didn't really need school 'cos everything I wanted to learn, I learned through other types of ways, like the milk round... things like that were running through me mind, they put me off as well...
>
> (male, 21)

What is putting this person off school is the example of a brother doing very well for himself by eschewing the normal education system and finding it easy to make money nefariously. He conveys a sense that the parents' concern for his education is more token than real, and that they believe that there is little direct connection between the conformity of schooling and success in life, at least at the financial level. But not going to school is given here as a personal decision. It might be the outcome of many subtle influences but it demonstrates the way in which some – even if they are only in a minority – pupils approach school, with suspicion and a lack of any real belief in the efficacy of education. In the end the sense of personal rather than parental disenfranchisement becomes profound.

> My mum can shout and shout at me all she wants, can't she but at the end of the day it's down to me whether I go to school or not. I can go out the door and just ignore her, which is what I used to do when I was young. My mum can't really do much can she...
>
> (male, 20)

Parents can be seen as helpless. Once a pupil (or a child) senses the fact that he or she *doesn't* need to follow convention, or to conform to other people's expectations and desires, the moral fabric or glue that holds society together, particularly in the earlier years, is lost. The usual habit of response to authoritative commands is obedience. They are seen as necessary and unquestioned. But when there is a realization that it is no longer an automatic requirement to follow rules, then all kinds of authority are placed in doubt. In the case cited, that sense of personal liberation and freedom, and the ability to go one's own way are so strong that they are presented with the immediacy of the present tense. But the son goes on to reflect on the fact that much of the advice that he then rejected was made the wiser through the advantage of hindsight:

> Like when I was at school people used to say to me, my mum used to say, school's the best day of your life. You don't know. I'd love to go back and all that, and I used to think 'Nah' but now I know it's true and that. My kids will go to school.
>
> (ibid)

One problem in the education system is that the benefits of the purpose of schools are so rarely discussed.[8] Instead there are the phrases of what seem all too conventional wisdom, like the idea that school is the 'best time', or in the son's case 'day', of your life. That assertion is not a strong reality to those who are suffering at school from academic or peer pressure, from a sense of normlessness that derives from a sense of personal failure and inadequacy, or from a sense of undermining that easily turns to anger. Those studies of young people who are unemployed or deemed in any sense to be 'failures' all reveal their sense that the purpose and meaning of school were never explained to them.[9]

Parents, schools and truancy

Clearly, all who play truant or who dislike school receive a significant amount of cajoling. They are told they ought to, or must, like or appreciate school. They are told in general terms that attendance is what is expected of them. But the rift between the rhetoric and the perceived reality can be wide. Indeed, parental insistence can be interpreted as part of the nebulous complicity of authoritarianism against which these young people react. The problem with these attempts, often belated, to impose commands is that they can be seen as a challenge, a battle of wills, a confrontation rather than an explanation or joint endeavour. And, when challenged, it can be seen as empty rhetoric:

> My parents used to always say 'go to school, go to school' and I used to run away. To me it used to seem like they'd try to make me go to school but they used to say 'oh school's good for you, you should go, you should learn something, it'll be good in the future for you' and all this and I used to think, 'no, no, sack it' you know what I mean, it's not my kind of thing.
> But you realize, don't you, afterwards.
>
> (male, 20)

It is at the moment that a command needs insisting upon or becomes an imposition that the implicit agreements, the endorsements, the sharing of behaviour and assumptions all seem to fail. The rhetoric has been heard too often and is no longer respected. It begins to sound like the kinds of things that teachers might say; once they are challenged rather than accepted, they sound like a kind of plea rather than the agreed acceptance of a shared responsibility. All authority demands compliance, or the perceived wisdom of endorsement. Once it is even scrutinized or questioned, let alone challenged, it becomes undermined.

In the typology of parenting, which includes the two extremes of laissez-faire or indifference and the almost bullying insistence of obedience – in Bettelheim's phrase, the cajolery of 'come on' – the over-authoritarian parent is, in fact, not a successful or extreme dictator, but more like an empty bully.[10] The phrases can sound insistent. 'You "ought" to go to school', 'It's "good" for you', 'It's for your "future"' are the kind that so easily provoke reaction. Trying to 'make' someone do something, like going to school, merely hardens their will, once it comes to that sense of confrontation, of alternative actions. The phrases continue but the will, and the authority that derives from agreement, is no longer there.

The main sanction used against recalcitrant pupils is punishment. It is both ironic and telling that those parents who think they are best emulating the stance of official bodies – 'do this or else' – impose punishment. They place themselves on the same level as an alienating official position. It is as if they felt that the louder they shouted the more they were on the side of authority. Whilst not being openly *against* the school system, as a representative of social organization, they strike up an attitude that is supposed to emulate it, an attitude seen as dependent on sanctions, or punishment, threat and retribution.

> 'cos then you get stress of your mum and dad then for getting detentions. They used to shout a bit and then make me stay in for the night or depending on what I'd done at school. Say I got into bad trouble at school, that was depending on how long I was grounded for as well, was getting punished at school.
>
> (female, 19)

The inflexible aspect of school as a disciplined, even harsh enforcer of rules is thus reflected in the home. Instead of an alternative regime recalcitrant pupils find themselves doubly attacked as if more sanctions could make all the difference, despite the fact that the previous punishments have failed to have an effect. The result of this harsh authoritarian attitude in this case was that the girl became too frightened to go to either school or home. She would play truant and then pretend she had been to school.

This is the opposite extreme from laissez-faire, that indifference whether through self-absorption or not, towards the behaviour and personality of children. Such authoritarianism does not necessarily show any greater or closer concern. Being 'shouted at' does not create the conditions for dialogue. It suggests more of a reinforcement of the school as responsible for imposing discipline. These are the kinds of parents who encourage schools to exert even harsher punishments on their offspring as if the school were almost wholly responsible for teaching social and moral values.[11]

Such heavy-handed impositions of discipline do not have the desired effect.

Just got a good hiding and grounded for a few weeks. But whatever they said just went in one ear and out through the other 'cos you just think it's a big laugh in school, most people do anyway.

(male, 16)

Being shouted at, or 'grounded', is not perceived to be an effective sanction. Instead it creates another barrier, an impersonal force which appears alien to the pupil and which is not taken seriously. There is a dismissive tone to the punishments and threats of punishment and being 'grounded'. In the same way, using home as a prison is unlikely to have any real effect. The usual way that children find of avoiding the sanctions of home repeating those of the school is simply to cover up what's happening. One girl simply stays away from both school and home, until she is so behind with her work she can hardly re-enter the system. What parents do not know they cannot punish.

Like I know if I didn't turn up for school, at junior school, me mum and dad and everything would be going mad. Like they never seemed to find out at secondary school; only twice I think I can remember, something like that. Shout at me or something.

(male, 17)

The extreme of authoritarianism is never seen to work. It is as alienating as indifference. Being shouted at, seeing the parents go 'mad', does not in itself change anything. Threats are seen to be empty, and avoidance the easiest of strategies. This includes the inner avoidance of families, as if the parents were in a coalition *against* the child rather than in a partnership with them.[12] When parental agreement is facilitated by general family problem solving, it has very different effects than when parents present themselves as some kind of enforcer of discipline *against* their children. Parents then become a zone of conflict, like the school, a force to react against.

Parental responsibility and schools

There are, then, different ways in which parents can be out of tune with the school, either by the conflict of different interests or through the conflict of ostensible reinforcement, bolstering the sense of estrangement from school. But parents can also themselves come into conflict with schools. Schools are a social system, representing the State. They have their rules and sanctions and expect and demand support from parents. They also see the parents as responsible for their children's behaviour. When there is difficulty the parents as well as the pupil find themselves up against the authority of the school. They can feel not only 'confused' but actually humiliated, and in turn feel themselves to be psychologically excluded from the school system and social services.

> Me mum was working in the school itself and she was getting loads of hassle over me. She was only a cleaner in school. But every time she used to go home at night she used to get dragged in the office and told about me, and she just got onto me when I got home and I just couldn't stop what I was doing. It was just like a habit. They didn't like it, no they hated it, always having to go into the office to see about me.
>
> (male, 18)

School has many aspects; it is a social centre for all kinds of relationships and a place for different levels of learning. It is also an 'office'. It represents officialdom, where not only the pupils but their parents are spoken to. That sense, at best of awe, at worst of exclusion, is strongly evoked by all the opportunities to enforce discipline. The sense of wrongdoing as a 'habit' is reflected in the constant repetitions of meetings in the office, of being 'dragged in' and hassled. Then the same tone of being 'got onto' in school would be repeated at home, to little effect.

Visits to the 'office', facing a senior teacher or the head over difficulties over their own children, are always dreaded by parents, when they are not avoided. Such visits can reinforce the sense of exclusion in children through the experience of the parents. Schools do not always treat the parents as equal partners.

> And they just used to turn round and say 'tough, you're suspended' and me parents would go up and me parents got sick of going up so they said 'well, we'll go up when we're good and ready...
>
> And like when she did go up teacher slammed his hand on the table and treated her like a kid, so she stood up and give him a mouthful, started accusing him of this, that and the other and I never went back to school then.
>
> (female, 20)

There are a number of cases where the pupils reflect upon their parents' humiliation. The way in which pupils are confronted by disciplinary measures and anger, and emotion hardened into and supported by official sanctions, is emulated in the similar treatment of their parents. The parents learn to resent the commands of the school and react against them as if they wanted to show some defiance against the law. Non-attendance at school is usually the first act of rebellion against the legal system. It is often the first confrontation with those in authority. A natural and widespread suspicion of formal officialdom is then deepened by the sense of being treated 'like a kid'. It does not take much to provoke an angry rejection.

The rejection of school comes out of a particular context. It is, like exclusions, the final act in a series of incidents. It does not arise suddenly. There will already have been a suspicion of school or even some show of hostility. In this case 'never' going back to school is treated not with shock but tacit approval.

> Dad just stood there and laughed. He had a bet with me. He says if you walk to school now, he says, without your mum going up, or me, he says, I'll buy you 20 fags. He says that's if you can't get in. He says if you can get in you owe me 20 fags. They wouldn't let me in. I sat there in the classroom and they said 'what you doing back? Your parents haven't been up'.
>
> (ibid)

There are also features here of a number of familiar characteristics, like the daughter deceiving her parents into thinking that she is in school when in fact she catches a bus and goes 'down town shoplifting'. She gets 'slapped' when her mother hears what she has been doing. She stays in bed as long as she can rather than go to school. But the most important culmination of all these events is the sense of being rejected. The school might have good reasons for not wanting her. Nevertheless it signals that the formal requirements of a social organization, like attendance and behaviour, have not been met, so that there is no longer a place for her. Whatever the school required of the parents, who also feel a mixture of humiliation and cynicism, the pupil sees herself as being placed outside the boundaries of 'normal' law-abiding society.

Truancy and the social services

Getting into trouble at school evokes feelings of rejection. The sense of not fitting into a social system, of preferring alternatives, is strong. There is also a strong sense in these accounts that the social system wants them to be excluded. From the point of view of the school the rejection of an unruly or difficult pupil is a relief. For the individual teacher the truancy or illness of a particularly troublesome child is a palpable psychological boost – detected by the pupils even if the teacher reveals it inadvertently. For the head teacher and senior staff the saving of time in having to deal with problems is immense. But once exclusion takes place the larger social system of welfare officers is brought to bear. School, and exclusion from school, is no longer a microcosm of society with its peculiar ambience and rules. It becomes, through the involvement of the larger social services, a part of larger society. What is clear from these accounts is not only the sense of rejection but a strong feeling that people no longer care for the child. The teachers are seen to be relieved. The social services appear to be indifferent.

> Social services was gonna send me to a boarding school but they must have forgot about it.
>
> (female, 16)

There are signs of attempts to follow up and deal with difficult cases. But from the point of view of the young offenders these attempts are badly managed, infrequent and inefficient. Of course, as the young people themselves say, it is difficult to enforce attendance. One can see the difficulties of handling such cases. But there is a strong sense that they are not wanted, and that only cursory attempts will be made to help them, or bring them back into the social system. There is a general sign of social exclusion.

> A teacher that comes to your house every morning and that, a home tutor. I had it a few times and that were it, 'cos a couple of times I weren't in so she just didn't bother coming again.
>   Me dad even 'phoned up to see if I could come back. They says we don't want you back and slammed the phone down. Well, they didn't even bother trying 'cos I mean it's up to them to sort out another school for you, if they're gonna kick you out... but all the rest of the schools refused 'cos they're all dead posh as well and they'd put a bad report in for me, so all the rest of 'em said no.
>
> (male, 16)

Both the parent and the son are rejected. The reputation spreads. But the prevailing sense is that the educational service as a whole 'didn't even bother trying'. It is this sense of indifference that is at the heart of their disaffection.

Even attempts to coax pupils back to school are interpreted as being half-hearted.

> The teacher come from school and talked to me mum like and I was upstairs like listening to me music, mum shouted me and just turned music up like, just couldn't be bothered to go there and talk to 'em... teachers sent me a letter through the post saying that if you promise not to smack any more teachers or mouth out any more staff, or kick any more pupils in, I'll give you one more chance at school...
>
> (male, 16)

But this is never followed up. The visit and the letter are not pursued by further action. One can see why there should be some reluctance in making a great effort to try to re-engage the pupil. As he himself puts it, there have been many incidents of 'smacking' and 'mouthing out' teachers as well as kicking fellow pupils. 'Not being bothered' is understandable, especially when it is shared by the parents and their children. There are few rewards in pursuing recalcitrant pupils and it is understandable that the social services are experienced by the pupils as fading away or giving up.

> Well, he [the 'welfare man'] was coming to me house in the morning to take me to school at one time and I done that for a bit and I was getting a lift off him. And then he stopped coming and I just didn't go again.
>
> (male, 20)

There are few signs of a vigorous attention to detail or the pursuit of a policy of social inclusion. The gestures that are witnessed seem more tokenistic than substantial. The social services are easily deceived.

> Just didn't go at all, like, they rung me up to speak to me mum, say I could go back to school and I answered the phone, he says M. is that you and I said yeah, he goes well I'm just ringing to let you know you can go back to school. And I told me mum and says oh they don't want me to go back to school. So I just stayed in bed. She was just waiting for a letter through the post saying that, er, she was going to get done you know 'cos me and me mum thought that she'd get done 'cos I didn't go to school. But none of that ever came through, so...
>
> (male, 19)

One 'phone call and one lie and then the waiting for the 'official' follow-up. There is even the threat of the law, or 'getting done'. But nothing happens. Is this the result of indifference or despair? Is it the outcome of a shortage of social services or relief on behalf of the education system? Is there a sense that these pupils *ought* to be excluded from school? Is the rejection inadvertent or a deliberate policy?

Whatever the complex reasons for this perceived failure in the social services, the sense of rejection is significant. But it is shrouded in the stronger sense of indifference, an indifference often shared by the parents. Whilst there are some parents who punish their children for not attending school, and more who, without success, cajole their children about the virtues of school, there are many others who openly display their indifference.

> Not bothered. Well, they are bothered, they just keep telling me like, you'll be moaning when the school bobby comes round and all that lot, and they didn't come round.
>
> (male, 16)

It is not only the social services who do not follow up cases. The parents also wait for something to happen and assume it is the duty of the State to enforce attendance. Their children can detect that being told to go to school is more gesture than belief. When they subsequently reflect on this the young offenders all wish that their parents had shown a greater interest. At the time the laissez-faire attitude seems to suit them. They know that their parents are easy to ignore.

> Me mum and dad used to be moaning at me to go to school. Me dad used to come to me in the morning and try and wake me up and I'd lay there and pretend I couldn't hear him. He used to say it's eight o'clock M. time to get ready for school and he used to shout in me earholes and I used to pretend I was asleep.
> Me dad used to give into me you see. He used to turn round and say 'Oh, let her have today off' and then when tomorrow came 'Oh let her have today off' and before you knew it it was about a week. And then you know the truancy woman she started coming round and she started moaning at me to go to school and everything but I ignored her as well.
>
> (female, 21)

Being 'moaned at' is clearly ineffectual. By the time that either permanent truancy or permanent exclusion occurs there have been a number of experiences that have led to this reluctance or refusal to re-enter the school system. One of these experiences is the sense of dislocation between home and school. Beneath the surface of cajolery, of being told you 'ought' to go to school, lies a gulf between the parents and the educational system. Sometimes it is exhibited in open hostility, and sometimes in humiliation. But it is pervasive and a symptom of dysfunction in the home.

Schools can appear formal and distant places. The parents of the young offenders are never seen as being altogether comfortable with the system. The fact that their main contact with it is when their children are in trouble does not help. But there are rarely any signs that their parents really care. They are personally troubled by the reports of bad behaviour but rarely work with the school in dealing with it. The indifference, the 'not bothering', remains.

> She used to tell me all the time to go and that but like I'd just go and I'd stay there for a bit and then just go somewhere. She just used to say there's nothing she can do about it...
>
> (male, 20)

> Yeah they were bothered 'cos I weren't goin' to school but, don't know, 'cos I never took any notice of 'em, so I wouldn't really know what they were thinking about or nothing like that.
>
> (male, 20)

By the time the pupil abandons the formality of school there have been many signs of the rift between his or her parents and the school. Sometimes the two are both seen to be against the child. Sometimes they appear to be against each other. But the real rift is detected earlier, and that is between the child and the parent. The parents are expected to be 'bothered', but on reflection the young man or woman does not even know enough about them to detect any sign of caring. Long before no notice is taken of what teachers say, no notice is taken of parents.

References

1. Cullingford, C (1986) *Parents, Teachers and Schools*, Royce, London
2. Vincent, C (1996) *Parents and Teachers: Power and Participation*, Falmer Press, London
3. Cullingford, C (1996) *Parents, Education and the State*, Ashgate, Aldershot
4. Ibid
5. de Jong, op cit, previous chapter
6. Hughes, M, Wikeley, F and Nash, T (1994) *Parents and their Children's Schools*, Basil Blackwell, Oxford
7. See all the research reported, for instance in *Child Development*
8. eg Cullingford, C (1997) *The Politics of Primary Schools*, Open University Press, Buckingham
9. eg White, R with Brockington, D (1983) *Tales Out of School: Consumer's Views of British Education*, Routledge & Kegan Paul, London
10. Bettelheim, B (1987) *A Good Enough Parent*, Thames & Hudson, London
11. qv Cullingford, C, *Parents, Teachers and Schools*, op cit
12. Vuchinick, S, Vuchinick, R and Wood, B (1993) The interparental relationship and family problem solving with preadolescent males, *Child Development*, **64** (4), pp 1389–1400

5

The best days of your life?
The personal experience
of school

Introduction

Schools are social centres. They are the meeting places for peer groups. They are also organized social institutions to which pupils must adapt. The social side of school is extremely important and perhaps often underrated. It is through the informal aspects, the breaks between lessons, that social relationships are learned, that certain kinds of behaviour and attitude are fostered. From the point of view of children, this side of school, the hidden curriculum, the chance to meet with others, is as significant as the formal curriculum.[1] Of course the two overlap. There are formal rules that derive from the need to organize groups into receiving the curriculum, and there are many informal relationships and events within classrooms. But whilst there can be a sense of threat through incapacity or failure within lessons, these do not have nearly as deep an impact as the threats that derive from outside the 'safety' of the classroom.

The memories that young offenders have of school are as much, if not more, to do with what happens outside the classroom as within it. Schools are associated in their minds with the activities they share with their friends, with the playgrounds as well as the classrooms, with opportunities to do all kinds of things other than learn.

> Pretty boring. Everyone just goes round by the PE hall to have a smoke... probably go over to the library for a bit... I'd go with me mates. Just go up there 'cos it's warm and that, 'cos they wouldn't allow you in the classes till they started, even in winter.
>
> (male, 16)

There are many associations of schools with bleak places, with hidden corners, with contrasts between cold and warmth.[2] And many of the rules that are imposed seem to the pupils as unnecessary, unjust or absurd, like having to take a coat off for five minutes of registration or not being allowed into the warmth. But what emerges quite clearly is the sense of being with 'me mates'. 'Everyone' does certain things, despite the rules of the school. For school is also where you meet your friends even if you do not stay there.

> We used to like go first thing of a morning and like get signed in in the register and get off, 'cos they didn't get on to it for a while. When we used to like get to school that's where we used to all meet. Then we'd just decide to get off. Like when we had science lessons and all that first thing of a morning. It was alright. 'Cos we used to sneak off for a smoke.
>
> (male, 20)

What we see here is the gradual separation between two styles of behaviour. Ultimately the two will split entirely, but the sense of psychological exclusion already takes place within the school. The 'sneaking off' for a smoke leads to thinking of school as a place in which laws, rules and expectations can be broken. The sense of the illicit, of being able to deceive and to get away with things is strong.

From the point of view of the formal curriculum the pupils in school are all individuals and as long as they behave, relationships do not matter. Relationships, social intercourse, are, in fact, the greatest threat to order. Whilst groups are an important element in the social organization of the school, there are distinctions to be made between using groups as a means of spreading resources, using groups as a means of furthering learning and seeing friendship groups as a potential source of disruption.[3] But to children the relationships they make in school are of the foremost significance.[4] School phobia and school refusal are nearly always the result of friendships being broken and relationships failing. This obsession with relationships derives from both the positive and the negative aspects, from wanting to meet friends and from fear of being bullied. Those parts of the school day where there are opportunities to meet and play are of vital importance to the pupils. Playtimes, particularly the dinner break, are significant aspects of school, even if the pupils worry about being sent out on to the playground in the cold.[5] Whether inside or out, it is the breaks that give them time properly to socialize.

The informal aspects of school

Breaktime provides all kinds of opportunities, both positive and negative. There is a separate peer culture in the playground.[6] There are all kinds of things that happen there that would never take place within the aegis of formal management and con-trol. This not only includes aggression and power struggles, but a different kind of learning. The problem is that whilst breaks can be used creatively, they are often associated with the more negative aspects of school. One reason for this rests on the dominance of the playground. The assumption behind sending children out-side for physical, if uncoordinated, exertion is that they need to use up spare energy, that too much confinement in the classroom is a bad thing. Children who are particularly active physically are less attentive when they return to class.[7] The contrast between the strenuous and hard activity of the primary school playground and the classroom reinforces the contrasts and distinctions between school as a meeting place, a rough and tumble of relationships, and as a centre of learning.

There are, of course, times when the two sub-cultures of school overlap, partic-ularly in the secondary school which gives quite different and many more oppor-tunities for bad behaviour. The constant movements along corridors from class to class, and the changing personnel in groups give the chance for more contact between certain pupils and for less direct contact with the teachers. But within the classroom there is also the possibility of an underlying culture of disruption.

> Too much disruption went off in class, so like I used to just join in with them… mainly lads when they used to flick rubbers so we just started doing it… if only there were less people in the classroom 'cos then if you've got problems you can go straight to a teacher can't you, instead of having to wait for an hour.
>
> (female, 20)

One of the themes that constantly emerges is the sense of boredom, of not being kept interested or occupied. This comes about as much from the structural cir-cumstances – the size and shape of the classroom – as from the interest or ability in the subject matter. It is into these gaps that disruption occurs, as if it were some-thing rather smart to be able to get the better of a teacher. In those circumstances it is tempting to 'join in' with them, or at least to react rather than ignore. Flicking rubbers might seem a small matter but it becomes symbolic of a larger disbelief in authority. It is the beginning not only of undermining the role of the teacher and the meaning of school but of the influence of the peer group. Such behaviour spreads, until it can become such a collective habit that the normal functioning of the school is difficult to maintain.

> I like it when it's quiet and there's just you and someone else if she's teach-ing you you can do it then. I can do it but if there's like 12 lads in a room trying to do something and we're all talking about it, it just gets to me and I can't handle it. The lads who I used to be with like they used never to be interested in work. They wouldn't let you. They'd try and stop you, they'd

start messing about, throwing things at you, paper at you, through the room, all that kind of stuff and then that just disturbs you then and you can't do nothing.

(male, 20)

This young offender describes his school as rough, and presents his feelings of helplessness against the sheer number of disruptive boys. But these were the 'lads' he used to be with. There is a juxtaposition between the desire for personal attention, the security of being taught and the constant distraction by the many.

I used to try to get on with me work but like everyone's messing about, throwing stuff around, except for all the goody-goodies but they're the ones who got all the top jobs...

(male, 16)

There seems to come a point at which the critical mass of disruption causes serious trouble and has a strong influence. Every single pupil pleads for the desire to get on with work, to have individual attention paid to them, and they complain about all those who are 'messing about', but despite this, under such peer pressure, they join in. They also have to admit, for all the protestations of innocence, that this is not just a matter of weakness but of choice. They wouldn't want to be – or they did not at the time wish to be – one of the 'goody-goodies'. They wished, instead, to be one of the 'lads'. Some are able to resist the temptation.

The pleasures of disruption derive from a number of sources. One is the previous attitude to schooling, derived from home, which suggests that it is intrinsically worthless or irrelevant or hard or just plain dull. Another is the sense of personal assertion, of wanting to confront any figure of authority. Another is the desire to show off, to demonstrate that some teachers at least can be got the better of. Then there is the sheer amount of peer pressure, to join in the gang. But an even more significant source of disruption is boredom. Boredom can come about from all kinds of reasons, from having to wait with nothing to do, to the difficulty of the work. But it becomes a complex prevailing attitude, a desire for distraction.

I weren't unhappy but I wasn't that happy. Didn't like school anyway. I'd rather just mess about or something. Noisy, all the lessons I had were noisy. 'Cos it was better than just sittin' there quiet. If there's a lot of messin' about the time would just go faster. It got you out of class and you could go out, have a smoke, something like that, messing about, so that was ok.

(male, 20)

Avoiding the discipline of 'sitting there quiet' or the boredom associated with work turns a school into an opportunity for collective disturbance. The peer groups become the more central focus of attention and the demands of teachers are sometimes marginalized and sometimes deliberately thwarted. Instead of resentment at rules and the dislike of being told what to do, rules became a kind of game; something to be challenged. 'Just messing about' is a kind of pleasure in itself; but it is made the more piquant by the way it challenges the context in which it takes place. 'Messing about' makes the time go faster because it is a type of game playing that challenges the status quo. 'Messing about' outside the framework of school can be a sign of trying to avoid the boredom of having nothing to do, of looking for a way of being amused. The peer group knows that the pleasure of 'having a smoke' is the more relished for its being forbidden. The sense of defining 'messing about' as a challenge to the authority and expectations of a school sets up the subsequent seeking of pleasure in challenging the authority of society.

The culture of disruption

Schools are microcosms of society, and central to the development of relationships, understanding of authority and the definitions of acceptable and unacceptable behaviour. An awareness of how society functions as a whole is derived largely from the observations of whatever is in the 'news', whatever the medium.[8] News is, after all, nothing more than a description of what takes place, often without analysis. The behaviour of politicians, the duties of policemen, the function of the law, as well as all the troubles with which they are supposed to deal are daily observed and internalized. But the news remains, to an extent, distant and impersonal. In a school the way in which society operates is not only observed but lived. The hierarchies and the battles for power, both private and public, are scrutinized daily. Just as the news has a bias towards what is difficult and anti-social, the unusual that upsets the norm, so what is observed in school with the most attention are the clashes, the abnormal, those events that break the ordinary routine. Schools have a social culture of their own. The interactions between peer groups and between teachers create a strong impression of how society operates.

The impression given by the young offenders of their schools is a very distinct one. It is of a culture that encourages disruption, a culture of disobedience, and a culture that nourishes fighting. The symbolic centrepiece of this culture is the playground, those spaces where pupils are left for the most part on their own and where they pursue their personal social lives through their interactions with others. The culture of the playground is set up in primary schools, so that long before there are serious signs of truancy, let alone exclusion, certain norms of behaviour are already imbibed. Playgrounds are the places where two very important activities are developed – socializing and the learning of rules.[9] Girls in particular are found to spend time working on their relationships, in terms of both friendships and enmities. Both boys and girls are seen developing the rules for games, of learning how to standardize and control their play.

Observation of children in playgrounds reveals why rules are developed.[10] In all studies of the subject what emerges is the physical aspect of play, the constant interactions of children that can look quite violent. There are some commentators who would accept that as nothing more than a symptom of childhood, that a certain amount of rough play and pretend fighting is normal. But close observation and reflection reveal a great deal of what should be unacceptable behaviour. Playgrounds are designed for physical activity, and some of this can be very rough.[11] It might be play, but it can look like bullying. Children might need the physical release of play but they themselves view playgrounds as essentially bleak and off-putting.[12] This comes about not so much because playgrounds are large empty spaces but because they are associated with experiences of fighting. There are two important points that are made in the research on this subject. The first is the prevalence of aggression.[13] Not only do children observe fighting but they report having the experience of an aggressive fight themselves. Whatever the reason, whether retaliation or disagreement over the rules of a game, fighting is part of the experience of playgrounds. The other important point is the fine distinction to be made between play or pretend fighting and real aggression. Observers find it sometimes impossible to know whether two boys, for example, are enacting some kind of fighting play, or whether one is bullying the other. Sometimes it is obvious; but the background to bullying is a subtle one of constant physical activity with clashes of bodies and of teasing and name-calling, a hubbub of quarrels and arguments.

The pervasiveness of bullying

The social life of school that takes place outside the classroom and beyond the immediate control of teachers is very important to the pupils, and formative. This can, and does, include not only arguments but fighting. The schools that the young offenders attended all seem to have developed a culture of fighting. Sometimes in contrast to the calm of the classroom, and sometimes spilling out even within the supposed formalities of lessons, signs of aggression, of anger and of fear seem to symbolize a prevailing atmosphere. Bullying, teasing and retaliation are constantly reported. The expectation that there will be trouble of one kind or another, that schools are like that, runs deep. It is as if schools are seen not only as social centres, the place where the peer group meets, but as centres of violence.

> I didn't get it every day, you know what I mean. Nice environment, know
> what I mean, nice place.
>
> (female, 21)

From a girl who was teased or bullied, the occasional absence of being bullied
makes the school 'nice'.

The opportunities for provocation are many both in terms of the physical environment and the personal relationships of adolescents.

> There were quite a lot of fights though; that's how I got into them and
> that. About people calling each other slags and that, calling each other
> names. Yeah, about people nicking pencils off each other and that, or
> somebody nicking somebody's boyfriend and stuff like that. Just childish
> things really. Start tripping you up and lift the leg over and you'd be flying
> and that, then you'd get all hyped up over nothing and start fighting with
> them.
>
> (female, 16)

The corridors as well as the playgrounds make an environment in which the
proximity of a large number of pupils can easily cause physical provocation.
This girl has learned fighting at school. She might dismiss the reasons for 'getting into them' as childish but it is clear that fighting is part of the prevailing
ethos of the school. This can be the result of a simple act like tripping someone
up or a more emotional provocation like 'nicking' pencils or boyfriends. The
result of emotional and physical bullying – name calling or fighting – is a constant sense of threat.

> Stupid things really, calling names, throwing things about, pushing things
> about, anything like that. I didn't like to be beaten if you know what I
> mean. I hate the thought of being beaten… so no one would play with me.
> I was always paranoid I'm not gonna talk proper and that. Don't know
> why I was like that, some lads, 'cos you never know if they're gonna whack
> you in the stomach or laugh at you or something. Every person that
> walked past I'd tense myself up 'cos you never know what to expect. Are
> they gonna run past and hit your stomach or clip you over head.
>
> (male, 20)

The reason for citing a 'culture' of violence is the fact that it seems to be constant.
There are so many different levels of physical interaction, from a gentle push to
being 'beaten up'. But it all creates a sense of threat. No one knows when there
might be the next name calling or being 'whacked' in the stomach. There is no telling when they might do something that gets them laughed at. The tension and the
readiness to retaliate are continuous.

In any community where violence is part of the standard experience and expectation, the need to protect oneself, to show that one cannot be bullied becomes paramount. Violence breeds violence. Retaliation becomes a norm. Indeed, for some it is important to 'get the retaliation in first'. In such an atmosphere gangs are formed. Some are known to be bullies just as others are easy victims. Often the same person is both. The desire to show off, to present a 'macho' image, to be able to 'protect' yourself means that there is a need constantly to keep such a reputation up to date and reinforced.

> Like when I was at school, like, my... er, I wouldn't say I was a bully, but, I could you know. I was the main lad you know? Just top fighter in my year 'cos I just grew up fast and like I had a big brother with me as well. Think he toughened me up a bit as well... used to get into a lot of fights and gettin' into fights every day, especially with older people as well...
>
> (male, 19)

The distinction between a bully, which by implication is how he describes himself, and 'main lad' is a fine one. Being the 'top fighter' meant that there would be fights 'every day'. This casual acceptance of the prevalence of fighting encapsulates the experience of school for a large number of pupils. Not all will be the 'main lad' but there are constant challenges to show who is 'tough'. In fact there is a certain pride in being able to hold his own against older boys and in being taught (and no doubt protected) by his older brother.

From the notion of being 'toughened up' comes the development of gangs, of more organized fighting, so that what has at the beginning grown out of personal animosity, the result of personal provocation and anger, becomes the carefully managed and deliberate organization of revenge.

> I've said something or someone said to me that they've said something, you just start fighting them. They were all in their little groups and that... I'd probably have to start fighting them all. I had a fight with one lad and like I was him. And then him, his brother and two of his mates like all jumped me when I went home from school. One of them just kicked me in the mouth, just cracked all my teeth. It just toughens you up doesn't it?
>
> (male, 20)

The development of personal quarrels, of saying something so that they 'just' start fighting, leads almost inexorably for some into the formation of little groups. Once these are organized to fight, the peer pressure that 'toughens you up' becomes that much more dangerous. There is a difference between 'groups' based on defined boundaries of friendship and shared interest and 'gangs' who not only define themselves as supporting each other but who define themselves *against* others. For pupils in school, however, almost any grouping, 'hard' or 'soft', can be depicted as a gang.

> Gangs. All different gangs. Softies used to stay with softies and hardies used to stay with hardies. I don't like bullying. Never have done. I disagree with it, but I don't walk around with all those soft dopey girls either 'cos you get pulled down. Erm, teachers look down on you, to say well you're trying to come down to their grade, acting thick and stuff like that, so I just stayed in middle, just knocked round with a few kids. Bullying, it were mainly lads and some of them like cock of schools.
>
> (female, 20)

To be associated with the 'wrong' pupils is to be avoided. Also to be avoided are the extremes, to be too clever or too stupid, too soft or too hard. For these young people, however, there is more attraction in being 'tough' or 'hard', in being street-wise, in having what is sometimes called 'attitude', than in being successful at school. The peer pressure of fashion does not just cover designer wear and music but being a leader, someone gregarious and popular, someone admired for displaying a greater concern with teenage interests than in pleasing the teacher. In this case the 'softies' seem to be associated with 'dopey', as if they are keeping as invisible as possible, avoiding many of the challenges of intellectual argument.[14]

'Gangs' are usually formed of 'hardies' since they have the greater need to 'protect' themselves against others. They arise out of the seeking out of those who are 'well hard', who protect particular people, and who therefore can dominate others. For some it is better to keep out of their way.

> Some of them were alright, and some of them thought they was well hard. They used to go around telling people, saying OK, 'cos say if somebody wanted to smack somebody else and somebody harder would come up and say, er, if you hit her then I'll smack you and all this lot. Just think they're hard 'cos they stick up for other people, that's why... 'cos if somebody can smack me then it's not worth hitting the other person then is it? 'Cos you'd only get a thumping as well, so it's not worth it.
>
> (female, 16)

Some of the fundamental attitudes of pupils in schools who are inflicted with the culture of violence are pointed up here. It suggests a prevailing atmosphere of incipient violence and threat, in this case with girls. Just as some boys are proud of being 'tough', so some girls are 'well hard'. The 'hardest', the strongest, wins. Each person knows the hierarchy of power. If they play this game right they will have protection from those who 'stick up' for other people, when they choose to do so. If the pragmatist realizes that she is not the toughest, that she has to avoid provoking or fighting certain people, then it is 'not worth' hitting that particular person. With others she can get away with it, as if that made it 'worth it'. Once gangs are formed within a school, that kind of culture tends to be taken beyond the confines of the school. They 'bunk off', further than the place they have their cigarettes, and look for greater challenges of confrontation elsewhere.

> There always used to be fights between our school and their school. The girls used to bunk off as well.
>
> (male, 20)

The cultivation of fighting in schools is the manifestation of complex social interactions where there are quarrels and teasing, loneliness and bullying. What all children report from school includes periods of real personal pain, of feelings of rejection and of humiliation. Schools can be breeding grounds of discontent. It is almost as if there needs to be an awareness of the dangers of schools to survive them. Much of what goes on in schools lies below the surface. Bullying is not an obvious phenomenon for most of the time. Indeed, some schools deny its very existence, in the face of irrefutable evidence.[15] Whilst the causes of bullying have not been all that fully explored, the fact of its existence and its prevalence has been returned to often, almost as often as the experiments with dealing with bullying before trying to understand it. Even with the narrowest of definitions, or the most obvious manifestations of bullying, it is a common and widespread problem. Every survey is a new surprise in terms of the extent of bullying.[16] But even this evidence does not really uncover the extent of the underworld of difficult relationships, of threats and subtle provocations. This is not to imply that all schools are havens for behaviour that is uncontrolled or that there is constant mayhem. From the research that has taken place, and from the analysis of the experiences reported here, there are two important conclusions to be drawn. The first is that the distinction between bully and victim is a nebulous one. The second is that the *feeling* of being bullied (or teased) is more important than the intention to hurt. Once the individual personal experience is explored in depth, we discover how young people are easily hurt, even if inadvertently, and we discover that what provokes bullying is not just a sign of being 'hard' but usually the result of a retaliation against humiliation, a sign of weakness rather than strength.

In the research on the prevalence of bullying there has almost invariably been an attempt to categorize it, either by comparing the incidence of bullying by boys or girls, or of the different types of bullying from verbal to physical. There have also been attempts to define what exactly is a 'victim' and what exactly is a 'bully', as if the two could be separated. There are many definitions of what constitutes one or the other, and more particularly what gives rise to the one or the other.[17] Boys might appear to be bullies more often than girls, but this is to take observed physical aggression as the norm. A bully might wish to cause hurt with intentionality but this is to put aside all the private feelings of the individual who is, as it were, 'yawned at' and ignored by those who are desired as friends.[18] Most self-report scales of bullying bring out the feeling that to confess to being bullied is to bring out a sense of weakness. It is not only those who fear retaliation who do not pass on information, although these threats are palpable and effective. It is because bullying is so much of a hidden, almost a counter-culture, that it is treated as something that is outside the orbit of interests of teachers. Whilst there are many examples of teachers' perceived lack of concern when they are told about incidents of bullying which need not be pursued here, the fact is that for the most part pupils would not even *think* of reporting what goes on. There is a whole aspect of school life that remains in the pupils' domain and from which teachers are excluded. Teachers are seen to have their own agenda and pupils consider that finding out what is wanted from them and how to meet their requirements is one aspect of school. The other remains essentially separate, and officially secret.

In the counter-culture of school bullying is the ultimate manifestation of festering relationships, of underlying tensions, the end of what has been called a continuum of acceptable violence.[19] It is difficult to know, even from observed physical behaviour, when someone is being bullied.[20] It is more difficult still to know when someone feels himself or herself to be a victim. Pupils like being in groups, of having a circle of friends. At what point does this group become a gang or a 'mob'?[21] Opportunities to bully in some form or another are many, and these do not link with any factor such as school size or ethnic mix.[22] Bullying is a far subtler and more profoundly damaging phenomenon than at first appears. It is not obvious. The secret pain that it causes can stay with the victim for years. These are not surface matters, not easily observable and only prevented by far more subtle approaches than contracts with the school to behave well or the fierce imposition of discipline – not that any means to eradicate bullying should not be taken. The problem is that there is a part of the culture of schools that is the testing of interactions between pupils, the explorations of relationships and the examination of the nature of power. Just as in adult life, bullying can become accepted not only as an inevitability but almost as a sign of legitimate command, a sign of strength, a part of the 'robust' style of management. If one considers the effects of bullying, the way that one person gets the better of others, one is able to see why there should be such a subliminal attraction to it. As we have seen and will see later, the 'weak' tend to be despised. The innocent suffer; that is what they're for.

The complex and emotionally highly charged nature of shifting relationships makes schools potentially and occasionally distressing places to be in. The possibilities of humiliation and of failure are always there. They are not confined just to a small group who seek to damage others. Bullying is pervasive, and not confined to a few extreme characters. The fact that teachers and lunchtime supervisors, when asked to distinguish in videotapes between play and aggression, could not always do so, suggests the subtlety of the distinction.[23] And these are observers of *physical* manifestations. They do not begin to explore the mental anguish or the intellectual taunts that lie beneath the surface. Even at the level of observation of playground behaviour, aggression tended to be interpreted as play, rather than vice versa. It is as if a whole dark side of school is hidden, subconsciously, if not from sight.

If we accept, as we have to, that there is a part of the experience of growing up that can be traumatic, there is a temptation to conclude that this is a necessary aspect of the journey into maturity. The research that is summarized here suggests otherwise. Bullying might seem inevitable but it is in fact unnecessary. The consequences of suffering are not just pitiful but can be permanently damaging. It is clear that some children are more vulnerable than others. But these are not just the weak, the failures or the despised. They are the ones who are the most vulnerable because of the nature of their earliest experiences, by the way in which they deal with, or react to, aggression. It is clear that in this sample of young offenders, all have found themselves to be, or feel themselves to be, victims. These are the people who have committed acts of violence. They have also been vulnerable to bullying.

Bullies and victims

One of the most important indications that there cannot be a clear demarcation line between bullies and victims, or a typology of one or the other, is that one of the most tempting aspects of 'victims' is their ability to be provoked. This is not just the fact that they are most easily hurt, or the fact that they have characteristics that are easy to tease. It is the way they can be made to retaliate; their very reactions elicit the cruelty of verbal taunting. One of the most used phrases in the personal experience of school is 'being picked on'. This can apply to anyone. There are very few, if any, cases where a pupil feels that he or she has never been unfairly 'picked on' either by teachers or by fellow pupils. The universality of the phenomenon suggests that it is for the most part coped with; but there are some who cannot cope. The victims are those most vulnerable to the sudden sense of personal exposure.

In all the accounts of school, bullying (a word never brought up by the interviewer) seemed to be at the centre of the experience.

> I used to get bullied myself in school. 'Cos of me hair colour, me glasses and, 'cos, erm, I've always been plump, put on weight and that. I were just somebody to pick on and if they were picking on me I knew they weren't picking on others so, and one day I just turned round and whacked one of 'em and they were shocked 'cos it was what me brother had learned me. I

just broke her nose… they get taunted, don't they, by other kids saying
you're dirty, you're smelly, or whatever.

(female, 20)

Anything that stands out as different, whether intellectual ability, interest or attitude or, more commonly, physical appearance, can be the target of an attack.
Wearing glasses, being plump, having an unusual hair colour all add together to
being selected as an obvious person to 'pick on'. It is as if the young offender feels
that they had to find someone and that she made the most agreeable and the most
collectively agreed victim. If it had not been her, she implies, it would have been
someone else. She then questions both why it should be her and why she should
put up with it. What seems in her own eyes a successful retaliation – they both go
laughing when sent to the head teacher – sets her on a career where the same physical reaction is at the centre of her life. Provocation leads to retaliation. The excitement of teasing is that it can elicit a reaction. And the reaction, desired or not, is like
the tables being turned; the victim turns on the bully, and those simple concepts of
'intentionality' are again broken down.

Bullying and victimization are contagious. It is as if a cultural disease had broken out in which the majority became infected. Not everyone succumbs but the
spread of a pervasive and wilful virus that catches so many people up in it is like the
viral infections of the analogy. All live in fear of germs but for the most part they
are controlled. With bullying the conditions are always there but need controlling.
It is not the particular individual who has a will to cause harm that counts but the
almost indifferent acceptance of the power of will that makes the 'disease' spread.
Thus bullies and victims are not only dependent on each other but caught up in
each other, and often interchangeable. This is not to say that there is any excuse for
the bully, but to clarify the fact that bullies thrive in certain atmospheres, and these
contaminating atmospheres make the distinctions between the role of bully and
the role of victim, like the passer-on of germs who is not affected and those that fall
ill, almost a meaningless one. Those who are clearly defined as bullies have also
been teased in their turn.[24] And, as has often become an almost retaliatory reaction
to the phenomenon of bullying, the hidden and deep sources of bullying derive
from weakness rather than strength, from a sense of insecurity and fear of being
rejected, rather than self-confidence.[25]

Whatever the development into the role of bully, which is complicated, there is
no doubt that certain children make easy targets as victims. The victims clearly do
not have the confidence of dialogue, of being able to turn an argument, or to ignore
one. It is not just the fact that they have some physical peculiarity that makes them
the target but that they have a kind of emotional vulnerability that allows their
weakness to be exploited. Having a peculiar colour of hair or being fat is no
weakness. It is merely an excuse to exploit the deeper vulnerability which is the

self-consciousness, the insecurity that makes differences so acute.[26] The actual circumstances in which bullying takes place almost invariably include not just an opportunity, as in a crime, but a realization that the victim is vulnerable. To this extent the act of bullying is crueller. It is only later that a burglar might think of the effect on the feelings of the victim, but in the breeding ground of bullying the awareness that damage can be caused is central. But the awareness is not so much of emotional damage to the victim as the excitement in seeing someone 'picked on' so much that he or she goes over the edge. As with the provocation of teachers, the horrid curiosity is to see how far you can go.

> It's just actually when we were doing our work and things like that I used to get picked on. Like, if a teacher weren't looking she'd sort of flick me with a ruler or something like that. It would be alright if the teachers were sort of there but as soon as the teacher used to leave then the bullying would start. I tell you what they used to do; name calling and they used to call me this name and I used to hate her and I used to get really mad when they used to say it and they just used to wind me up and wind me up all the time and I'd start crying and they'd carry on and carry on, you know, 'til they'd really get you mad and you'd do something.
>
> I was really fat when I was at school. I've had eating problems. I was always paranoid about my weight. I got bullied. They'd all start pulling me hair and hitting me. That was just over the fags and things like that. They all used to work in like gangs there.
>
> (female, 21)

What starts as furtive provocation, an attempt not so much as to see what harm can be done as how far one can go without being spotted, gradually and subtly escalates into something more serious. The teachers need to keep control. The assumption is that without their protection all manner of things might take place. It is one kind of society set up against another. Far from assuming responsibility for their own actions, the underlying message is of confrontation and control, an almost inevitable clash of values and systems. It passes from name-calling to hair-pulling. Suppose the girl could have ignored that particular name that so hurt her? What made the peer group so relish the idea that she was vulnerable? She mentions being 'paranoid' about her weight. The paranoia exposes all kinds of temptations for her peer group, temptations for them that lead to disaster for her. There is no doubt about the depth of feeling in being 'wound up'. The crying is real. So is the 'madness' that is the ultimate outcome. Vulnerability at home is joined with vulnerability at school. But it also leads to means to retaliate, from the point of view of the victim, and to retaliate effectively. We begin to see how the threat of gangs, of 'getting at' particular individuals, gradually leads to the need for self-protection, both personally and collectively.

Bullying and criminality

Bullying is both pervasive and complex. It is deeply rooted in the culture and experience of school, and spills over into the life outside. There are as many different types of bully and motivations for bullying as there are different types of victims: for instance, those who respond aggressively, those who show great distress and those who pretend bullying does not exist.[27] There are anxious bullies as well as provocative victims. There are those who are bullied occasionally and those persistently bullied. The problem is that bullying is often hidden and rarely reported to the teachers.[28] The unhappiness of the victims, often feeling friendless and rejected, often remains obscure. There are many different reasons for bullying, from sheer curiosity about provoking a reaction or boredom to a far deeper, more obscure sense of anger that is directed towards particular people. What is clear is that whilst *all* children report being bullied at least once, there are some who are persistently victims, for reasons that they themselves understand. But victims do not necessarily remain passive. All the motivations that cause distress and anger can lead either to aggression against others, or being 'picked on' or both.

> I used to get picked on and that, called a pikey, called a gypsy, 'cos my clothes and that were second-hand. There was people there who had like a bit of money, their parents had a little bit of money and stuff, they used to dress really smart.
>
> I used to like school first but then I used to get bullied. I used to hate going, used to bunk off and stuff. Allen, he used to hurt me and that physically, you know kick me and stuff and say like 'oh you pikey' and that. I was too scared at first... and the people I hanged round with you don't mess with them sort of people, you know they play tennis and all that... oh and we used to be like, we used to bully people as well... it's probably you know I wanted them to know how I felt, you know, when I was younger... just take, just nick their bags and stuff like that and just take everything out their bags, like pens and stuff and throw their books away... I know it sounds terrible. It's just like authority 'cos their parents were rich, they just used to get a buzz out of nickin' other people's things, just for the buzz of it.
>
> (female, 21)

So many elements are brought together in fostering a sense of grievance and revenge. There are factors of class and poverty, a sense of being socially discriminated against and seen as different. Being called a 'pikey' and being kicked led not only to understanding the motivation behind such attacks but to a hatred for the reasons for that motivation. A strong sense of antipathy to classes of people, with their habits and their money, is gradually formed to such an extent that the form of revenge that is pursued is the most long-lasting antisocial one of all. What can begin as simple revenge, throwing the contents of bags away, can then become a habit that in itself gives pleasure. Stealing gives a 'buzz'. What is born out of dislike of fellow pupils because their parents are rich and because they despise her soon becomes, as she herself puts it, a rejection of 'authority'. And once the habit of rejection becomes the excitement of stealing, that can become a permanent habit. Out of such small beginnings, and large personal motivations, criminal activities are formed. The aggressive victim is no longer frustrated and provoked, but herself becomes part of a gang that decides bullying does pay and that 'you don't mess' with certain sorts of people.[28]

One of the strong links between bullying and crime is the fact that there is an element of pleasure to be derived in having kudos, as well as profit, and a sense of indifference about the consequences, the inability to see deeply into the point of view of the victim. It is as if a normal kind of dialogue, of social relationship, is missing. Seeing how someone reacts, finding distress amusing, is more of an act of playing with other people as if they were objects than a means of communication. There are always ostensible reasons for bullying, but it is the act itself that gives a 'buzz'. Some might be obvious victims, what DH Lawrence called 'murderees' as if they attracted their own fate. But if some are 'picked on' much more than others, they are the targets because they are most obviously 'different'. Everyone has at one time or another *felt* that they were 'picked on', sometimes by the teacher. For some such an experience is persistent.

> I started getting bullied as well. I didn't like it at all. Take things off me, steal things out me pockets, just silly things in them days. Erm like me school books, they used to rip me school books up, me work and that… just bullies. I had a fight with her little sister and that was it. I was beaten up for that. I used to sit in the classroom 'cos I used to get bullied. I looked funny. I must have looked like one of them that you can bully, you know what I mean. 'Oh let's go and bully Tracey today'. I don't think it's right for them to start fighting me, unless I've done something wrong.
>
> (female, 21)

There is a strong sense of injustice, of unfairness. The fact of arguments and quarrels and even fights is an accepted part of the social life of school, including the power battles that they imply, but what gives rise to the sense of deep grievance is being teased and bullied for no apparent, or no good, reason. It is one thing to have a fight and get 'beaten up', and another to merely 'look funny'. What are dismissed as 'silly things', almost part of the everyday life of school, are in fact more deeply distressing than the victims would at the time admit. The sense that it is not 'right' underlies the arbitrary nature of bullying and the way that it grows out of the rough currency of social interchange.

The reasons for attracting the attention of bullies can be physical, or they can be social.

> Well, me dad's been in jail so I got a lot of trouble for that... I denied it, made it worse for myself... I got a lot of hassle 'cos me dad was inside and they didn't know half the story and I didn't tell no one...
>
> (male, 17)

Class difference, an absence of money or a hidden past or different background is as potent a reason for teasing as physical appearance or personal habit. Even without an ostensible reason, teasing can be pursued by the attraction of seeing how some would react.

> Just sometimes the way people just looked at me sometimes, erm if they said oh your hair's a mess or one of your socks have fell down, or there's a ladder in your tights or something like that, I used to go off me head...
>
> (female, 19)

The worry is that in such atmospheres there is little pity for the victims. Those who have never learned to be able to develop the dialogue of reason, or who have easily provoked tempers, can easily find themselves in the pervasive culture of aggression. Fights abound. Anything that makes someone 'go off me head' can be used to promote the excitement of 'trouble'.

> Just one of them things. Just can't put up with it. If they say it [he has a one-legged father] it was either that or am not good at erm maths, English and things, if they called me about me work or I used to, me writing 'you can't spell, you're thick' and things like that... They used to think I always caused the fights. There was a lot in school, they used to just get bullied... fighting with me and some other lads, me mates. It was just names, being young... name calling and that.
>
> (male, 18)

The desire to provoke, the deliberate seeking out of potential victims, those who can be most devastatingly hurt, suggests a lack of sense of pity, or mercy. The kind of society being revealed here is cruel as well as competitive. It seems to relish other people's distress. It develops the notion that to do harm, to upset the system, to disobey and to ignore rules is a sign of power and even fashion. It also suggests a lack of insight into the feelings of the victims. This might seem surprising, given that all the young offenders have experienced being bullied and know how it can hurt emotionally as well as physically. But at the same time there is a separation from personal feelings and insight into other people's feelings. The cultural phenomenon of the excitement of seeing outbreaks of aggression or lawlessness overcomes more detailed analysis. It is like an absence of thought, as if no one had even tried to reason out the consequences. The schools reported here make rough communities where aggression and anger are almost accepted as part of some rite of passage, or at best simply ignored. It is as if a collective passion was added to the 'rough and tumble' of play.[29] And there is little concern for victims.

Bullies, gangs and competition

The absence of concern for those who are bullied gives some insight into the nature of social groups, and the way they can create a collective atmosphere that overcomes the individual. Whilst there are many examples of the effect of such a collective subconscious, like inter-ethnic conflicts and nationalism, the beginnings of such prejudice lie in the home and are developed in school.[30] Even when children are asked whether they do not feel pity towards the outsiders, the victims, they are at best ambivalent, at worst, dismissive. Whilst they feel that bullies should be punished, they support hostile behaviour towards those perceived as weak.[31] They see victims not only as undesirable but as attracting the bullying they receive. They almost approve of the perception that bullies are expert at seeing who they can safely bully.[32] Children simply do not seem to care about the suffering of their victimized peers.[33] This is partly because bullying has become deeply embedded in the culture of schools, as if it had become almost a 'norm'. Bullies tend to be in larger groups than other pupils, as if they were deliberately creating a micro-society of their own.[34] Every gang defines itself through its difference, and this creates the need to create enemies, whether it is another social or ethnic group, or the formal structures of school, or society as a whole. The pity of it is that gangs are given so many opportunities.

There are many aspects of school life in which pupils can be hurt or humiliated. Many of these lie outside the formal systems of school. These could be defined as the 'delivery' of a curriculum and the circumstances in which this can be brought about. The problem is that one of the greatest sources of disquiet, discontent and unhappiness lies at the heart of the educational enterprise. All pupils are expected to do well, to achieve set targets. They are in a competition, both against set criteria and against each other. There is little pity expressed for victims of bullying and teasing, however humiliated they feel. One major source for the development of bullying lies in the failure to be able to do academic work. It can be one small aspect of the curriculum as a whole, but the potential to hurt, to see a weakness, lies in the work itself.

> And I never mentioned it 'cos I was ashamed of myself 'cos I couldn't tell the time… I still can't tell it very well. I wish the people had been different,

the pupils, more kinder, more supportive... some of the work at school I found really hard and I couldn't do it, so... and that used to put me off as well... all the others used to be there writing and I couldn't. Teacher had to help me all the time. I used to feel stupid.

(female, 21)

One cannot blame the teacher for attempting to help, or the fact that some pupils are faster learners than others, but in the ethos of any school there is a sense of wanting to do well, or at least not doing so badly as to be exposed. In all schools pupils know how well they are doing compared to their peers. Furthermore, they tend to label themselves and others as 'clever' or 'stupid'. For them, not *doing* well is the same as *being* stupid. They become ashamed and hate being exposed. One of the major dark satisfactions for the bully is being able to expose the victim not only as having defects of background or appearance, but being intellectually inferior, thereby letting down both the formal and informal sides of school.

'cos I've never been right good at spelling or owt like that. Class eight is if you can't spell and that and I had to be in there and like I got a lot of hassle for being in that class. Not just teachers, friends as well... 'cos I couldn't read and like if you have spellings at end of week... you have to read them out and like I couldn't remember one of them.

(male, 17)

The 'hassle' from the teachers is official; but the real humiliation is what is seen by the peer group. Having to demonstrate failure before the whole class is worse than recognizing it. Schools can become constant reminders of inadequacy.

Boredom with school

Matching the individual's needs with the requirements of the formal curriculum is a delicate and difficult business. It depends not only on the sensitivity and intellectual prowess of teachers but on the ways in which each individual pupil approaches the demands of the school. It is perhaps surprising how many pupils submit to the school, and are determined to adapt, despite the temptations of dropping out. Of course the majority of them see the long-term purpose of school which, in their eyes, is to enable them to acquire a worthwhile job. It is, perhaps, for this reason that they put up with all the difficulties that they have to go through. But if this purpose, or assumption, is undermined at home, then one of the sustaining forces that enable a recognition of a worthwhile place in society is undermined. Schools can appear strange and forbidding places, not only because of what takes place

within them but because of the ways in which work and academic demands generally are presented. One of the undermining emotions that support the temptation
of truancy is simply that of boredom. This can lead to pupils questioning why they
are doing work that seems to them essentially meaningless.

> I did everything I got told to, but it got too much. I just did work that got
> put in front of me. I'd do it like but if I got bored with it I'd just like sharp
> pen and I'd say oh pissed off with this like and just throw me pen or snap it
> or summat.
>
> (male, 16)

The difference here is that the pupil refuses to put up with it, when the majority of
his peers would carry on doing what is 'put in front of them' whatever they
thought or felt about it. The majority accept without question. They acknowledge
a system in which they are there to fulfil tasks that are set before them by the teachers. They are there to guess what it is that teachers require. Once, however, this
tacit assumption is disturbed, boredom turns into disruption.

Dissatisfaction with school can come about because of the sense of intellectual
or academic failure. Often those who drop out feel themselves to be inadequate or
humiliated or both. But there is no direct link between academic failure and exclusion. The questioning of the demands of the school goes deeper. The outcome is
labelled as academic failure but the causes are different. There is something about
the relationship between the individual pupil and the education system and the
way it operates that causes a disjunction. Some pupils, after all, confess that it is
their own approach and temperament that cause difficulties.

> I were a right little bugger, you know what I mean. I didn't like school
> much but like it were alright. I can't read very good. So that's why I've
> skipped it out. I didn't like paper work, don't like paper work, know what I
> mean.
>
> (female, 21)

In fact it is not so much the approach that pupils bring to the school that causes difficulties but the nature of schooling juxtaposed against them. Not being able to
read immediately causes a problem. The emphasis on 'paper work', the imposition
of writing, a perennially disliked demand that school makes, is another barrier for
many.[35] Most manage to negotiate their way through boredom and inability. But
there are some to whom the demands of school, on the formal surface as well as
below it, are implacable, and impossible.

When the experiences of schools are described by those who have failed, what is
striking is the tension between the idea of schools as systems and the idea of the
school as groupings of people. The crucial factor in the eyes of the young offenders

is that ultimately the school is a 'system'. It has people in it, and preferred teachers and friends. It also gives rise to personal clashes. But it is the informal and systematic imposition of a regime – of expectations, rules and what seems like arbitrary judgements – that really strikes them. As the next chapter demonstrates, personal relations with teachers are an extremely important factor – a flash point between the personal and the public – but it is the impersonality of the school system as a whole that is the underlying context. Whether the individual pupil adapts to it or not, it is the way in which schools are forced to operate, as systems with rules and sanctions. They are inclusive systems from which there can be no easy escape. They wish all to conform but are very easy to dismiss, mostly personally and privately but sometimes more obviously. What is interesting from the accounts of these young people is how often they suggest that schools are dealing with impossible circumstances, and that schools are under-resourced. Concentrating on these particularly estranged individuals might seem to demand the most lavish of resources, but it is the system as such rather than all the people in it that concerns them. This is an important distinction even if the final outcome is a clash with a particular teacher.

> Most of the schools I've been to, all they have is this place, like units, you know what I'm on about, units for the stupid people. They should have more classrooms in schools, separate classrooms, where you have like three teachers between about ten pupils and see when you go to school you have one teacher between so many pupils in a classroom, all's he does is stand at the top of the classroom, shouts out this, that and the other and most of the time you're only copying from books and you learn nothing, you don't learn nothing. Or they just give you a textbook. Two, add three, you write it down… it's simple 'cos you're just copying.
>
> Those that aren't interested in work because they're not getting the attention they need. There should be teachers there to give them the attention they need.
>
> They give you like lower work like for younger people and from there you'll start workin' up, instead of letting you learn the proper stuff, like the hard work. They were just giving you dead easy work, what you could do and you weren't learning nothing.
>
> Well, you're thick aren't you? 'Cos all them are in the top classes and that and you're just a dunce, 'cos you're down in the unit.
>
> (male, 21)

If we begin to analyse schools from the point of view of pupils, a different pattern of interpretation, indeed, almost a mirror image emerges. All the concerns of the system are to do the best, in terms of standards, for everybody. At the same time, schools are in competition. There are league tables. Failures are reported, at the school level, with relish. And those individuals who are the casualties of the system feel their own culpability deeply. The remedial unit is the symbol of abjection. All the other pupils know who are the failures. And whilst such units are created out of concern, and run by people who have concern, they are seen by other pupils as sinks of failure, draining away the stupid ones. Units are for the stupid. Special treatment and reduced pupil staff ratios are associated with failure rather than success.

The problem for those who do badly at school is that it is only then when they find that special attention is paid to them. All these witnesses appreciate smaller classes and the personal attention of teachers. But that is not part of the normal system of the school. The daily impression of the school is of an unwieldy impersonal system with large numbers of pupils ferrying themselves from overcrowded classroom to overcrowded classroom. The young offenders recall the routines, the lack of a sense of dignity. From their point of view schools are off-putting. The teachers are depicted as 'shouting out this and that'. And the tasks seem designed to keep them occupied, as part of a routine; 'copying from books', 'you learn nothing'. They 'just give you a textbook'. The assumption that these failures make is that they were never given the attention they needed when they most needed it. It was not part of the normal routine of the school. Given the class sizes, the demands on teachers, the necessity to deliver the curriculum, to test the pupils, and given the state of the buildings, one can see that this perception of school is a kind of backcloth to disaffection. The lack of personal attention or interest is linked to doing 'dead easy work', merely being occupied. Into these routines comes boredom, and boredom looks for distraction. And at the same time there is a parallel sense of distinction, between the 'swots' of the 'top classes' and the dunces. The gap becomes wider and wider. The contradictions inherent within the system – of every pupil having an entitlement on the one hand and of all schools being in competition and judged against targets on the other – are part of the daily experience of pupils. They are aware that they deserve and need individual attention but also know that what they seek distracts teachers from their main task. They are a nuisance, an extra burden on resources, and however sympathetically schools try to deal with them, they understand this fundamental fact.

Reactions to the demands of school

This picture of school, painted by the disaffected, is actually shared by all pupils. Most of them cope and adapt.[36] They learn what teachers want them to do and submit to whatever 'is put in front of them'.[37] It is not, then, a biased view fuelled by excuses. Many of them realize that they came to school with negative attitudes, that they were not fundamentally interested to begin with. They never suggest that their failure or their disaffection is simply the school's fault. They bring their own responsibilities, and weaknesses. But it is clear that schools find it difficult to help. A difficult pupil who has learning problems will not be easy to deal with.

> What pissed me off the most were when I... 'cos I can't read very good do you know what I mean? I can't write very good and it just does me head in that.
>
> (female, 21)

There could not be a more powerful barrier to attainment than a sense of failure and humiliation, and the inability to carry out the routine tasks. If these depend on 'copying' and on 'doing' whatever text is put in front of them, then there is not even a feasible starting point. The inability to read not only undermines the tasks that teachers set but becomes a challenge to the very way the system operates. Teachers are disappointed and other pupils unpitying. The individual is isolated as well as bored.

Schools might appear as a particular system, but each individual responds differently. And whilst schools are a system, they each have their own ethos.[38] Whilst we have dwelt on the negative experiences of the disaffected, we should not suppose that this side of their experience is the only one they have. There are certain things about school that are off-putting: bullying and the potential for humiliation, boredom and the potential for failure. But there are also parts of the school that are enjoyed. There are certain friendships, certain teachers and certain subjects that stand out. The majority of these young people had good moments as well as terrible half-hours. They all cite those parts of the academic side of school that they liked. They might be selective, and reject anything that makes the kind of demand they resent, but they talk of the pleasures of learning, as well as seeing friends.

> I used to love science and business studies. Erm, I weren't too keen on English or anything like that... I used to love doing course work... 'cos it was something different from what we'd ever learned before and we had to find out all the information ourselves and we weren't told nothing... and I used to love doing that 'cos it gave us some sort of initiative to use our brains.
>
> (female, 19)

We have already witnessed the resentment of routine, at doing what appears boring and meaningless work. Several display a desire to be challenged, to be made to 'use their brains'. They all long for something out of the ordinary, 'something different'. In fact it can be the contrast and the variety of demands in a school's curriculum and the style in which it is presented that can cause a problem as well as a solution. Pupils all learn to like some subjects more than others. Sometimes it is because of compatibility with the subject, and sometimes the relationship with the teacher. Those who follow their own interests to an almost pathological degree either submit to the fact that some subjects are boring but necessary or draw out the contrasts in such a way that they become selective in their attendance. Long before permanent truancy, these pupils 'bunk off' particular lessons. The stages of progression towards exclusion are gradual. At first the disaffection with the school, or with some lessons, is inward. 'I can't do that.' It is a refusal even to try. The next stage is the avoidance of a lesson for any number of reasons: incomplete work, a dislike of the subject or the demands of the teacher. Once that taste of personal choice is relished, the avoidance of lessons spreads from just those that are particularly disliked to any that are not their favourites.

These young offenders have their favourite lessons. These might be few and the exceptions but they also dominate the interests of the pupils. They want to become specialists in a system that expressly forbids it.

> Gym and Art… probably 'cos I was more relaxed, a more relaxed lesson and more time maybe to talk to other people in class. Say, like lessons like Maths, English, you had to work, you know? Like the teachers made you be quiet and work but like in art and that you could talk a bit and do the pictures and that.
>
> (male, 19)

The National Curriculum demands that all pupils take the core curriculum and then foundation subjects on the grounds that they should be 'broad and balanced'. The rationale for it is that no one should be allowed to specialize early. Maths must balance English. The National Curriculum also demands that pupils undertake set tasks. When so much needs to be learned there is little time for 'relaxation'. Maths and English are taken seriously. 'You have to work.' Art, on the other hand, allows both a sense of personal expression and a quite different approach to work. The contrast for some pupils could not be greater.

Certain lessons appeal to pupils because they feel that is where their talent lies. Others expose their limitations and bring out their resentments.

> I used to hate Maths and English. I used to go home in them. I used to like Art, Biology, Science, er and Woodwork and that. I've always liked doing things like that, practical rather than… I like making things and things like that, rather than doing sums and… just writing essays and stuff like that, but I didn't really like it, the comprehension where you just had to read questions and read passages out. I didn't really take much interest.
>
> (male, 19)

For someone who likes 'making' things, doing practical work, including experiments, some subjects will naturally stand out as being compatible. The problem is that in the mind of the pupil other lessons seem like a waste of time. Such lessons are often part of the core curriculum. It is that part that has to be taken most seriously by the school, that is the most inspected and most scrutinized from Standard Assessment Tasks and League tables, that is most disliked. Maths and English evoke associations with meaningless routines. They are the first to be avoided. When one subject dominates the interest, all others become of no particular interest.

> I used to concentrate on art all the time and you know try and get as best I can… so I wasn't really interested in anything else. 'Cos everyone used to say oh you're really good at art and that. I just forgot about everything else.
>
> (female, 21)

Certain subjects, often associated with a particular style of learning, are sought after and preferred. They contrast with the 'mainstream' subjects in such a way that the ways in which the core curriculum is presented, and the demands that it makes, become the more associated with the burdens of routine, and the strictness of control. Schooling is seen by some as an essentially off-putting experience. The discipline, the work, the seriousness; all these were in contrast with the excitement, the 'buzz' of life outside.

> School: it were morbid. Used to walk in classroom and there'd be people sat with faces, long and like all in their own little worlds. Then some of them would be doing stupid things and you'd think oh god please get me out.
>
> (female, 20)

To some the whole ethos, the whole experience of school, becomes meaningless and unpleasant. They begin to question why they are there. Their sense of estrangement is complete. Instead of accepting the need to work, to carry out duties, to follow instructions, they begin to wonder why they should submit to all these demands. They no longer see the point.

> I started not bothering going. I just used to find it really boring. I just couldn't be bothered. I'd rather have walked round town and things like that or stay with me mum and dad than just sit there in school. I didn't like the writing and I didn't like most of the people what was there… I wish the people had been different, the pupils… more kinder and more supportive, and I wish I… worked harder.
>
> (female, 21)

There is a point where *some* pupils cannot be 'bothered' to submit to the boredom. Whilst they might regret it afterwards, they cannot see the purpose of school at the time. Boredom is associated with not liking the set tasks, like writing, and there is also a sense of the school as an alienating institution in terms of the people in it. But even when the school remains a social centre, it can be experienced as something to be rejected, to be hated.

> If I could go back to school now I would but when I was at school I hated school. I don't know why I hated it, I just hated it. It's just school. But I just didn't like school. I got on with everyone at school. I used to have a laugh with everyone, used to get on with everyone, in our year.
>
> (male, 20)

There is something about the 'school' as an institution, beyond individual teachers and lessons, that appears to some pupils as being oppressive. Schools always carry in them, like all formal institutions, a tension between collective rules and individual personalities. Whilst the worst and defining moments in the experiences of these pupils depend on individual personalities, the background of the organization in which individual relationships occur is like a brooding presence. There are many different reasons for truancy, from personal laziness to social reasons, like the attitudes of parents. But the most common reasons are school based; the sense of low self-esteem and the way in which the school responds to it.[39] Given the conditions of schools in terms of class size and the pressures of inspection, it is not surprising that demanding pupils are difficult to handle. And there is something about the physical, social and academic environment that can appear extremely unattractive.[40]

> Getting detention and having to get there early in the morning and the school bus... the little ones 'cos they used to scream and run about and just do your head in at the end of the day.
>
> (female, 19)

Schools are unlike any other institutions, although many have suggested that the closest analogy is the prison.

> It's just like school this place.
>
> (male, 20)

The pupils are expected to conform. They are given strictly controlled tasks. There are rules to be followed, enforced by the threat of punishment. Some people – the adults – rule the rest. They are in charge. They set up the expectations and try to make sure that they are met. There are some pupils who find this manifestation of authority oppressive.

Just didn't like it, getting told what to, told what to do and that, just didn't.

(male, 20)

Just being told what to do it's always been my problem… so that was my image.

(male, 17)

The more you grow up you lose patience, I think, or I did anyway. Listening to people, er, wanting to do me own thing.

(male, 19)

These are the ones who, for one reason or another, have not learned the dialogue of negotiation. They see themselves being made or forced to do things. Discipline becomes a matter of will. Mutual collaboration is replaced by confrontation. The sense of being 'told what to do' is reacted against, and the more it is resisted the more weighty are the pressures. Some end up with a reputation, an 'image', so that confrontation is never far away. The alternative is simply to 'do my own thing'.

Once the school is perceived as oppressive, as something to be confronted rather than complied with, there is only one way out. The problem for the minority who do chose to exclude themselves is that they share their sense of the school as an often troubling place with the other people's awareness of the school as a place run by and for teachers. Pupils feel that they are not at the centre of the enterprise. They see the strain on teachers and understand the demands constantly made upon them from outside. They detect the fear of inspections and the nature of hierarchies.[41] Even in a school that does its best to include the children in decision making, the pupils feel that their voice is not heard.[42] Whilst only the minority of pupils, for their own reasons, fail to adapt to school life, there is something about schools and the way they are run, despite the often heroic efforts of teachers, that is essentially alienating. There are good moments and quiet corners, but there are also many oppressions, from fellow pupils and from tests. In studies of delinquency, there are many factors in schools that are shown to have damaging effects. The characteristics of the school and classroom environment and peer group experience can combine with low self-esteem and low levels of self-control to make a combustible mixture. Most pupils learn to adapt. But for those who do not, the intervention programmes are too late.[43] What could have been prevented, partly through the awareness of what the school is like in the perception and experience of some pupils, becomes an issue in itself. The very intervention can be interpreted as a disruption, an interference and another oppression. Schools are, in fact, a catalyst in which social problems can intensify.[44]

The painful experience of school should be seen as an outcome of the 'system', however broadly defined, rather than any deliberate personal agency, or desire to make them difficult. Schools are functional testing grounds, but supposed to test intellectual achievements and academic competences. But they also test character, and stamina, even if inadvertently. The daily experience of school can be summed up in the gaps between work, in the little events that the orchestration of a large number of people can throw up.

> Always fighting and that. I used to have fights nearly every day... just get little divs get on your nerves, just end up punching them. Spittin' on your back, things like that and you walk in and you'll hear somebody laugh behind you and then somebody else'll say you've got spit on your back, you know who it is, and it's just childish... that's what I don't like, people taking the piss.
>
> (male, 16)

References

1. Cullingford, C (1991) *The Inner World of the School*, Cassell, London
2. Ibid
3. Galton, M and Williamson, J (1995) *Groupwork in the Primary School*, Routledge, London
Bennett, N and Dunne, C (1992) *Managing Classroom Groups*, Simon and Schuster, London
4. Davies, B (1982) *Life in the Classroom and Playground*, Routledge and Kegan Paul, London
5. Blatchford, P (1998) *Social Life in School: Pupils' experiences at breaktime and recess from 7–16 years*, Falmer, London
6. Blatchford, P and Sharp, S (eds) (1994) *Breaktime and the School: Understanding and Changing Playground Behaviour*, Routledge, London
Blatchford, P. (1996) Taking pupils seriously: recent research and initiatives on breaktime in schools, *Education 3–13*, **24**(3), pp 60–5
7. Pellegrino, A and Davis, P (1993) Relations between childrens' playground and classroom behaviour, *British Journal of Educational Psychology*, **63** (1), pp 88–95
8. Cullingford, C (1992) *Children and Society*, Cassell, London
9. Boulton, M (1992) Participation in playground activities at middle school, *Educational Research*, **34** (3), pp 167–82
10. Smith, S (1997) Observing children on a school playground: The pedagogies of child-watching, in *Children and their Curriculum: The Perspectives of Primary and Elementary School Children*, eds A Pollard, D Thiessen and A Filer, pp 143–61, Falmer Press, London
11. Evans, J (1994) Problems in the playground, *Education 3–13*, **22** (2), pp 34–40
12. Titman, W (1994) *Special Places, Special People: The Hidden Curriculum of School Grounds*, World Wildlife Fund, Godalming
13. Boulton, M (1995) Playground behaviour and peer interaction, *British Journal of Educational Psychology*, **65** (2), pp 165–77
Boulton, M (1996) Lunchtime supervisor's attitudes towards playful fighting and ability to differentiate between playful and aggressive fighting: an intervention study, *British Journal of Educational Psychology*, **66** (3), pp 367–81
14. cf Pye, J (1989) *Invisible Children*, Oxford University Press, Oxford

15. Besag, V (1989) *Bullies and Victims in Schools: A Guide to Understanding and Management*, Open University Press Milton Keynes

16. Whitney, I and Smith, P (1993) A survey of the nature and extent of bulling in junior/middle and secondary schools, *Educational Research*, No. 35, pp 3–25

17. Olweus, D (1991) Bully/victim problems among school children, in *The Development of Childhood Aggression*, eds D Pepler and K Rubin, Lawrence Erlbaum, London

18. Sir William Taylor likes the anecdote that the greatest stress on baboons is not being chased by a lion (and presumably subsequently eaten) but being yawned at by a superior baboon.

19. Arora, C and Thompson, D (1994) Defining bullying for the secondary school, *Education and Child Psychology*, 4 (3), pp 110–20

20. Schäffer, M and Smith, P (1996) Teacher's perceptions of play fighting and real fighting in primary schools, *Educational Research*, 38 (2), pp 173–81

21. Munthe, E and Roland, E (1989) *Bullying: An International Perspective*, David Fulton, London

22. Whitney and Smith, op cit

23. Boulton, (1996), op cit

24. Mooney, A, Creeser, R and Blatchford, P (1991) Childrens' views on teasing and fighting in junior schools, *Educational Research*, 33 (2), pp 103–12

25. Dodge, K, Coie, J, Peltit, G and Price, J (1990) Peer status and aggression in boy's groups: developmental and contextual analyses, *Child Development*, 61 (5), pp 1289–309

26. Perry, D, Williard, J and Perry, L (1990) Peer's perceptions of the consequences that victimized children provide aggressors, *Child Development*, 61 (5), pp 1310–25

27. Stephenson, P and Smith, D (1989) Bullying in the junior school, in *Bullying in Schools*, eds D Tattum and D Lane, pp 45–57, Trentham Books, Stoke

28. Boulton, M and Underwood, K (1992) Bully/victim problems among middle school children, *British Journal of Educational Psychology*, No. 62, pp 78–87

29. Perry *et al*, op cit

30. Cullingford, C, in *Politics, Groups and the Individual*

31. Randall, P (1995) A factor study on the attitudes of children to bullying, *Educational Psychology in Practice*, 11 (3), pp 22–26

32. Lowenstein, L (1995) Perception and accuracy of perception by bullying children of potential victims, *Education Today*, 45 (2), pp 28–31

33. Perry *et al*, op cit
Whitney and Smith, op cit

34. Boulton, M (1995), op cit

35. Cullingford, C (1991) *Inner World of the School*, Cassell, London

36. Cullingford, C, *The Human Experience*, op cit, previous chapter

37. Kounin, JS (1970) *Discipline and Group Management in Classrooms*, Holt, Rhinehart and Winston, London

38. eg Rutter, M, Maughan, B, Mortimore, P and Ouston, J (1979) *Fifteen Thousand Hours – Secondary schools and their effects on children*, Open Books, London
Mortimore, P, Sammons, P, Stoll, L, Lewis, D and Ecob, R (1988) *School Matters: The Junior Years*, Open Books, London

39. Reid, K (1985) *Truancy and School Absenteeism*, Hodder and Stoughton, London

40. Lewis, C (1995) Improving attendance – reducing truancy, *Educational Psychology in Practice*, 11, (1), pp 36–40

41. cf Cullingford, *The Inner World of the School*, op cit
42. Greenfield, C (1996) The Teaching and Learning of Citizenship in an English Comprehensive School, Bristol University EdD
43. Gottfredson, M (1984) *Victims of Crime: The Dimensions of Risk*, HMSO, London
44. Hollin, C (1992) *Criminal Behaviour: A Psychological Approach to Explanation and Behaviour*, Falmer Press, London

6

The immediate causes of exclusion

Introduction

The number of exclusions from school increases each year. This focuses attention on the underlying causes. One explanation is that exclusions are an inevitable response to difficult and disruptive pupils who come to school already disaffected. Another is that they react against the way in which the education system is being steered, with more targets and assessments, more prescription and more measurement. Schools face conflicting pressures. On the one hand they need to improve their standards in order to rise in the 'league tables' and this means excluding any pupil that damages the likelihood of success. On the other hand one of the measurements of failure for which a school can be held to account is the number of official and recorded exclusions and unauthorized absences. The gap between the actual instances of truancy and the official figures is often wide. Truancy is recognized as a growing problem but it is probably even greater than is generally recognized.[1]

This is not the place to analyse the connection between education policy and disaffection from school. Here we want to trace the complexities, the different influences, personal and public, that lead to exclusion. This kind of disaffection is a gradual process, not a sudden one. Whilst home background is significant, the individual schools and the way they operate also have an influence. Every year there is an increase in the number of pupils excluded, but a small number of schools account for the majority of exclusions.[2] The reasons for the exclusions are mostly to do with aggressive behaviour – assaults on peers or teachers. But these are the final, overt, culminating actions that derive from all kinds of causes, from a sense of personal inadequacy and not being able to keep up with school work, to the feeling of being humiliated either by academic failure or by the incidence of teasing and bullying.[3]

Long before the final exclusion the pupil has become disaffected with school. The sense of estrangement has been well developed. There is almost a sense of inevitability, and certainly anticipation, that one day they will get away from school, whether of their own will or because they are forced to. With hindsight, of course, they regret it, and wish they had both behaved better and been treated differently. Even at the time they see what they half-despise as 'swots' setting themselves up for a successful future. There is a kind of disjunction between their rational understanding that the skills that schools are there to promote are necessary for their future employability and security, and their emotional antipathy and boredom. The school is a formal place that is presented as a necessary training ground for the future. Some are seen to put up with what takes place because of the long-term benefits. Others cannot accept the conditions; they cannot 'hack it'.

This disjunction between personal feelings and reactions and the whole system of school is very significant. At the heart of disaffection there is a clash between the private and the public. For these pupils relationships have always been the more important for their being difficult. They have made emotional connections. The relationships between peers can be strongly felt, positively or negatively. Nothing is more of an emotional relationship than nagging, teasing or bullying. These are attempts to get 'under the skin'. The constant interactions between groups and individuals are part of a personal and social pattern of school life. Beneath the surfaces of school are all the private tensions and ambiguities, the desire to be liked and the fear of being hurt. But the 'surfaces' of the school are also important. These are the rules, the expectations, the means by which the curriculum is organized and delivered. There is always a potential clash between personal desires and formal expectations.

Reactions to teachers

At the heart of this clash is an ambiguity about the role and personality of the teachers. Teachers are seen as people with their own feelings and problems, their own personal characteristics. Some are liked and others fiercely disliked. Some appear interesting and approachable and others are connected with boredom and incessant demands. Whilst teachers are clearly people, they are also playing a role. They impose discipline, whether they want to or not. They represent the order of the school. They are part of an homogenous unit, an overall policy and rule. The majority of pupils are able to accept that the teacher is both an individual personality and someone fulfilling a role. The best teachers accept the impersonality, the disinterestedness of their task, whilst also revealing something of their personalities. They do not try to be liked but see their main task as enabling the pupils to learn. They can be strict. And when they are strict it is because they see it as necessary, not because they feel like it.[4]

The majority of pupils who know how to relate to teachers accept the distinction between the public and the private; the role of the teacher and the fact of their different personalities and moods. They know just how far to go, and what the parameters are to acceptable behaviour.[5] They appreciate the teacher who is both exact and fair in the impersonal imposition of discipline and who can share a joke. This kind of relationship between a teacher and a class depends upon the teacher having a concern for all the pupils equally rather than having favourites, or more particularly certain pupils who are disliked. The balance between the public role and private personality is crucial, but it is not always understood by some pupils. These are the ones who resent the rules of the school and the enforcement of discipline. They also take it personally. They assume that if a teacher tells them to do something they are being personally 'picked on'. They assume that if a teacher shouts at them it is because he or she is angry. So they live with the recognition of the impersonality of rules, the social system of a school as an organization, but see individual teachers as personalities imposing these rules. The irony is that the more they perceive formal relationships as personality clashes, the more they see teachers as part of a 'system', and the more they hate them in a general way. There could be an analogy with the way in which the same minority subsequently view the police. They are hated as the 'fuzz', as generalized as possible, but their interactions with them are personal and emotional.

These disaffected pupils lack a sense of how to have a dialogue which is impersonal, and which depends on the transactions of life in public. Just as they veer from violent friendships to violent enmities, so they seek out particular teachers either for approval or because they react strongly against them. It is as if personal motivations were attributed to an inflexible law. Those who impose their will become enemies. This ambiguity of outlook is at the heart of the reactions against teachers as part of the system. What takes place is not just the imposition of social order but personally directed. It is not perceived as 'fair'. The whole social system then becomes the personification of impositions. Those who are part of it are demonized. The proper distinction between role and person, between structure and agency, is never made.

At the very time when 'all' teachers are associated with an alienating system, the strength of feeling about individual personalities ensures distinctions in reactions and behaviour. All pupils have teachers they prefer, and those they dislike. They pass on messages to each other about those who can keep discipline and those who can't, about those who are interesting and those who are dull, about those who can explain and those who stick to routine tasks. To the minority of pupils, however, the liking or dislike of individual teachers and the routine they impose tends towards the pathological. There is no easy-going tolerance of the foibles of particular characters, no acceptance of the limitations or innate absurdities of those who cannot properly communicate with their class. To them the differences between teachers (and tasks) are extreme.

Whilst teachers are generalized as people who are part of an implacable system, they are also responded to as individual personalities. The contrast between those who are liked and those who are disliked is strong. It is important to recognize that all the young offenders could recall teachers they particularly appreciated, for all kinds of reasons. There had been times when school work was, at least in part, good fun and interesting. Whilst some recall disliking all teachers almost on principle (to their subsequent regret), the majority appreciate particular teachers, either for the way they listened or the way they taught.

> Mrs F. that's our English teacher, taught English, taught about wildlife and all things like that. Er and Mr F. my form tutor, although he could be a bit stroppy at times, I think he preferred the girls to us for some reason.
>
> (male, 20)

Some teachers are approved. They provide the happier memories. Each one is judged, and their inclinations observed. Having someone who could be 'a bit stroppy at times' or who is more lenient towards the girls does not rule them out of appreciation.

The sense of personal empathy, of being able to strike up a relationship, is very important. Those teachers recalled with approval have certain characteristics. They either make the work interesting or relate closely to the individual or they do both. The sense of teachers having time for their pupils, and of treating them as individuals is paramount.

> Some teachers understand you and that. They understand how you feel and they're made to work that way. That's what they work for, to understand what we're like and that.
>
> (female, 16)

The desire for understanding and for personal recognition is strong. There is an irony in the half-recognition that such treatment is 'what they work for', part of the duty and role of being a teacher, but also it is taken personally. Instead of feeling rejected the pupils perceive that some teachers have 'time' for them.

> They always had plenty of time for you. If you had any problems they was there and it was really a close school where everyone was close to everyone. The teachers were always there. They used to be strict but you could have a laugh with them as well.
>
> (female, 19)

Here we have the recognition, once again, of the role that underlies personality. Before something goes wrong that tension between a necessary 'strictness' and a subtle bending of the rules, 'having a laugh', is part of the happier part of school life.

The desire to be 'understood' or 'listened to', to have a warm and secure relationship, can be very strong.

> There were Mrs T.... she was oldish. She ended up retiring just before I left. She were lovely, her, she were just like a grandma. If you got problems she used to sit down and cuddle you, things like that.
>
> (female, 20)

Especially for the girls there is a sense that a teacher can be someone who is like a personal friend (or 'grandma'), someone to talk to. Above all they wish to see their 'problems' acknowledged and understood. The desire for a personal and individual relationship implies that the normal routines of impersonal classroom control are more antipathetic. The longing for closeness, for personal contact, does not fit with the demands of routine work. It is the sense of the personal that is so dominant.

> I used to get on really well with this teacher Miss H. and she was the form tutor for the whole of that age group. I used to get on really well with her. I used to sit and talk to her and stuff... and she said... if you need anything just ask me. She was really nice.
>
> (female, 18)

Getting on well, being listened to, and being able to say what is going on privately is especially appreciated. It also contrasts with the routine demands of school: whole class teaching, the delivery of the curriculum and the reliance on old-fashioned methods. These individuals are looking for an alternative to the impersonal social demands of the school.

The contrast between some favourite lessons, those alternative and oblique opportunities to flourish, and the sense of insidious and creeping regulation and routine, becomes gradually more acute. It also becomes associated not just with some preferred subjects, like art and PE, but with the concentrated approach to work. The way in which certain subjects are taught is as important as the subject itself and linked closely to the personal style of the teacher.

> I remember the woodwork teacher. He was alright 'cos he was dead easy going. We used to have a laugh and that, crack jokes and like I got on with him alright.
>
> (male, 19)

Certain subjects give scope not just to creativity and individuality but to the engagement in a dialogue of a kind that feels much more like that of the peer group. 'Having a laugh', cracking jokes and being relaxed are in contrast to the demands of writing, of meeting set expectations. The boredom with certain lessons is presented against the mitigating factor of interesting tasks.

> Miss H…. she were like really nice. She used to do us about jobs and like we had to go through drawers and stuff like that, see what job we wanted and then she used to have a talk with us and that and hers were the only lesson I used to behave in.
>
> (female, 20)

The possibilities of behaving well depend on that subtle and sometimes seemingly arbitrary combination of the subject and the approach of the teacher. 'Having a talk', giving individual attention, is linked with a subject that appears to have meaning.

The moment that a subject is interesting it becomes 'easy'. The barriers of hostility, suspicion and most of all, self-abnegation, are broken down. Looking for jobs, perusing the files and talking are a far cry from the machinations of the standard assessment tests. There is room for personal manoeuvre and private relationships. Some subjects, almost inevitably the pupils' favourite ones, lend themselves to this.

> Used to like science, the lesson; it was ok. 'Cos like you'd be doing things like experiments and things like that. It wouldn't be the same thing every week so like I used to enjoy it.
>
> (male, 20)

Differences from the imposition of a set routine, and the chance to interact with others on a personal level, become increasingly important. For some, the astringent demands of the standard curriculum with measurable outcomes and common tasks become more and more estranging. Those sometimes happily remembered freedoms of primary school and the joys of learning are supplanted by the rigours of imposed expectations, of targets and of not meeting those targets. Alternative approaches become almost a haven in the mechanistic routines of general policy. What is attractive seems easy. What is unwillingly undertaken is always so much more difficult.

> I liked the English teacher 'cos he was nice. He was about the best person I liked in the school to talk to and that. Erm, and the work he used to give us was quite easy.
>
> (female, 21)

Sustainable work is linked almost inevitably with being talked to. It is no surprise that what is liked seems 'easy' and what is most alienating is difficult. The question remains whether this is purely in the minds of the pupils or whether there is something about the way the schools operate that makes them distant, difficult and obscure. For the pupils the good side of school (and that is firmly true of primary schools) is the warmth and concern of teachers. But then schools become larger, particularly from the pupil's point of view, and that personal contact with particular teachers becomes more problematic and more rare.

The development of disengagement from school

An assumption is sometimes made that the sense of security or insecurity is all to do with the developmental stages of the child.[6] Primary schools appear to be warm and all-embracing. They are certainly small by comparison to the secondary school. And it is clear that truancy and exclusion are almost exclusively the province of the secondary school. But this Piagetian assumption is to lay the blame on the individual, on adolescence, in the atavistic assertion that as people grow up they change, sometimes for the worse. The connection between age and exclusion is clear. What is not so clear is whether the underlying difficulty lies with the individual personality or the system, or the combination of both. One parameter of experience that deserves exploration is the social conditions in which people find themselves and whether they can put up with them or not. Secondary schools are fundamentally different in their organization and therefore in their ethos. The teacher as the centre of authority and the arbiter of welfare for the class is replaced by the teacher as representative of what is to be imposed, as the person whose responsibility is to the subject that he or she presents. In the minds of pupils this is an important distinction which rests not on their developmental stage but on the way in which schools are organized. From the point of view of the young offenders there are certain effects that strike them as significant. One of these is the estrangement, the separation of teachers as personalities, trying to care, trying to enable, and teachers who care more about what they are meant to teach than the effects on the learners. For those who wish to learn, the teacher as a fountain of knowledge is more than adequate. For those who do not, the same source of wisdom becomes an alienating being.

All this is gradual. The crucial years of the expression of disengagement are in the secondary school, even if the seeds have been sown earlier. They are not just to do with adolescence, but the circumstances of the school. The sense of psychological exclusion is a growing one, and there are all kinds of influences at work that enforce it.

I remember I got on well with all the teachers. They were alright, all the teachers was… Me mates said you can do this you can do that, you can swear at this teacher and you can swear at that teacher, so after the second year I just started getting into pure trouble.

(male, 20)

The process of disengagement from the norm is a slow one. Dropping out of particular lessons and finding it easy gives a taste for trying it out more often. Seeing what peers do and get away with becomes a definite attraction. All these are pupils vulnerable to alternatives to the formal systems of the school. They have learned clearly about what they like. Despite positive attitudes to school, they are resistant to certain aspects of the school's demands, like the tedium, the rules and sense of personal diminution. The factors are many. But the underlying cause is the disjunction between their sense of the school and the way the school presents itself to them. The increasing rates of exclusion are well documented and the ostensible reasons clearly outlined.[7] There are some obvious vulnerabilities and a clash between the individual and the school. Disliking rules and the work, disliking teachers and peers, the ostensible reasons, as well as the real ones, are many. But at the heart of all the disaffections is the central cause of dislocated relationships: the failure to be able to engage with others on an intellectual basis. 'Intellectual' means nothing erudite, but the meeting of minds.

Understanding others depends on being able to conduct relationships on more than one level, in differentiating between the formal and polite and the intimate or personal. It is the way in which these different transactions interact that the socially excluded find difficult. Those who are behaving in a manner that accords with their role and status are perceived as behaving in a personally directed way, driven by emotion rather than duty. Those who are trying to be approachable, to create a friendly dialogue, are seen as functionaries, saying things they ought to say because of their position. This means that schools are not experienced as simple or total systems. They are not seen as symbolic of the state or other social organizations but are far more complex. There is not, in fact, a conscious resistance to the ideologies of society.[8] Instead, the growing resistance to school is to individual or isolated parts of it, to the curriculum or to the pedagogic styles of teachers. There is a differentiation between which parts of the complex system are to be resisted.

The result of this personal experience of the different levels of schooling and the different types of people and approaches in a school is that the process of disengagement is a gradual one. There might be those who resist the whole notion of school as some kind of structural representation of society, but these are rare. The evidence that emerges from the experiences of the excluded is that the whole process is far less immediately confrontational. There is no sense of the recognition of the school as a symbol of an alien society, promoting class or capitalism.[9] The rejection of school begins with selected parts. It is discriminating. For every person who wants to avoid school completely there are 20 others who say they avoid particular lessons.[10] There are large numbers of pupils who have played truant from single lessons. It is easy to get away with. It is not usually recorded. Once it is seen to be both possible and rewarding, it is easy to apply the same technique to any lesson that seems to be threatening or demanding. Sometimes it is occasional. Sometimes it is habitual. Always the reasons are given as dissatisfaction with particular lessons, usually English, Maths, PE, French or Sciences.[11]

The constraint against truancy is much more to do with the sense of letting parents down, or being found out, than any deeper sense of guilt or duty.[12] The idea of *wanting* to miss certain lessons is as widespread as the dread of facing some teachers. All pupils have subjects that they wish did not exist, in which they feel inadequate and exposed. They are not good at the subjects and do not want to be good at them. When a pupil gives up trying there is little point in attendance. This is the seed-bed of truancy. Many pupils submit to the necessity of attendance, of going through the painful episodes of school. But the temptations of giving in, of finding the social expectations too constricting, are strong. Once that sense of cohesion with the social order, that almost unexamined assumption that social duties, like attendance, need to be met, is undermined, then a quite different way of thinking is introduced. By then no amount of subsequent control and punishment makes any real difference.[13] In all the evidence accumulated here there are almost no signs that what has been called the 'truant-catching industry' makes any positive difference. Despite all the unrewarding efforts of the welfare officers, the harm has already been done. And by that stage interagency rivalry also ensures that the help given will be far too late, as well as too little.[14] Once a pupil feels rejected by the school, or rejects the school, subsequent interest in him or her appears to make little difference. The support of other agencies needs to be given within the school rather than as some kind of bureaucratic afterthought.[15]

The school is a complex social organization and an unusual one in which the demarcation lines of power and helplessness are clearly drawn, at least on the surface. At one level the schools operate for the sake and order of the teachers, and the pupils are there to submit to their requirements. This is why some commentators have drawn the analogy with capitalist industries, of managers and workers, or officers and men. But schools are also places that are not dependent on clear sanctions, like losing a job, or being court-martialled. They rely fundamentally on the acceptance of rules, on recognizing the importance of delicate social control, and the acceptance of that control. At the same time they are places filled with the most volatile and changeable of power shifts, of constant redefinitions of friendships and enmities. The peer groups, the rivalries, the bullying and teasing, are an undercurrent in school life. Sometimes these undercurrents rise to the surface and involve the teachers.

The imposition of discipline

The teachers have their duties to perform, and these include sorting out problems of discipline. This can be a difficult, time-consuming and delicate matter. The evidence is conflicting and the tempers raw. The volatility of the pupils and their desire to bring in the teacher as arbiter makes for a breeding ground for disappointment and a sense of betrayal and disaffection. It also draws attention to the place of teachers in the social hierarchy of the school. They are caught up in decision making, in judgements and in immediate responses. The way they are perceived, therefore, becomes the more important. They are people as well as roles. They are no mere 'deliverers' of their subject but essential disciplinarians. This is not an easy job and it is no surprise that the young offenders have particularly potent memories of certain teachers, and sometimes of teachers as a whole. One image that abides in their memories is of teachers struggling to impose or maintain control. They are remembered in a symbolic way.

> All I can remember was them shouting at me all the time, sending me out of the classroom, that's all I can remember.
>
> (female, 16)

> The headmistress, like you couldn't talk to her, you know, just normal, she'd start shouting at you and that.
>
> (male, 20)

The sanctions which teachers have over misbehaviour are not that strong and constantly eroded. This diminution of power is not just the fact that all kinds of punishments are no longer acceptable but rests on the deeper one of the loss of moral authority. The instinct to question the way in which society operates and is controlled is growing. Teachers therefore attempt to impose order in difficult conditions.

The symbolic memory of teachers as 'shouting' is both the result of attempts to control and the signal of despair. Shouting is both confrontation and plea. It means the imposition of will and the recognition that there is an intractable situation that demands intervention. Such circumstances immediately distort normal relationships. Teachers become policemen, trying to impose order, relying on the generalized social acceptance of their position, their function and authority, and the subtle way in which they can make this 'acceptance' become imposed. The memory is often of a teacher who is on the edge of control, who has difficulties in imposing authority.

> I hated the teachers. This one, Mr O., don't know, just didn't like him. He'd hit you if you did anything wrong or that, just messing about and that in class. He just went mad and started shouting and that...
>
> (male, 16)

The question is at what point does the imposition of authority become one of personality rather than control? The ambiguity of role and person, as enacted in the responses of pupils, is also incipiently perceived by them in the actions of teachers. There are some who are perceived as antagonistic.

The vulnerability of teachers and their defensiveness are a deep consequence of their so often difficult, indeed absurd, task. One has to question whether any person should ever be put in the position of exerting control over recalcitrant and unwilling pupils who are not being punished but are supposed to be there for their own sake, for their own fulfilment. The answer to this question lies, of course, in analysing the way in which teachers find themselves in such a position, accepting it as a duty without exploring the wider social dimensions of their role. Whatever the position, however difficult, the teachers are seen as powerful rather than helpless, as motivated by hatred rather than concern. Those circumstances of the battle of will, of one against many, of the upholder of law against the individualism of a whole host of pupils, create a spectre of the fully charged personal antagonism that can humiliate. Teachers are seen to expect standards of academic achievement. That is their job. The whole edifice of published tables and assessment targets highlights the fact. This is acknowledged and recognized on an emotional level not so much by the teachers and the pupils' parents, but by the pupils. That point at which they psychologically exclude themselves is the point of public failure. The teachers who are so negatively remembered are associated with humiliation.

There are many opportunities to fail. Some pupils are poor readers and others feel innumerate. But personal failure is brought out in their perception through an association with a particular teacher.

> Miss M…. she used to like stabbing you in the elbows, yeah, wi' fork. If you had your elbow on table and all of a sudden fork'd jab you in elbow. I did it back to her once and I say do you like it. Hated her. Very bossy. And like if you's didn't turn out right she used to patronize you, you didn't try hard enough… 'Cos even though you were trying she ought to say well at least you tried. Makes you feel better for starters even if you have to throw it in the bin.
>
> (female, 20)

Of all the resentments that linger in the memory of school, the most pointed is the sense of humiliation. This comes in a number of forms. One is the sense of being patronized, of being treated like a 'little kid'. Another is the perception that teachers are not interested in pupils, that they have no time for them. And yet another is the sense that when a teacher pays attention to them it is for the wrong reasons. This teacher is described as hurting in a humiliating and provocative way, as being 'bossy' and, crucially, of never giving praise or encouragement. All that is recalled is of being accused of 'not trying' and having work thrown in the bin. But it is the sense of being patronized that penetrates into the pupils' abiding resentment, and is perceived as the most provocative attitude in the role of teacher.

> There was a couple of alright ones but like the rest of them had a bad attitude. Just like talking to you like you're a little kid and that... If the teachers had a different attitude... dunno, they should talk to you as if you're a normal person instead of treating you like a big kid.
>
> (male, 20)

Whilst the tone of teachers is generally resented, there are also moments of what seems like deliberate humiliation. In the experience of pupils it is bad enough to find certain subjects or skills difficult. It makes them automatic targets for teasing. Competition reveals their limitations. Their slowness of learning causes problems for teachers. But to some extent the difficulties in school are caused by psychological barriers. One of the inexcusable experiences of school is the public demonstration by a teacher of the inadequacies of individual pupils.

> Some teachers used to make me go into the classrooms and spell words on the board that I couldn't, that they knew I couldn't spell, to show me up and I didn't like that either.
>
> (male, 17)

> Because they embarrass you 'cos they know probably you ain't very good at reading and that, they'll just pick you out of the whole class and say stand up and read that paragraph to the class and all that and you say no I'm not doing it and they say right if you're not doing it you're going to the exclusion room so I just grabbed my bag and just walked out and everyone was taking the piss and that.
>
> (male, 16)

The moments that connect the sense of being humiliated and completely giving up on school and 'not bothering any more' are those when the pupils anticipate what will happen. They begin to expect teachers to take against them, to embarrass them or to 'pick on' them. They are already on the defensive as if there is nothing that they can do about it. Once that sense of inevitability sets in, once it is no longer a single act of a teacher but what appears like a continuing policy, then the school becomes an impossible place to inhabit.

> I used to just go to the exclusion room every time we had a language lesson 'cos I knew for a fact that if I went to the class he'd end up sending me there anyway... he weren't bothered, he were right out of order he were.
>   Most of the teachers stick you up.
>
> (male, 16)

What starts as isolated incidents and unpleasant surprises can easily become a set pattern. Both the beleaguered teachers and the recalcitrant pupils anticipate what will happen. The great temptation on both sides is not to care, to find the disengagement and the lack of dialogue to their advantage. The pupil avoids humiliation and the teacher avoids disruption.

Truancy and exclusion

Some individual pupils become marginalized. They feel themselves no longer to be a natural part of the school. They begin to presume that they belong elsewhere, that they no longer fit. At that stage truancy, not only from individual lessons but from school as a whole, sets in on a permanent basis – unless exclusion comes first. The sense of no longer being important to the school, of being on the periphery, of being ignored, as well as humiliated, is strong.

> Most of 'em, I didn't like 'em. I used to think they had their favourites. And I used to sit there and they just sort of blanked me out and talked to the others all the time, so I'd sit there most of the time on me own, nobody to talk to, so I used to sit on me own and then I used to think oh god I'm not coming tomorrow...
>
> (female, 21)

In the conditions in which teachers have to operate, with large classes, constant accountability and set targets, disruptive or difficult children become an extreme challenge. They are not just an extra demand, another call on the psychological skills of the teacher, but a source of major difficulty. Each of the young offenders wished there had been more individual attention – but they also wish that classes had been smaller so that this could have been possible. From the point of view of the teacher, the absence of a difficult pupil is an immense relief and this is bound to show. In these circumstances the sense of collective exasperation becomes like a palpable fact, interpreted by the individual as a desire to get them removed.

> I think the teachers, the school, didn't really want me there either... I didn't do nothing much to get expelled. I seen people get away with worse, but I think they just wanted me out of the school anyway and they knew I wasn't trying.
>
> (male, 19)

There is always a subtle balance between the sense of being emotionally excluded, of perceiving the negative reactions of teachers, and the desire to escape the conditions of school, of 'not going through with this...'. Before the incident that ultimately precipitates exclusion there are multiple instances of misunderstandings, confrontations, humiliations and dislike.

Those who are most vulnerable and feel themselves the most helpless feel any criticism that much more strongly. They are also subliminal targets for criticism, as if some form of humiliation were an inevitable outcome even if not deliberately sought. Just as victims of bullying are those most easily provoked and whose reactions are uncontrolled, so those alienated from school find themselves in the most difficulties. It is almost impossible to separate one from the other, as it is almost meaningless to make crude distinctions between 'victims' and 'bullies'. The criticism by teachers of school work is meant to be helpful but certain pupils find it undermining. These same pupils connect an individual incident with a global negative self-judgement, as if they were essentially incapable or constantly incompetent.[16] The tendencies to react negatively have already been well established before the traumas of the secondary school. But these negative reactions are a mixture of a lack of fundamental self-belief and an aggressive response to any confrontation. What has been set up in early childhood comes to fruition in adolescence. Those who react most aggressively to teachers also assume that teachers are angry with them, that the role of authority is imbued with personal animosity.[17] Everything is taken so personally that there is a constant and abiding assumption both of a lack of self-worth and of the need to strike out against such judgements. The incipient respect for teacher authority is gradually usurped by a reaction against it. Those who have respected their parents gradually develop a sense of autonomy and start to challenge such authority. When there is little parental authority or control, any kind of imposition or discipline is the more easily challenged.[18]

Once the acceptance of authority is questioned, all kinds of consequences follow. It is almost a surprise for some pupils to find out how powerful they can be. There are so many implicit assumptions on which authority rests. As in the case of revolution, if the majority really wish to impose their will nothing can stop them. There are times when schools are noted as being on the edge of a significant disturbance.[19] But this is successfully clamped down on because the collective sense that rules matter, and that all should function in a well-regulated society, is at the heart of the way schools operate. If it were not for such mutual sense of self-control teachers would be even more vulnerable than they are. Children are very quick to detect where authority lies. They instinctively search out and challenge weaknesses and vulnerabilities, not only in their peers but in the teachers. Whilst adult authority is generally accepted as greater than peer authority, the force of peers easily overcomes the non-authority of the adult.[20] That loss of adult authority comes about when pupils detect, without sympathy, how vulnerable teachers can be. Their personalities, their own concerns, come to the fore.

> Some teachers are alright, but most of them it's like when they have prob-
> lems and that at home, most of them bring it in to school, take it out on
> people.
>
> (male, 16)

Here is an example of personalized interpretation being turned inside out. The
world as the pupil understands it, according to his own nature, is projected on to
others. Teachers are no longer figures of authority but weak individuals, con-
sumed by their inner passions and private concerns. The difficulty is that teachers are on a knife-edge. They are supposed to display impersonal authority and
anonymous judgements. And yet they are also sought out as personal responders,
as sympathetic individuals who are charged not so much with discipline as with
caring. They are bound to be perceived as not capable of carrying out their tasks;
and the crucial fact is that they are perceived as not being able to do so, not
because the task is impossible but because they themselves are in some kind of
personal vendetta. The social system is impossibly implicated with personality.
The result is that teachers also feel vulnerable. They are not confident in their
ability to deal with bullying.[21] They are threatened by any events that are outside
their immediate control in the classroom. The sharp edge of disaffection is the
cut made between the private and the public, between the person and the role.
This is one that is generally understood by pupils. Those who do not see it, for
all kinds of reasons, become disaffected. At first it is with individual teachers,
but as disaffection becomes personalized, it spreads to the whole anonymous
system.

To those aggressively inclined, to those who feel at the end of their tether and
those who cannot cope with the demands of the school or the influence of their
friends, teachers are seen in a personal light, as if their remarks and their tone were
born in deep exasperation. Whilst they are not seen 'in role', they are depicted and
reacted to as part of a 'system'. Whilst most pupils, the 'jokers', know how far to go,
and when to desist from crossing the boundaries of discipline and expectation,
some pupils, sometimes after a long time and sometimes quite suddenly, seem to
snap, to lash out against the particular teacher who represents the system of rules
and orders. For some, the inability of knowing when to stop, or how to control
outbursts of anger, the problem is habitual.

> Just hitting teachers and everything, fighting with all me mates, best mates
> as well… I've given a hiding to teachers, given them a hiding as well. They
> put me in classes where there was a teacher who could control me, you
> know, a big enough teacher, you know, I couldn't hit, they put me in
> classes like that.
>
> After a couple of years I realized like they're doing it, they're starting off
> by calling the teachers this, that and the other and I was finishing it off and

going further than that, but they were getting the best of it 'cos they were-
n't getting done, it was me at the end of it.

(male, 21)

When a pupil needs physical constraint there is clearly a deep-seated problem. The
habitual fighting even with 'best' mates is not only deeply ingrained but suggests
almost a pride in being stronger and more aggressive than others. But this is a significant example of the way in which some pupils can be led on by their peers, deliberately tempted into trouble. There are always those who go further than anyone else,
who copy what seems to be a popular and daring psychological sport, and who attract
all the blame. Suddenly there is real trouble, and no admiration from the peer group.
The pupil trying so hard to win popularity feels himself exposed again.

The point of no return

The final point of exclusion is often associated with fighting. Months of frustration
and pent-up anger and resentment suddenly boil over.

> I didn't get on with this teacher and he was just naggin' me like, and just
> naggin', naggin' and that, and I couldn't take it so I just slammed the
> work down and just walked off, just walked over to him like and just said
> 'look keep buggin' me like I'll, you know, start on you like'; sat down. He
> says 'Glad to tell you if you do that like I'll get you arrested and all like
> that'. So I says 'will you' and just ran up there and just jumped up and
> head-butted him, glasses flew off, stamped on 'em, all teachers piled in,
> slapped me over the shoulder, he hit his head into the wall, and they all
> just done me.
>
> (male, 16)

The scene is depicted clearly. The point at which a school has to use physical force
is the point at which a pupil has been lost. All this, however, stems from just one
named teacher and one major incident. It is also the culmination of what is felt to
be unnecessary and unexplained 'nagging'. Pupils are always being told what to do.
That is what school seems to be for. The collective assumption is that the teachers
are there to impose rules, and academic demands, rather than share them. A quite
trivial incident can light aggressive instincts into a fire.

> I remember punching one in the stomach. 'Cos I walked in the class and I
> had me coat on and like he just started dragging me out of the class like by
> the hood of me coat, so I turned round and punched him. I got suspended.
>
> (male, 20)

Whilst one can understand the feelings of teachers and the sense that there are few constraints, it is never a good idea physically to engage with pupils. Despite government advice that teachers should do so, any physical approach to aggression merely provokes a physical response.[22] In this incident a school rule is being broken, a rule that the pupil clearly does not see as sensible. Reason and reasonableness disappear. One can understand the exasperation of the teacher; how is he to insist that the rule is obeyed? He feels he cannot ignore it or the whole organization, the whole system of authority, would collapse. But there should be no surprise at the reaction.

> Well, teacher'll come in, you probably have your coat on, he'd say take it off and me mate he didn't take his coat off and he says take it off and he says I'll take it off in a minute, he says you won't, you'll take it off now, and he tried to rip it off his back so me mate started fighting with him and that... and then he dragged him in the office; three teachers battered me.
>
> (male, 16)

It is every teacher's nightmare to find himself or herself in a direct conflict of will. To an explicit order the answer is no. Of course, there are techniques that bypass such scenes, but such incidents can happen easily. It is worth rememberingthat schools continue to function because such confrontations are rare. They are generally avoided on both sides. For if a whole class decided to disobey, or even a group, the teacher would be helpless. Schools rely on tacit agreements, on fragile conspiracies of obedience. Out of such a small but symbolic incident emerges pent-up anger and resentment. The coat has to be taken off 'now', not in a minute, not just because that is the school rule but because it is the teacher's will. Personal confrontation is born out of resentment at being told what to do, and the way in which one is spoken to.

The resentment at a particular teacher, the individual *bête noire*, that leads up to conflict, is built up over time. It does not always end in violence, but the incipient anger lies there ready to be enflamed. Sometimes the teacher provokes fear, and sometimes loathing.

> She started bullying me first thing in the morning and I just pulled a knife on her... I used to start crying at first but in the end I just got the knife to her.
>
> (female, 21)

Such violent acts are not arbitrary. They are usually directed against particularly disliked teachers, the ones that the pupil longs to disobey or the ones that seem to be 'picking on' them. The pupil sometimes even waits for revenge.

There was this teacher and I really hated her. She was really out of order...
she used to say like right horrible things and that to me. I can't really
remember some of the stuff she said but she had a Jaguar, yeah, this car,
and I was jumping on the bonnet on it; I think she grabbed hold of me or
something and whacked me, not round the face or anything, just whacked
me shoulder or me arm or something, and I ran off home screaming.

(female, 21)

This happened early and is connected in the girl's mind with her hating school and
with 'nickin' stuff and that from school'. For her the teacher remains unsympa-
thetic, 'just horrible'. There are many angry and hating relationships amongst
peers. Most have enemies. But when the enemy is a teacher it can be devastating.
The sense of helplessness adds to the hatred, the sense of powerlessness to the
resentment.

Certain incidents stand out from the monotonous routines of school or from
the daily frustrations. These include the good lessons, the favourite subjects, but
also the unhappinesses that culminate in an outburst. In the end the rage suddenly
becomes uncontrolled, even if it is triggered by a small event.

'Cos I had a Walkman it was, in class and the teacher told me to pull it off
and that and I was young at the time and I wasn't listening to her so I
answered her back and she just dragged it off me and it like broke, it fell on
the floor and broke, so I just like went mad and told her to fuck off and, er,
I got expelled then.

(male, 19)

'Just going mad' is a phrase that will reappear. It is the unleashing of pent-up anger
and the last resort of the irrational. Swearing at teachers is something that schools
take seriously; it is symbolic of the loss of authority, of disobedience mixed up with
a lack of respect, confrontation and spite.

I just stood up and said 'oh fuck off, I've had enough of you' and I just
walked out and everyone burst into hysterics. He kept having a go at me...
he was really horrible, he just, he used to grumble and all that about everything you done... He just done my head in.

(female, 18)

This is a person who 'everyone used to take the piss out of', perhaps a case study in
teaching failure, weakness and resentment.[23] But in the end it 'does her head in'. It
is like 'going mad'; there comes a point when such pupils cannot control themselves. If the confrontation is verbal they 'answer back'. If it is physical they hit out.

Nearly all of these confrontations are between individuals, even if there is an
audience. It is a result of a relationship not with a class or a group but with a very

personal sense of threat, one to one. Whilst pupils talk about teachers, they cannot resist the temptation collectively to undermine them if they can. But there are only rare occasions when they deliberately 'gang up' on teachers. A lot of pupils resent teachers and imagine revenge, but very rarely is it carried out systematically. When it does happen it is startling even to the young offender. A real taboo has then been broken.

> I dunno, I think it was something daft, over the teacher called one of the lads a thief or a liar or something, so there was two of them. One of them was in the toilets and er the other one went in the class and said 'here me mate's being sick in the toilet' and the teacher went in and his mate was in there with this pick hammer thing and whacked him with it. It's out of order, couldn't believe it, it's not the type of thing you expect to see in a school like, is it. They had some grudge against him. No one liked the teacher who it was, 'cos he was always dead nasty. No matter what a teacher can't do nothing to you that bad.
>
> (male, 19)

Even in the smouldering world of difficult schools there are certain events, as well as people, who are 'out of order'. It is a telling phrase, since there are certain kinds of order which all young offenders expect. There is an underlying sense of justice and fairness that despite their tempers and their experience they recognize as vital. It is the background against which they measure what has gone wrong. The sense of disappointment, of outrage, is strong. If there were no such insight into 'order', there would not be such a sense of anger. The actual cause for violence, like bullying, is often looked back on as being something 'daft'. With hindsight there are few provocations that merit such violent reactions. With hindsight many of the extreme events in school border on the absurd.

Alienation from school

For these young people who have 'failed' at school, their recollections combine the miserable with the absurd. At the time it was serious enough, with potential humiliation and fear from peers as well as teachers. But looking back they all give the impression that school did not have to be like that. It could have been markedly different. Hindsight can be an important commodity. The analysis that is brought to the social side of the school, both formal and informal, and to the academic purpose of the school does suggest at once how fragile is the school's social infrastructure and how narrow the line that divides success and failure. This is not to suggest that the 'school' by itself is responsible for all that goes on. The difficult pupils bring particularly delicate problems, and difficult temperaments, with them. It is the concatenation between the social ethos of the school and the way that it is interpreted that causes difficulties. Disaffection has a number of different levels; the sense of not being wanted is almost as powerful as the final act that invites exclusion.

> Don't know... pushing the teacher I think... some of them were ok but like didn't like any of them really. When they tell you what to do, like, I didn't like that... She weren't too bad but she slapped me once so I didn't like her.
>
> A PE teacher, that's the one I got expelled for. Got his head pushed and I didn't like him... but I was always like, don't know, wild towards him. Didn't like doin' what I was told. I'd argue about it.
>
> (male, 20)

Fighting with teachers and disliking them is the final outcome of disaffection. Teachers represent both the symbolic functions of the state, authority and order, sanctions and control, and individual personalities, those who are disliked and those who dislike in return, those who 'slap' and those who make a pupil 'wild'. There is no sense that this wildness is just the fault of teachers, but a breakdown of relationships. Pupils recognize their own responsibility whilst at the same time defining their feelings of helplessness, as if their character, combined with the circumstances, were too much for them. Thus we find they confess to being unable to cope with provocation, however trivial, and the demands of the teachers, however slight.

Exclusion from school derives from a fundamental challenge to the way the school operates, to the rule of authority. Fighting is clearly the most visible and extreme form of this challenge, and physical assaults on teachers the most dramatic. It is the final expression of frustration. It is not the only reason for exclusion. There are those who are expelled for drug dealing and those who feel that they were 'got rid of' because they were simply too difficult to handle, by not working and for disobedience. But fighting, whether with teachers or peers, is normally the core reason for exclusion. Sometimes it is a reaction to provocation.

> I used to fight with the boys all the time, that's why I got expelled. Got done of ABH, GBH on a boy, put him in hospital, just smacked him, punching him in the face and dragged his hair across the floor. 'Cos he tripped me up and I went flying and that. 'Cos it's not right though is it? Tripping a girl so I went off my head.
>
> (female, 16)

The inability to control a violent temper marks the experiences of many of the young offenders. It is a characteristic born of their experience, of the incapacity to develop a rational relationship unaffected by extreme emotional demands. It is not simply a genetic characteristic. They know that they are easily provoked, that they are easy targets and that they contain both anger and frustration. Usually their violence is in response to some act. It can be the culmination of a series of incidents when, as with their reactions to the final provocative action of a teacher, their sense of grievance bursts out. The inability to negotiate, to know when to stop, to be patient are both looked at ruefully and also, to some extent, defended. 'It's not right is it'?

> If you didn't turn up for school they weren't really bothered. It were truant-ing as well mainly, but fighting was a big problem. I just get worked up with little things, like so I just started fighting again and being stupid and I got expelled from there again and the police had to remove me from school.
>
> (male, 17)

Getting 'worked up', going 'off my head' are all indicators of a common experi-ence, the sense of bewildered psychological insecurity, of not being able to see their place in the framework of the school, its rules and expectations. There are estranged pupils who long to be able to be a part of the school, in their own way, but who somehow cannot do so. Whilst it is easy for them and popular for them to play truant, there is a part of them that also regrets what they are doing. The peer group pulls them away, but the school also pushes. They see which lessons and which teachers they like, but they cannot really feel ontologically at home. Many of the hidden meanings of school do not make sense of them. Most pupils detect both what the ethos of the school means and what it demands. It is rarely made explicit. For the minority the demands of the school remain both hidden and meaningless.

There are times when the violence that causes expulsion is deliberate:

> I used to rob loads of dinner tickets… out of the dinner hall and someone grassed me up so I battered him over it. This lad were just going on and I weren't having that so I just punched him and I got chucked out.
>
> (male, 16)

Usually, however, the fighting is a result of a reaction, a strong emotional impulse that the individual feels he or she cannot help. This does not mean they do not feel responsible but it suggests a disjunction between the emotional personality and the control of behaviour. It is as if some second, alien force had taken them over, as if they felt out of place in their surroundings and out of place with themselves. The phrase 'done my head in' and doing what are deemed to be meaningless tasks leads to a sense of disequilibrium. The school is then no longer a natural place to be. Being 'bored' with school can at one level simply mean having to submit to routine tasks like counting and writing. But at a pathological level it becomes a deep antipa-thy to all that school, as a social organization, stands for.

Didn't get on with them, was always fighting and that all the time, just arguing all the time. It was me and me sister really. Me sister would start arguing with one... then one of her mates would come and tell me she's fighting with the teachers and I'd just start fighting with them as well then... it were smashing fire alarms. Dunno, just bored.

(male, 20)

One could argue that there are some pupils who will never properly fit in, whose boredom leads to 'smashing' things up and fighting. There are those whose backgrounds suggest, whether brother or sister, that they are not easily suited to adhering to the regime of schools, given both the temptations from peers and the potential for discomfort, for being shown up as incapable of doing well in at least some subjects. But from the point of view of those who have failed school there are certain aspects of school that they find inimical. It is the way that teachers or head teachers talk to them. It is the amount of time spent waiting. It is also the abrasive relationships with others, inside and out of the classroom. And it is, above all, the gradual realization of the school as a monolithic set of rules and instructions, a place where people need to be de-personalized or the whole nature of authority would be jeopardized. It is the submission to the demands of the school or people in the mass, or the control of groups, or the needs for conformity that they find difficult. This is why the alternative set of relationships formed by the peer group becomes so attractive.

References

1. Most of the information remains officially 'hidden', for obvious reasons, but three anonymous local education authorities and countless schools have privately suggested that their figures are carefully 'laundered'.
2. Imich, A (1994) Exclusions from school: current trends and issues, *Educational Research*, **36** (1), pp 3–12
3. Chaplain, R (1996) Making a strategic withdrawal: disengagement and self-worth protection in male pupils, in *School Improvement: What can pupils tell us?*, eds J Ruddock, R Chaplain and G Wallace, pp 101–15, Fulton, London
4. Cullingford, C (1996) *The Effective Teacher*, Cassell, London
5. See Sluckin, A (1981) *Growing Up in the Playground*, Routledge, London
6. Piaget, J (1926) *The Language and Thoughts of the Child*, Kegan Paul, London
7. Gersch, I and Nolan, A (1994) Exclusions: what the children think, *Educational Psychology in Practice*, **10** (1), pp 35–45
Keys, W and Fernandes, C (1993) What do students think about school? A report for the National Commission on Education, Slough, NFCR
8. McFadden, M (1995) Resistance to schooling and educational outcomes: questions of structure and agency, *British Journal of Sociology of Education,* **16** (3), pp 293–308

9. McFadden, op cit
Bowles, S and Gintis, H (1976) *Schooling in Capitalist America*, Routledge and Kegan Paul, London
Gramsci, A. (1977) *Selections from Political Writings*, Lawrence and Wishart, London
10. O'Keefe, D (1994) *Truancy in English Secondary Schools*, HMSO, London
11. Stoll, P (1994) Truancy in English secondary schools, *Education Today*, **44** (1), pp 35–37
12. Ibid
13. Carless, P, Gleeson, D and Wardhaugh, J (1992) *Truancy: The Politics of Compulsory Schooling*, Open University Press, Buckingham
14. Ibid
15. Irving, B and Parker-Jenkins, M (1995) Tackling truancy: an examination of persistent non-attendance amongst disaffected school pupils and positive support agencies, *Cambridge Journal of Education*, **25** (2), pp 225–35
16. Heyman, G, Dweck, C and Cain, K (1992) Young children's vulnerability to self-blame and helplessness: relationships to beliefs about goodness, *Child Development*, **63** (2), pp 401–15
17. Trachtenberg, S and Viken, R (1994) Aggressive boys in the classroom: biased attribution of shared perceptions?, *Child Development*, **65** (3), pp 829–35
18. Smetana, J and Bita, B (1996) Adolescents' conceptions of teachers' authority and their relations to rule violations in school, *Child Development*, **67** (3), pp 1153–72
19. Measor, L and Woods, P (1984) *Changing Schools: Pupil Perspectives on Transfer to a Comprehensive School*, Open University Press, Milton Keynes
And see the story of the Ridings School, Halifax.
20. Lampa, M and Tariel, E (1986) Children's conceptions of adult and peer authority, *Child Development*, **57** (2), pp 405–12
21. Boulton, M (1997) Teachers' views on bullying: definitions, attitudes and ability to cope, *British Journal of Educational Psychology*, **67** (2), pp 223–33
Eighty-seven per cent wanted more training.
22. Guidance published by the Department for Education and Employment in 1998.
23. Cullingford, C (1997) Children's response to teachers, *Topic*, **19** (11), NFER

7

Peer groups: the alternative society

Introduction

Schools have often been likened to prisons. This analogy is also a common one in the minds of those in prison. But schools are easy to escape from. The association with prison comes about because of the sense of being incarcerated in a closed society. Once within the confines of the school, the pupils are supposed to stay there, to be told what to do and where to go. They therefore begin to think of the school as a closed institution, not so much in the physical as in the mental sense. They observe people operating in particular ways, following predetermined patterns, submitting to the will of those in authority. This view of schools emerges clearly and consistently from those who are disaffected. They easily see themselves either as being forced to be in the school, which makes escape the more attractive, or as being inwardly rejected by the school. For them there is a more attractive alternative.

In leaving school, whether voluntarily or not, there are both 'push' and 'pull' factors. The 'push' is demonstrated in verbal and physical abuse and humiliation. The 'pull' is that of the peer group. Even those who enjoy school find the siren voices of some of their friends difficult to resist.

> It weren't the school. It was the people I was with and I always felt guilty for not going to school... They never went to the school and they're the same age as me and like they seemed to be living so exciting lives and I was there stuck at school everyday and like I used to be going to school in the morning. They used to have loads of money all the time and I thought why can't I do this? Then I tried to do it both together and that didn't work so I tried robbing without going to school...
>
> (female, 19)

The peer pressure that is being described here is, of course, of a particular kind, the pressure not to conform, to seek out far more immediate attractions. The temptation to acquire money easily is made stronger by witnessing the success and the display of those who have been 'out robbing'. They seem to live such 'exciting' lives that the daily routines of school seem even more dreary. In the end the pupil can't fulfil both calls, either physically or, more importantly, psychologically. The power of the group that has a lot in common, and that is bound together outside the school setting, is very strong.[1] Academic failure in school and peer rejection by those who are working create antisocial friendships.

The growing habit of 'skiving' or 'bunking off' school is not only a matter of rejection but of seeking a more exciting alternative.

> Just didn't end up going. Just the people I started going out with, just didn't end up going. Just used to like go to the shopping centre by ours, just like hang around there, just loads of us, liked just decide to get off.
>
> (male, 20)

The problem is that one type of boredom, the entrapment of having to do certain kinds of work that is monotonous and appears meaningless, is replaced by another, that of seeking something exciting to do. Just 'hanging around' is soon replaced by challenging authority in different ways, authority being security guards instead of teachers. Those who would not normally dream of leaving school during the day nevertheless find the temptations proposed by friends too attractive to resist. Again and again the decision to play truant is made by a group. It is hardly ever an individual decision. Even when it is, there tends to be a group waiting. Sometimes people come from outside the school to tempt pupils away. Sometimes it is a sudden agreement.

> I were planning to stay at school, like me mate coaxed me into it, so we caught bus and went down town shoplifting. I didn't know we were going shoplifting at the time, but like when we got down town I saw her putting stuff in her coat and I thought 'oh my god'.
>
> (female, 20)

We hear a great deal about 'coaxing'. There is no doubt that before there are clear examples of antisocial behaviour and criminality the peer group finds means of weaning away from school those who are susceptible. There are many accounts of being 'tempted' as well as being misled. And once entrapped by association it is difficult to turn back. Being the disinterested witness to a robbery, or shoplifting, is one thing, but seeing it being carried out by a friend is quite another. It creates a sense of guilt by association, responsibility by not invoking preventative measures or calling in the authority. One of the crucial codes of this alternative society of friends is not to 'grass' on each other. There needs to be a code of loyalty, and that binds the witness to the act.

Escaping the demands of school

Those who still wish to work and who are committed to school find themselves tempted to enjoy an alternative style of behaviour. There are many who find school so boring or so meaningless that they are subconsciously seeking a way out. It all depends on the collective outlook of the peer group.

> Well, the lads who I used to be with like, they used never be interested in work... with school mates, they were like wagging it.
>
> (male, 18)

Both the characteristics of adolescents' friends and the quality of their friendships affect their attitude to school and this can be negative as well as positive.[2] The peer group can have powerful psychological weapons, for those who are not armoured against them. Examples of how to escape disliked activities are one. Threats of being bullied are another. Being teased, being found wanting or unworthy is possibly the most powerful.

> Just being with all me mates and that, just getting in with people. 'Cos if you didn't run off they'd say ohhh, you know pick on you and stuff like that... They'd say oh you're not hanging around with us no more then, they'd say stuff like that... gutted. So I'd go and run off with them.
>
> (female, 16)

Those with fragile self-images are especially susceptible to being cajoled into joining in with the gang. Some want to show off their popularity, prowess or individuality. Others want to avoid being teased or bullied. One of the motivations behind 'picking on' people is not so much the melancholy pleasure of seeing someone else in distress as in making them do what you want them to do. Peer groups need members; it is like a contagion some find difficult to resist.

There are many who do not even think of resisting. The alternative activities that are presented by the antisocial peer group seem exciting and attractive. They seem to stand for 'freedom'. This is especially clear in the accounts of females. The males, with their macho self-image, emphasize their prowess as well as their excitement. For the girls the excitement of freedom, of a different way of life, still retains that edge of glamour as they recollect those heady days. Freed of the numbing routines of the everyday and the ordinary, they relish a completely different

way of life, of constant excitement and riches, of routines overturned and a different pattern and style of living endorsed.

> People helping you out and stuff like that. I loved it there. Just running off
> all the time and getting drunk and smashing windows and nicking cars. I
> used to be into that all the time. I just loved it, just being with the people I
> mixed with and that 'cos we always used to run off all the time and that and
> I could do what I want to when I was there. Just like mixing with my
> friends and that, messing about, running off. I felt free. I love me freedom
> and that so.
>
> (female, 16)

Freedom. Being with the people she mixes with. Running off, out of the entrapment of the classroom and the school, doing what she chooses to do rather than
what is demanded of her. The peer group offers support for all these things. The
individual takes part in shared and collective decisions, but feels a personal ownership of what happens. Nothing appears to be imposed from outside. The peers
'support' and do not suppress. The irresponsibility, the lack of constraint, all
bound up in the term 'freedom', seem a wonderful alternative. Looking at the different lifestyle that seems so attractive makes it, for some, almost irresistible.

> I think it was the fact that they could do whatever they wanted and get
> away with it and 'cos I didn't have that at 16. I felt dead stupid when I was
> with them 'cos they could like go in like eight o'clock in the morning and
> stay out all night if they wanted and I wanted to be like them. It was more
> the freedom that I wanted and it seemed to me like the crime that they
> were doing would give me the freedom.
>
> (female, 19)

Freedom, again. In the circumstances it has an ironic ring. But this does not diminish the fervour and the relish of its attainment, a world away from the enclosures of
school. Having personal responsibility, doing 'whatever they wanted' without
being stopped or punished: that seems to be the alternative to the regime of the
school. It is as if the young offender's friends had somehow escaped. They had
shed the constraints. And to keep up with them, to avoid being made to feel 'dead
stupid', she had to do the same. The power of peer pressure is not just negative, in
forcing someone to follow, but attractive. She wants to be like them.

Being 'like them' means parodying or copying a way of living that is the antithe-
sis of the fixed routine. This does not mean that there is no routine at all. There are
still 'typical' days. They are just very different.

> Whereas my typical day was, get up, erm have a piss, get ready, go out, do
> some robberies, erm burglary or whatever else, nick a car, go home again,

get changed again, go and see my friends, spending loads of money or whatever, travelling all over, visit friends in the nick in the afternoon, go home, get changed again, go out robbing again, go home, get changed, go to aerol's or something like that, all that time I'm taking more and more drugs so I'm out of my head anyway.

(female, 19)

Freedom or distraction? What on the surface appears to be plenty of variety, and a new routine of changing clothes, is underneath the taking of more and more drugs. In such circumstances, of being 'out of my head', the routine demands imposed by school are replaced by the routine necessities of yet another fix, or 'piss'. Stealing a car or carrying out a robbery are almost washed clean of their implications. It is constant movement in which seeing friends, like changing clothes, is a recurrent and underpinning theme. Those who accept the alternative way of life are just as bound up in it as those who remain back at school. But this appears to be so much more liberating at the time, so much more free of constraint. The more people are accustomed to a routine, imbued in a way of life, the more what is at first exciting becomes habitual. What at first is witnessed or observed gradually becomes absorbed and parodied.[3]

Types of conformity

Conformity to expectations and doing what everyone else is doing is a powerful motivating factor. It can be a force for good or bad. Obedience to rules and fulfilling perceived duty can be both an explanation and an excuse for either the most honourable acts or the most despicable.[4] The school demands conformity, but so do peers. The choice between the two can seem a stark one, but the way in which the choice operates upon the individual is a matter not only of chance but of many intervening factors. There are clearly some children who have all the high-risk associations that will lead to the influence of antisocial peer pressure, from parents to communities. There are certain children from certain backgrounds who are most likely to be maladjusted.[5] When the peer group and the shared expectations are all in place, antisocial behaviour is constantly reinforced.[6] The peers meet and bolster each other. They live close together. They find places to congregate. They tend to share certain characteristics that lend themselves to more hostile acts, on the one hand displaying symptoms of unhappiness or disturbance, or on the other finding a solution in excitement, like drinking.[7] There is almost a typology of those who are most at risk from following the patterns of delinquent group behaviour. They are all to do with the absence of constraining social forces, of a lack of stable social relationships.[8] There is very little of the antisocial carried out solely by the individual. The accumulation of examples and the implicit support of others are crucial.[9]

The powerful influence of peer groups has often been recognized but perhaps less often really understood. At one cultural level it is obvious. That people are formed by shared tastes as well as creating their own is clear, as well as the desire to fit in to their dominant expectation.[10] But the psychological necessity for certain types of approval over others remains to some extent unexplored. What tips a person who is seemingly happily entrenched in one form of conformity to reject it for the sake of another? Most studies of the strength of taste and the attempts to satisfy the peer group deal with single, shared and commonly understood positions. We are 'branded on the tongue', brought up in certain circles or societies. The demands of a common culture and inheritance, and the moulding by its prerequisites, are strong. But what of those who have not one homogenous environment, but two alternative ones or more? Whilst it is easy to suggest that the socio-economically deprived will always have their own way of thinking and language and not submit to the imposition of an alternative conformity, the facts do not bear out such an assertion.[11] Whilst the influence of the community, really peer pressure, is strong, it is not automatic. The majority of children from those deprived environments do not succumb to their peers. The way that pressure operates is far more subtle.

It is too easy to explain all behaviour purely on the genetic basis of personality. Whilst most recognize their own weakness and responsibility there is also a shared acknowledgement that environmental factors are very important. At one level this is obvious. Criminal activity depends not just on motivation but on opportunity. At the same time it is the result of an expectation of what people do and a knowledge of how to do it. Those who steal objects need to know where to sell them in order to make money. The majority of citizens would not have the faintest idea of where such outlets might be. That there are places where one can find drugs is clear, but most people would not know where to look. Knowledge and familiarity arise from certain places and certain circumstances. One barrier to criminal activity is broken down. But more significant is the collective cast of mind.

> Everyone, everyone my age round my area guarantee they all rob and like I don't know one that don't. You've got nothing to do, you got no money for no fags so you just go round and if you see something in a car you think well, there's money there and I could just get it.

> (male, 16)

'Everyone' doing something is not just conformity but sanction. The peer pressure is not just individual but collective. When the assumption is that all are criminals, crime becomes habitual. Many of the young offenders, the men in particular, talk about the conformity of crime, how all the people where they were brought up were 'criminals'. All wish to go out with their 'mates'. Some 'mates' can easily lead them astray: 'started to go round with me mates. That's when I started to go criminal'(male, 19).

There is nothing done as an individual that is not heavily, almost mercilessly, influenced by others. This takes nothing away from the status and dignity of being individual. All influences are a personal choice and as much rejected as accepted, and refined. But the desire to please, to join in, to be liked, is strong.

> When I was in the seniors, other lads were doing it, and I've always been one, if they're doing it, I've got to do it, no, I wanna do it. I've got to do it, so I was doing it, started off shoplifting, up to robbin' sheds and then started burglaries.
>
> (male, 21)

The desire to please, to fit in, becomes internalized. Following the example of others quickly becomes translated into personal desire. He knows his own bent towards copying others but he assumes that by doing so he makes actions his own choice. In many of the accounts there are clear indications of the moment of choice, of being cajoled into an alternative path. Such a choice is never inevitable.

Choice is not just the result of chance, but grows from the awareness of alternatives. The pull factor of peer pressure, whatever it takes, is not juxtaposed solely against the push factor of the school. There are other alternatives of rejection.

> The people I liked to hang around with, they never used to have anything either, see, the people who had everything, they'd like keep to their group and I'd keep to another group.
>   And the people I hanged around with you don't mess with them sort of people.
>
> (female, 21)

Definition of the self against others is compounded by wider social definitions. If there is a popular or trendy group it defines itself as such in opposition to outsiders, to those who do not belong. It can also see itself defined against other distinct groups, and even come into being as a kind of protective measure. The individuals feeling themselves to be 'different' are bolstered when there are also others who are on one side of a psychological or social dividing line, whether this is based on personality or possessions. In this case the young offender's own group is defined at once as the 'wrong crowd' and the one that did not have money for smart clothes. There are both a sense of solidarity and defensiveness, a feeling of shame, and an urgency of anger. The 'us' is defined against 'them'. Sometimes the groups are formed simply by daily experience, by the compatibility of certain personalities, and by the antipathy to others.

'Cos they're all from like don't know normal quiet areas and I couldn't associate with them: it was like five or six who I could get on with and that was it.

(male, 20)

Most personal and collective cultures define themselves in opposition to others.[12]

Whilst opposing factions define themselves in subconscious enmity, and sometimes overt distinction, the real point of the group is the sense of warmth and protection it affords. The sense of the social embrace, the pervasive and lubricious
support of a large crowd, affords the opportunity for atavistic security. The group
is the fulfilling alternative to the divisive and dismissive aspects of school.

Everyone hangs around with each other like big group of you; everyone
just gets on with everyone. I just didn't like school. Sometimes like I
wouldn't go to school, would wait until school finished and then wait outside the gate for everyone, walk with them like.
When you're young you're just buzzin' off not going to school.

(male, 20)

The big group, everyone getting on well with each other, is held up as a contrast to
the usual experience of school. No one makes demands that cannot be met. At last
school is finished and it seems like a blessed relief.

The attraction of being with mates, free of school, is that of not being forced or
expected to do anything that is not self-indulgent.

I went back to me old ways like hanging about with me mates, doing, you
know, stupid things, you know what I mean, like getting drunk and doing
this that and you know what I mean just doing nothing, actually, nothing,
really just wasting time.

(male, 20)

The group reinforces certain habits. It might seem, in retrospect, like 'wasting
time', doing 'nothing', but it seems at first comparatively liberating. He has been
warned about being caught up in the 'wrong' crowd, but old ways, old habits, die
hard. It is like a contaminating influence, the sense of belonging to a crowd of
mates or thinking of things to do; it is both a definition of belonging, of being *in*
and being admired, and a definition *against* what they ought to be doing. The group
is deliberately antisocial. The group pattern can also affect a whole community.

Like round our area it's just like there's sweet packets everywhere… all the
kids. There's too many kids in our area. They all walk round smashing
things up and the council just say to us when we've gone you can smash it
up again if you want 'cos we're only getting paid for it anyway.

(male, 16)

There comes a point where even those in some kind of ostensible authority become imbued with the notions or habits of the gang as if there is nothing that can be done about it. It is 'all the kids', too many of them to control, that create the antisocial norm.

The attractions of esteem

The pressure to follow group norms comes about partly because of the habit of conformity, partly because pupils would be teased or bullied if they did not cohere to the standard pattern, and partly because of a desire to show off. Given the alternative styles of behaviour, of submitting to the expectations of authority, or of conforming to the behaviour of the group, the latter appears to many to be more admired. It is then people who stand out, who behave in ways that dominate, that others would like to emulate even if they dare not do so. The reputation, the image of being outside the standard conventions, is for some very important.

> So I just lived up to my reputation... this is a bad area as well and that's where I started all me drugs and thieving and robbing and all that. Right, so that was my image and I just when I started doing it everyone saying 'alright D. lad'. I got a lot of respect for it so I just thought I'd carry on doing it.
>
> (male, 17)

The desire to please, to live up to expectations, can be directed towards teachers or, in those places where there is an alternative culture, the peer group. There are many different types of peer group, with changing circles of relationships, with varieties of size and with different standards of expectations. But one should not underestimate the pressure of the 'alternative' society. Image and reputation are important. They depend on the audience. For some, pleasing the teachers is crucial. For others, gaining respect for being antisocial is more attractive. One of the strongest motivations is fulfilling other people's expectations. Once a reputation is made it is difficult not to keep it up, even if there is a desire to change. The peer group goads and cajoles. It does not easily allow for any change of action, like beginning to take work seriously. This is why so many of the young offenders regret that they did not have enough independence of mind to resist that pressure.

It is only afterwards that that crucial motivation is recognized for what it was: gaining esteem in the eyes of peers, demonstrating unconformity and independence. It seems at the time like a sign of freedom, of strength, of not following standard rules and behaviours. The irony is that it is in its own way a deep conformity, a bending of the will to what certain others expect.

Just showing off all the time, that's all it was, just showing off all the time, had to be better than the others, had to be better than everyone else.

(male, 21)

'Like then I went out banging clothes and that, then 'cos me mates were round, I was just, I was doing it showing off in front of me mates.

(male, 19)

'Showing off' in front of some people is to demonstrate the breaking or abandoning of other conventions. This rests on the assumption that those who adhere to rules are somehow 'soft'.

And the people I hanged round with, you don't mess with them sort of people.

(female, 21)

Those children who are highly rated tend to be those who are willing to engage in aggressive behaviour, who can 'stand up for themselves'.[13] The quiet and the demure are associated with softness and weakness. They would not think of being aggressive on the grounds that it could lead to negative outcomes. Those who show off, who want to be admired, have no thought of the consequences. They exhibit self-confidence and independence, as if no one could 'mess' with them. But they also are driven by the desire to please, to fulfil expectations.

I started mixing with older people then, and from there it went worse... I wanted to think that I was more grown-up you know being around older people and like I was only young and I just wanted to grow up fast you know? Just wanted, I wanted things to happen fast... going to pubs and that, staying out late and basically being lazy. I did have friends, yeah, just like people I used to, er, not real friends but just people who used to look up to me.

(male, 19)

There is no peer pressure for young people as powerful as the small differences in age, in being respected by older people. Going out with someone older, being taken seriously by those in the year above, is very attractive. The younger ones look on the older ones with admiration. Of all the people who it is hoped will 'look up to me', the older ones are the most important. And being more mature is associated with doing all those things that only adults are allowed – drinking or watching restricted movies. Maturity is associated with discontent at 'childish' restrictions.

Showing off is a strong motivation for antisocial behaviour. It presupposes an admiring audience, and being noticed. It also defines itself against the usual expectations of the formal society of school. But once there is that great divide peers can become important at another level. They share the same tastes and habits but they also provide understanding. Adolescents select as friends those who share their own characteristics. The aggressive and the antisocial will cling together.[14] There comes a time when only those who have had similar experiences can really sympathize with each other. The peer group reinforces itself when the individuals within it cannot really relate any more to outsiders. The experiences become too different. This can come about for all kinds of reasons.

> At one time I thought that I couldn't socialize with no one unless I had a drug… if I'm with friends I'm alright.
>
> (male, 17)

The gap between more formal relations, or normal dealings with people, and basking in the succour of friendship grows.

> I've been through everything with her, and that and no matter what I wouldn't stick up for the other person. I'd stick up for her 'cos I think a lot of her… They were funny and that, made me laugh, cheered me up. They'd been through what I'd been through and they understood how I feel and that.
>
> (female, 16)

> Whether they're there whenever you need them, if you've got a problem you can talk to them, if they've got a problem they can talk to you. They're always cheery… and they've got to be hygienic 'cos I can't stand sitting next to a smelly person…
>
> (female, 20)

Those seeking understanding turn to those who have 'been through' similar experiences, thereby reinforcing the shared behaviours. Only those on the 'inside' can really know what the problems are. So the peer group provides not just approval and tacit compliance but sympathy. It mixes the ability to share a joke with shared understanding, without criticism or demands.

The society of gangs

The bonds of friendship are varied. They include shared tastes and a common language. They can also be dependent on shared behaviour. They can be permanent or temporary. They can also be negative as well as positive.[15] Peer groups influence behaviours as well as attitudes. The desire to be liked and admired is paralleled by the desire to avoid being disliked or despised. Friendships depend not only on the identity of the friends but on the quality of the friendship. There are two perspectives in the study of friendship: a focus on the nature of the friends and a focus on the quality of the relationships. Both affect the way in which pupils adjust to school.[16] The peer group as described here is an extension of individual friendship. It extends sharing ideas and attitudes to a collective norm. And it also demands certain loyalties. Just as these people want to show off to their peers, so they feel they must not let them down. Once enclosed in an antisocial world there is that 'honour amongst thieves' that they should not break the boundaries, especially by not giving anyone away. There is nothing so despised or hated as those who 'grass'.

> When I realized lads were the thing then I changed. All the lads accept us as one of the lads… like most of the girls, you can take them out and they'll grass them up like they've done to me. I'm mad about that at the moment, all I was thinking about before is I wanna get out and just go mad at 'em, but I thought if I do that they'll just grass me up again and I'll be back in. So I just have to leave that thought.
>   The way I see it is if you're going out robbing with someone, you both going out with the same risk and you expect one of them not to grass you up like say to the police oh well he did it or she did it. It's like an untold law if you go out robbing with someone you don't grass them up and like that's the way it's always been and like I've never grassed anybody up.
>   (female, 19)

There are certain 'untold laws' that bind the groups together. The great fear is that the enclosed pattern of friendship is broken out of, or broken into. The peer groups share their secrets as well as their behaviours. Nothing creates so much anger as being 'grassed' upon. It is an extension of gossip, only an even more dangerous one. In schools what clearly upsets pupils, worse even than bullying, is being teased or accused. In previous chapters we have noted the hatred caused by people being called 'slags' or other such terms. It is an extension of teasing into false accusation. The next extension is being reported to teachers. Nothing creates more indignation than finding out that a fellow pupil has told those in authority what is going on – like stealing dinner money. And the further stage of the pattern is telling the police, of trying to pass the blame to someone else. Within prison and outside, 'grassing' is not forgiven.

> I know he's done a few jobs. I just, I'm just not a grass. That's what they say, things like 'it's not worth it'. If they all found out I'm a grass when I get out they'll probably come after me with knives and stuff like that 'cos I've seen that sort of thing happen before. I'll sort him out myself when I get out.
>   (male, 17)

The pressure to conform to the 'untold law' of the group is very strong on a number of levels. The breaking of that law invites retribution and many of the most violent incidents between gangs come about because the taboo of peer behaviour is broken. The gang is a self-enclosed unit. Once inside, it is difficult to break out. The prison of expectation and habit, of conformity to peer group pressure, is as strong as any other. This is why the young offenders reflect so much on what will happen once they are released. What will be the threats and the temptations they will face? They know that their peers await them, and assume that they will not have changed.

Once caught up in a 'gang' and a set of behaviours it is difficult to escape. When a whole community seems to be at one in the way it operates, there seems little choice. But entering into the antisocial community can swivel on a decisive moment. Whilst the whole area is 'bad', it needs an action, a trigger, to get someone to enter into the world of crime.

> I met this lad called R. right and I don't know really. One day I just seen him over this fence and like I just knew I'd seen him about and I just asked him to lend me a quid to get some dinner and I asked what you doing and he said breaking into this house and I thought fucking hell I can't believe he's breaking into a house so I walked away, went to shop and on the way through he called me over, he says, grab hold of these for me and he give me video and he give me half the money. I got about 60 quid. Then day after, seen him again and he says do you wanna come with me again and do another one and get half the money and it just started from there.
>
> (male, 17)

The starting point might seem accidental. Incipient criminality is turned into crime. One could argue that it was only the opportunity that let this boy into the temptations of gaining money (and respect) through burglary. But he was also ready for the temptation and quick enough to take up the offer. He had seen 'the lad' before, well enough to ask for money. The problem is that what has been started is very difficult to stop. The moment of choice is very significant. But it emerges from a readiness to act, a desire to please, to show off, as well as a kind of desperation. And once inside that other world the pressures of conformity are strong.

The moment of turning to crime cannot be separated from criminality. It is embedded in the vulnerability to temptation, in the readiness to please and in an essential insecurity. There is that moment when the individual succumbs to pressure and no longer says no.

> I kept saying no and he kept saying it won't hurt you... and I didn't really like it but him and all his friends were into it and like I kept saying no after

that. And then, er, I started sniffing gas up with one of his friends and I
liked the way it made me feel 'cos it made me escape from reality sort of
thing… so I tried it, smoking draw.

(female, 19)

And once started, this is a habit, like thieving, that is difficult to give up. All the
friends are 'into it'. It is as if, out of a deep insecurity, there was a lack of
will-power. For all the showing off, the need for the crowd and the desire to
impress are a sign not of 'machismo' but of a lack of self-esteem. Being tough is an
action of the body to hide the defects of the mind.

This conformity to the will of the peer group is recognized by the young
offenders. When they acknowledge their own weakness they do so not to deflect
blame, or to suggest that it is not their own fault, but in the spirit of realization.
This is proved by their recognition that they are likely to be too weak to resist
temptation, whether they want to or not. When they emerge from prison they
would like to lead a quite different life. But they know this is an ideal, unlikely to
be realized, not just because of the strength of peer group pressure but because of
their own amenability to it. What they want to do, and what they hope to do, is
deeply affected by peer pressure: and this is recognized.

Depends what company I'm with… I want to 'cos I know the life of a
smack head.

(female, 21)

Knowing what is dreaded is not enough. It all depends on the 'company', the
temptations, the inability to say no. The pressure of the familiar community, and
the ease of returning to established patterns of behaviour, is strong.

Just all me mates I think. I mean everyone else was doing it… 'cos I know
if I carry on living in L. I'll just get into trouble again.

(male, 20)

This is recognized as a fact as well as a regret. When 'everyone' does it, to stand
against them is difficult. It is even recognized as the technically correct term.

I don't know I suppose it's peer pressure isn't it, 'cos you're all together in
a group. The girls I used to hang round with, they was really popular. I
thought it was funny at the time. You just go along with it. I suppose if
they're your friends and stuff… Mixing with the wrong crowd again.

(female, 18)

The 'wrong crowd'. This is a phrase that keeps reappearing. It is suggestive
both of the difference between right and wrong, correctness, social norms and the

alternative, and of different conceptions of personal or social morality. The 'wrong' crowd are those who bully or cajole, who lead into temptation. They are also clearly antisocial. They do harm. But they are powerful and when the young offenders look back on their previous behaviour they do not mislead themselves into the assumption that they have been transformed.

> Probably end up back in here, knowing me. 'Cos I'll get in with the wrong crowd... They used to nick from shops and do burglaries and stuff like that and I'm hanging about with them now and writing to them still and everything. So I'll be out with them again.
>
> (female, 16)

Conformity, obedience to the norms, and the desire to please are as strong if the circumstances are deviant as when they are regular. The 'normal' to some is not the 'norm'. Each group owns its particular sense of 'normality'. This does not mean that it is, in the usual sense, conventional. The probability of reoffending is strong and recognized. Good intentions will so easily be undermined.

> It's just like when I get out I've gotta like push myself to do it, haven't I. That's the hardest bit about it... like the people I hang round with they're the sort like who take the piss and like it's hard to get away from them... probably the crowd, the crowd I was hanging around with.
>
> (male, 20)

The pressure can be applied with features of threat and attraction. People can be manipulated in all kinds of ways, made to conform against their own desires and their own instincts not just because a path of action is attractive but because they will be threatened with worse alternatives.

The power of the peer group depends on the powerlessness of the individual. These people acknowledge their own weakness. They know they are easily suscep-tible. They blame themselves as much as the 'crowd' in which they are entangled.

> Yeah, I am easily led... and like I started the way I did because I couldn't say no because I wanted to be like people, and the way they was and things like that. And like now I've got to be firm with meself to say no...
>
> (female, 19)

The problem is that this young offender is not the only one easily led. The conta-gion spreads faster than temptation. She wants to be like people but even if she did-n't there is the fear of being led, of not being able to resist, however 'firm'.

> I was really close with her and then when I started seeing her now she gets weary, 'cos everytime I'm with her then like all the twockers and things go

back to her again and she can't, she's like really easily led... and she's scared to death when she sees me. She'll say 'oh God, not again, please go away' 'cos she just don't want to get into trouble again.

I started going out with one of them and I met his friends and erm but I got really drawn into it and like she stopped and then I couldn't stop now. I don't know why but I just felt as though I wanted more and I wanted to do more... I was really getting worse and worse and everyone was like all the people who I met like T. and all his friends and he was saying oh god, she's going mad now, look at her like we turned her into this and like they all really worried about me.

(ibid)

At what point is there no turning back? At what point can temptation no longer be eschewed? One of the girls fears the association. The other one is so caught up in what she is doing that it even appears heinous to her friends. And yet both are 'easily led'. Both will commit more crime given the connection and influence of the 'twockers'. Is the one who is so much more overdoing it, even to the embarrassment of her fellow conspirators, simply trying harder to please? Or is she realizing her inability to keep self control? The initial responsibility is with her friends. They have, indeed, 'turned her' into what she is. For she was, and is, susceptible to that kind of influence.

Between the desire and the fulfilment falls the shadow. The will to change habits, the wish to be no longer incarcerated by keeping clear of punishment and the law, is strong. And yet there is always that underlying recognition that the peer group is powerful, that there will be pressure to return to previous habits. If crime in itself is not attractive, the sneering of erstwhile acquaintances is deeply disturbing.

I want to stop. I do. I don't wanna keep coming back and keep coming back. I want to stop. I do. I don't wanna, like I mean I rung him up the other day R. and I were talking to him on the 'phone and he said are ya coming out to do some burglaries. I've got some jobs lined up and I'm going yeah, yeah, I'll come and do some: then I just put the 'phone down and thought what did I say that for? When I'm under the influence with him. I want to do it. It's just him, I don't know.

(male, 17)

For all the good intentions it seems inevitable that this young offender will keep 'coming back'. The influence is too strong. Putting the 'phone down is so much easier than facing the pressure of an actual presence. The immediate reaction is to give in, and it is only afterwards that he wonders why he is so easily led. He wants to stop but will not be able to. The pressure will be too much.

There are all kinds of ways of manipulating what are essentially vulnerable young people, malleable beneath their aggressive exteriors. In prison they have time to dwell on what it will be like when they emerge. They have their hopes as well as their fears. They have their weak determinations, weak because their sense of reality is too strong to allow them to be anything ultimately but fantasies. Some way or another they see the same influences being successfully deployed.

> Yeah, I'll go round with the same people. I'll tell them I'm not doing that, I'm not doing the other with you. If they're 'oh come on J. we're nicking a car', nah, see you. I'll just go into house and play on computer. If they come round and say 'come on help us nick this, help us nick this wagon full of spice' or summat, nah, nah, see you, shut door, play music... and I'll go round back and say 'nah, not bothered'. 'Oh you're chicken, cluck, cluck', and all the lot as they do goin' s s s s s really getting on me case and next minute I just say 'oh go on then' and they go 'hey' and we'll go and nick a GTE or summat.
>
> (male, 16)

In the end the resistance will be broken down. Appeals for help are not as powerful as accusations of weakness. The whole scenario is clear, from the half-hearted attempts to do something else, like play on the computer or play music, to the constant and incessant and successful badgering. And so he falls again. The tone of voice, the phrases used and that sense of being pushed beyond the end of the tether are all captured laconically, dramatically and completely. The threat of the world of the peer group is constant. It can be cajoling, ostensibly attractive, or a more direct and punitive coercion.

> Instead of getting up, doing whatever and the every day, I've got the risk of either one of my enemies seeing me, either beating me up or kidnapping or killing me... I mean I've always got that risk every day, as soon as I step out of my bed, as soon as I open my eyes in the morning that's the risk that I've got.
>
> (female, 19)

The real world to which young offenders return is a threatening one. It does not necessarily mean one of direct bullying, enemies imagined or actual. It is threatening because of their own susceptibilities, their weakness in the face of peer pressure. Their erstwhile circle will embroil them again, and try to make their lives a match for what went on before. They know they will meet the same people. They know their own habits and securities, the way in which they will relate only to those of similar experience. The alternative world, of order and knowledge, of work and family, is like a closed book. They want to open it. They fantasize about its contents. But they also know that their peers will bind them up. What is most important, however, is their ability to recognize this. They might, by themselves, be able to do little about it. But even if they are liable to be drawn back into that netherworld of gangs, they are in fact as susceptible to the alternative. In the back of their minds is an alternative reality. It might be expressed as a fantasy but it points up the fact that what they have experienced includes what is a more conventional, a more ordered, and at least potentially happier world.

> I just wanna meet someone that, you know, normal, that a good sense of humour I mean not someone that's like a right straighthead or something, someone that goes out and has a good time and that... a nice friendly man, easy to get on with.
>
> (female, 18)

But 'I'm bad at choosing men, all the boyfriends I've had are off their heads'. What kind of hold on reality is that?

References

1. Dishion, T, Andrews, D and Crosby, L (1995) Anti-social boys and their friends in early adolescence: relationship characteristics, quality and interactional process, *Child*, **66** (1), pp 139–51
2. Berndt, T and Keefe, K (1995) Friends' influence on adolescents' adjustment to school, *Child*, **66** (5), pp 1312–29
3. Farver, J and Frosch, D (1996) L.A. stories: aggression in pre-schoolers' spontaneous narratives after the riots of 1992, *Child Development*, **67** (1), pp 19–32
4. Milgram, S (1974) *Obedience to Authority: An experimental view*, Tavistock, London
5. Kupersmidt, J, Griesler, P, De Rosier, M, Patterson, C and Davis, P (1995) Childhood aggression and peer relations in the context of family and neighbourhood factors, *Child*, **66** (2), pp 360–75
6. Dishion *et al*, op cit
7. Windle, M (1994) A study of friendship characteristics and problem behaviours among middle adolescents, *Child Development*, **65** (6), pp 1764–77
8. Bursck, R and Grasmick, H (1993) *Neighbourhoods and Crime*, Lexington, New York
9. Sampson, R and Lauritsen, J (1993) Violent victimization and offending: individual, situational and community-level risk factors, in *Understanding and Preventing Violence*, Vol. 3, eds A Reiss and J Roth, National Academy of Sciences, Washington DC
10. Bourdieu, P (1984) *Distinction: A social critique of the judgement of taste*, Routledge and Kegan Paul, London
11. Cole, M (ed) (1988) *Bowler and Gintis Revisited*, Falmer, London
12. Braithwaite, J (1989) *Crime, Shame and Reintegration*, Cambridge University Press, Cambridge

13. Quiggle, N, Garber, J, Panak, W and Dodge, A (1992) Social information processing in aggressive and depressed children, *Child Development*, **63** (6), pp 1305–20

14. Cairns, R, Cairns, B, Neckerman, H, Gest, S and Gariépy, J (1988) Social networks and aggressive behaviour: peer support or peer rejection?, *Developmental Psychology*, **24** (3), pp 815–23

15. Hartup, W (1996) The company they keep: friendships and their developmental significance, *Child Development*, **67** (5), pp 1–13

16. Berndt and Keefe, op cit

8

The world outside: domestic reality and fantasy

Introduction

Being incarcerated in prison affords plenty of opportunities for reflection. The young offenders brood on their immediate past, their earlier experiences and their futures. Since they are not seeking to please, to convince a parole board, for example, that they are ready for rehabilitation, their thoughts are honest as well as equivocal. Whilst there is a great deal of regret, this is never a feeling left in isolation. There are no signs of a complete determination to change their ways and start again. Regret is tempered with realism. They know that the same temptations await them, that the same fraternity will welcome them back.

There are two significant reflections that bind their future to their past. One is that sense of personal weakness. They do not suppose that their previous habits will suddenly cease. Even if they wish to start on a steady life of work, home and family, they are aware that the exciting alternatives of easy money and the 'buzz' that goes with it will remain strong and perhaps prevailing temptations. The other reflection is that they will also return to places of violence, to a sense of personal threat. Once in that world, once known to be an integral part of it, it is not easy to escape. Some even take thoughts of violence, of revenge on those who 'grassed them' with them. Whatever the regrets or good intentions, rehabilitation is never going to be easy. Whenever the young offenders dwell on their experience of life outside school there is a sense of great equivocation. There are many ambiguities, and telling contradictions. They exhibit that crucial psychological trait of being able to hold two contrasting feelings or beliefs at the same time.

> 'Cos you know once you've done such a long time in prison you think right I'm sick of these. You have a certain attitude. I mean you can have it and you can't have it, you know what I mean. It depends which way you

think about it, depends which way you want to go about it when you go outside. 'Cos like if you're fed up with the officers and everything else and the police and everything else you think 'no, when I go out I'm not even gonna bother with the probation. I don't even wanna know him…' to you it's like they're bothering you all the time.

> (male, 20)

'You can have it and you can't have it'. The problem is that a certain attitude can prevail. The sense of being bossed or interfered with will lead to a predictable reaction. The intention is to settle down, to 'get off me backside and change things', to 'start education, learn something'. And then domestic normality will prevail.

Set up a little business and settle down with me girlfriend, know what I mean, get a little place of me own, have a little car and that's my future.

> (ibid)

That might indeed be his future, the lesson learned. But it is, unfortunately, unlikely. This is not because he is branded or labelled as criminal but because he acknowledges his own nature and experience. He has made the same vows before.

I never used to think about the future or if I did think about the future it'd be something like 'oh I'll go and settle down with me girlfriend' you know what I mean, not thinking about, er, the money problems and where I'm gonna live and everything like that… and I used to think 'yeah, that's a good idea, get that idea stuck in my mind and that, and just go out'. Well, I did go out and I did what I wanted to do and nothing works out. It was just like I went back to me old ways… I come in this time and I thought well this is what happened last time and if I do the same thing the same thing's going to happen again.

> (ibid)

The young offenders problem is how he can break the vicious circle of temptation and habit. He is like Hartley Taylor Coleridge, who used to vow for years unequivocally every morning in his hangover that he would never touch a drop of alcohol again. Each time, from the perspective of prison, 'settling down' seems like a good idea. His hope is that he can escape all the realities of facing other people, like the probation officer. He finds it difficult to deal with or react to others.

Like one time you're talking to 'em and they're alright and another time they just turn around and bark at you… and you think well, so I dunno. I guess life just goes on. It's like they've got mood changes, know what I mean.

> (ibid)

The idea of settling down with his girlfriend and having a steady job is a modest ambition and deemed preferable to yet another almost inevitable stint in prison. The problem is that for most of the young offenders the straight life is also associated to an extent with boredom. What they would really like is some extra money that comes from marginal crime without being caught. They all cite examples of people with qualifications who are unemployed. They point out how dull some jobs are and how badly paid. They refuse even to contemplate doing certain tasks like working in factories or shops. And they all are obsessed with money and what it can provide. The sense of regret and the desire to lead a different life is sincere. But so is the love of easy money.

Alternative definitions of social norms

The sense of equivocation comes about partly because of the contrast they see between the boredom of domestic reality and the excitement of the antisocial and partly because they see themselves as at once criminal and innocent. They suggest that what they have done is not as bad as what other people do. They would love to be able to get away with things. For all their lack of self-esteem, and their uncertainties which are typical of many adolescents, the fear of failure, the lack of a positive self-image, they are resolutely themselves.[1] They retain their sense of right and wrong. They have made clear distinctions between different kinds of acts. They discriminate between different teachers, and have a strong sense of the immorality of violent bullying, even if they take part in it. They are, in fact, typically human with all the usual weaknesses. They are not some different 'type'.

> Worse than me, they're like just worse than me. Like you look at me and you think I'm just a criminal and that, yeah, but myself I think I'm not. I know I've broke the law and that. I'm a criminal in one way but in another way I'm not. But them they go out thieving and that, burgling and all that kind of thing and I don't do none of that.
>
> (male, 20)

Doing a criminal act does not lead any of the young offenders to brand themselves as a 'criminal' as if only one way of life were open to them, as if they had consistently to carry out antisocial acts. There is even amongst the more 'hardened' criminal fraternity a strong sense of a hierarchy of different types of crime. At its most extreme this is demonstrated by the violent antipathy to child molesters. But even amongst habitual burglars there are distinctions to be made between what kind of property to single out, discriminations between robbing individuals and robbing institutions.

Ambivalence towards crime prevails. The sense of right and wrong is smothered by actual temptations and opportunities. And there are always those margins where what is legitimate fades into what is not. Just as at school where fighting and bullying are unfortunate but every day occurrences and where ABH or GBH are rare, the more the patterns of behaviour are studied the less easy it is to draw a line between them. At what point does a fight get out of hand? How much pain needs to be inflicted? Given the pattern of the young offenders' lives and the way they have become drawn to criminal activity, there is bound to be a sense that certain actions like 'twocking' are exciting, and that others, like petty theft or shoplifting, are comparatively trivial. And vandalism is a widespread crime that people get away with.[2] The world to which they will return is in many ways a murky one.

> I'm supposed to be going back to work with me Dad, but if he's out of trouble, he's not inside, that'll be alright 'cos it's good money. It's not illegal what he does but it's not legal if you know what I mean? You can't really get sent to prison for it unless he charges too much. He works on roofs. He, he's a con man, well he's not a con man, he doesn't con the people he works for he cons insurance 'cos like he'll say it cost four hundred pounds. They'll pay him four hundred pounds, he'll give them an insurance bill for four hundred and fifty so they're making fifty quid as well, they'll get that back, but really he's done no work at all, well he has sometimes, it depends. Whatever he charges it'll cost a quarter usually... but no one's losing out, the only people who are losing out are insurance and it don't matter to them really know what I mean?
>
> (male, 17)

This is a typical justification of a widespread myth that large corporations are impersonal and therefore constitute a fair target. It somehow does not count as much as a crime against the person. Whilst this young offender's father is supposed not to be sent to prison for what he does – 'it's not illegal' – prison is where he is at the time, and where he has been on several previous convictions. Being a con man is seen as on the margins of the law, 'neither legal nor illegal', as if there were a degree of fraud on the margins of all profitable private enterprises.

The problem for the young offenders is that crime is associated with easy money. A steady job is all very well but it does not necessarily pay well. Even when there is a strong desire to lead a 'normal life' there is an assumption that this will be dull, or boring. The ambiguities between one way of life and another can be very clear.

> And then when I'm older have kids or something like that. That's what I want but I don't. I sometimes think about it and like when I'm sitting in my room and I'm getting letters off the lads I'm going out with now;

> they're still part of what I'm trying to get away with, get away from. I'm trying to like say to 'em I don't want it anymore. The lifestyle I want I mean you've probably lived a life that I wish, I'm not trying to put you down but it sounds, it seems a bit boring compared to what I've been living like but I'd rather be boring than dead.
>
> (female, 19)

At one level the image of settling down to 'have kids' is standard. But the moment it is said it is also denied. 'That's what I want but I don't' succinctly sums up the dilemma. The young offender can think about an ideal but when she receives letters from the lads her reactions are equally ambivalent. They are part both of 'what I'm trying to get away with' [sic] and 'get away from'. The chances are that they will absorb her back into the fold. They offer both excitement and familiarity. She might try to tell them that she does not want that life any more but still find even that difficult, let alone acting on that wish. The real problem is that the lifestyle she wishes is actually 'boring'. She might not wish to put the person 'down' but she does so to the way of living. And whilst she might prefer to be boring than dead, these both become extremes, each one as unlikely as the other. She has settled in her world of ambiguity.

The feelings and thoughts both about the past and about the future are very complex. Every sense of regret is tinged with the realization that the young criminals are likely to carry out those very actions they regret. This is not to suggest that the regret is superficial. Whatever the attractions and the excitements of the time there is also a clear definition of alternatives in their minds, between those who settle down to work and those who, by discarding the normal system, end up not only outside it, but incarcerated by it. Regret is inevitable, even if it concentrates on the result of the action rather than the actions themselves. They have been caught and are being punished. This is something they have to accept. Indeed, there is little protest.

> Like the things I did on the out, burgling and that I should be here like, I know I should 'cos I've wrecked their lives, but dunno what else like. People who wreck people's lives should be punished.
>
> (male, 16)

This does not mean that because this young offender knows how it feels he will automatically become a reformed character. He found burgling easy and might do so again except for a shift of attitude or temperament.

> When I think about it, easy, but I've lost me bottle a bit now though.
>
> (ibid)

A realization of the consequences of their actions leads young offenders to rethink the alternative opportunities they have had. The contrast between those despised, hard working, 'soft' pupils who ultimately are successful and themselves is constantly drawn out. They convey a sense of wanting to try again.

> Get me head down and do some work, get a job when I've finished this sentence.
>
> > (ibid)

The poignancy behind the new intentions is the fact that they could have felt like that earlier. It is as if the sense of the purpose of school, of enjoying learning, was put to one side, unexplained. The sense of regret at not understanding the relevance of schooling is widespread.[3] Those who have failed at school subsequently realize how different it could have been. They know both that they have made choices and that these choices have often been arbitrary, matters of chance. They met a particular temptation or quarrelled with a particular teacher. Their careers have not been the outcome of a determination to be antisocial. They sense that, given their temperament and social outlook, they are caught up in a string of events that they would subsequently have liked to undo, impossible as that is.

> If I could turn the clocks back I'd do it all over again. I'd make a good start I would. I always keep saying that, I've said it about ten thousand times in 'ere, if I could turn the clocks back with what I've done to be in here I wouldn't have done it.
>
> I'd try and take up all the exams and that. A levels and GCSEs and stuff like that and then it'll make me feel better inside and I can get a better job can't I? I know that I'd had a good go at it, that I'd had a good try.
>
> > (female, 16)

At the time in school all the drudgery involved in passing exams does not seem worth it. It is only with hindsight that there is a sense that there was an underlying purpose to the tedium and the discipline.[4]

Regrets about the past

The regrets that are expressed centre not so much on lost opportunities, the young offenders wishing they had taken advantage of what was on offer, of being deeply engaged in the common activities of school, but on the lack of qualifications and their consequences. There is a feeling of waste, of wishing that they had been more deeply motivated and had concentrated on the tasks in hand. This is reflected by the absence of any outcome. All the insights into the purpose of school emerge only when they see what they have missed. The question remains what schools. could do about this. This sense of loss is not confined to the offenders or the unemployed. It is shared by those who are taking exams, who have not dropped away from the system.[5] Just as the tone of the official report tends to be moulded by the phrase 'could do better', so pupils in school realize that they could have made more use of the opportunities much earlier if only they had detected their relevance. This lack of understanding of the whole purpose of school is itself reflected by the concentration on qualifications. Instead of explanations of what everyday of schooling is for, the common goal appears more of a threat. If you don't work you will not acquire the necessary qualifications, and if you do not have these you will not have a lucrative job. It is no wonder that the regret focuses so often on the want of qualifications.

> My brother will be surprised when I get out 'cos I won't be a labourer when I get out. I'll have qualifications... I'll be able to do it all myself when I get out.
>
> (male, 16)

Qualifications and self-esteem are closely related. The young offenders want to surprise other people as well as themselves when they get out. They see the contrast between success and failure.

> 'Cos if I had qualifications I'd get myself one of these jobs where you need the qualifications... like me cousins. I call them snobs like but at least they've got an education in front of them, that makes me look stupid 'cos they've done something in their lives and I've done nothing, left school and all that, just wish I'd have got 'em now.
>
> (male, 21)

The view of the linking of qualifications, jobs and money is at one level a pragmatic one. But it is also a distinct way of seeing the world as divided, between those who are 'snobs' and have an education and those who look 'stupid', those who achieve, who have 'done something' with their lives and those who are failures, between those who have money and those who do not. Pragmatism is joined with a deep insecurity and normlessness. The contrast between those who have money and those who do not is especially important since there are shorter cuts to the acquisition of wealth than qualifications and a steady job. The importance of money to the young offenders cannot be underestimated. It gives them power and a sense of self-respect. They have something that others, for all their hard work, do not. They spend it freely and liberally when they have it to assert their sense of self-importance, to display their own abilities and to question the normal social standards and etiquettes. A good job is one that pays.

Anything that pays alright money. I wouldn't work for hardly anything. I wouldn't go on YTS or anything. Don't think it's worth it. You can get the same amount of money on the dole. You're not guaranteed a job at the end of YTS. Up me dole money. I would go out and commit crime then. Most people do it 'cos they need the money, some do it 'cos they get a buzz off it, but most do it 'cos they need the money.

(male, 19)

Having money is itself a 'buzz'. This young offender is not talking of spending according to the income but getting whatever he wants. The love of money is clearly not a result of need but of greed. Why should other people have better possessions?

The overlapping worlds of work and crime

Some of the young offenders suggest that there is almost a need to rob, that it is the only way for them to have an income. And the only way to prevent them responding to that need is to be incarcerated.

In here you've got everything you want... they don't need to go out and rob someone else, or rob someone else's pad...

(male, 18)

Reason not the need. The drive to have instant access to money, to acquire riches at will is in contrast to the actual necessities of life, those essentials that are associated with a steady income and an ordered routine. The 'need' to have money is an inward drive. It is not circumstantial. The connection between poverty and crime is a subtle one because whilst a case can be made for the significance of conditions in certain communities or neighbourhoods, the real connection is psychological. Just as the habits and influences of the peer group are more influential than the actual living conditions, so the sense of 'need' springs out of self-assertion, insecurity, impatience and an oblique and uncertain view about the normal means of the acquisition of money. These young people have not only rejected the standards of society, and been rejected in their turn, but have consciously sought an alternative reality. For them the desire for money is as real as a 'need'.

The world of work and the world of crime are juxtaposed against each other and can overlap. The ambiguity of the news of young offenders arises out of their almost schizophrenic attitudes to both. There are two routes to the acquisition of money and the power that money brings in terms of status, relationships and indulgence. One route is dull, safe, correct and not very lucrative. The other is dangerous but effective for a time, and gives far greater rewards. Sometimes the two actually go side by side.

> Thinking about getting a job, but like there's not a lot of money to be made in it or anything, so I'll probably be still doing the same things what I'm doing but not as much… so that I'm working and just bringing money in as well, off other things, but not enough to get caught again. 'Cos like I hope I'll be out a bit longer.
>
> (male, 20)

'Just bringing money in' makes burglary sound routine. It is also a little 'extra'. The young offender sees no contradiction between work and criminal activities. The motivation to work is, however, not just the matter of avoiding detection a bit longer but a genuine desire to have a job. There is a regret that the monetary rewards will not be enough to feed his pleasures and that as a result he will not be able to resist the temptation to 'do the same things' that he is in prison for.

Most of the regret of not having enough qualifications rests on the acknowledgement that without them lucrative work will be hard to come by. All that will be left for them will be the drudgery of manual labour. This is not bad in itself, for what is most crime but manual labour, but the combination of a lack of money and boredom is too much for them, or too little. Just as having a low-paid job is no real improvement over going on the dole or on youth training schemes, so certain jobs hold so little attraction that they would be avoided even if available. Again, the same contradictions abound, between attitudes to money and attitudes to work:

> I can see how they do need money and that, 'cos they've got no money and that. They don't wanna work, half of them. They wanna come straight in to a decent job and have a decent wage. They don't wanna work in factories and that. I know there is jobs there if you want to work but you might have to get a pretty crappy job to start with, but if you wanna work there's jobs there. If I was doing some job that I really did hate then I couldn't.
>
> (male, 20)

This young offender's description of the criminal mind, the desire for money and the temptation to acquire it without trouble is one that they would all recognize. It is also a reaction against some of the dull necessities that are demanded of people. If the routines of school, the demands of the curriculum and the inflexibility of rules have been rejected, partly because they seem like an imposition and partly because they are boring, then it is no surprise that the same strictures and the same rejection are directed towards employment. There are jobs there, as he points out, but he knows he 'couldn't' abide them. He knows he should. But the question is if ultimately he 'wants' to work. He sees that others don't.

There are, again, both 'push' and 'pull' factors. The description is of a routine world that is alienating, full of 'crappy' demands, unenticing and unrewarding, and the alternative one of self-indulgence at a number of different levels. Even that insight into what *ought* to be, or what the experience of law-abiding citizens is like, does not mitigate the temptations of crime, driven by greed.

> It was like when I was really young, that's when I started wanting more and wanting to be... It's like I felt I was on me own... when my house got burgled I thought I don't like this feeling so I'm not doing it no more so I stopped doing them and started doing commercial burglaries, then I was getting 80,000 for that, like that's like one night's work so I thought I can do it again. It was just easy money.
>
> (female, 19)

'Easy money'. This is such a contrast to their picture of ordinary jobs and ordinary lives that most people take for granted and have not found themselves questioning. The sense of estrangement from school is then projected onto the ordered world of employment. Just as school is seen in an ambiguous way, dull and meaningless, and yet offering rewards through qualifications, so work is both a necessity and something to be avoided whenever possible. The young offenders have tasted alternatives, and questioned the social system, and it is hard to return to the mental habit of acceptance, or order and stability.

Order and stability are defined as a 'normal life'. They clearly see themselves as abnormal, counter to the lives of the majority. Normal life is often seen as exactly what they themselves did not have as children. It remains, however, to at least a part of their awareness, desirable.

> Normal to me is like living with your mum or living on your own. You've got a job. You go out Friday's and Saturday nights, you've got proper decent friends. They don't take drugs, they don't steal or anything like that. They've got no involvement in crime.
> I want a normal life.
>
> (female, 19)

Normality is the avoidance of certain things, like the wrong kind of friends, drugs and crime. But it is also defined in terms of a traditional family scene, nearly always centred on the home.

> Just a nice clean home. Just a wife and a couple of kids and her cooking me teas. No, they should go out to work, as long as she gets someone to mind the kids...
>
> (male, 20)

The description of 'normal life' is a parody of the nuclear family; even if the wife goes out to work she is responsible for cooking her husband's teas. Wife or husband, a couple of kids and a nice little house, that is the domestic ideal.

> Just to be stable and that and have good friends, sort of a home, have my own home. Just a nice house, a three-bedroomed house, just to be happy I suppose. Children, a house, a bit of money but not much. I'm not really bothered. A man.
>
> (female, 18)

The symbol of stability is not just the steady job but the clean, regular house inhabited by the traditional family. However much this contrasts with young offenders' own experience, or perhaps because it does contrast with their own experience, this imagery has a strong hold in the imagination. Sometimes it can be exaggerated:

> Just a good job, director or something so I can tell everyone what to do to be in charge and have a really nice house, have children, just be happy and that, my own house, big house, five-bedroomed detached house in the country and then an apartment in London.
>
> (female, 21)

That is a happy fantasy, the stable family stretched into a rich one. But it is also acknowledged as fantasy, in contrast to actual experience.

> [Mum] She was on social but she works now, she works in a factory, she gets, I think, 125 pounds a week which is not a lot really.
>
> (ibid)

Most of the depictions of normal life are surprisingly modest, associated with having enough money rather than too much. That is part of the young offenders' difficulty. 'Enough' is a flexible concept.

Visions of normality

'Normal life' is also associated with a stable relationship. In contrast to their own experience and as a direct result of it they state their desire for a 'man' or a 'wife'.

> Me mum says eventually I'll meet the right person and I'll settle down and all that lot. But that seems so far away, seems like forever.

I want to meet a man who's not in crime, whatever, never even heard of drugs.

(female, 19)

That, together with 'security' and a 'really nice modern house' and a 'big garden for the kids', seems to this young offender the basic necessity: the stable partnership. This comes about because of her experiences. One of the few emphatic gender differences is the way in which the girls find themselves caught up in disastrous relationships, often dominated by a ruthless man. At first this person will appear attractive, with power and possessions. There will already be a tendency to be attracted to someone of that type, so it is not something that happens out of the blue, suddenly and inexplicably. The twin ideas of power – of toughness and money – will already be firmly set up in the mind. But after a while they find themselves trapped.

Sounds stupid now when I said it... love at first sight man. I like him a lot but I didn't know he were married till six months later. I felt used. Thought I was second best all the time but like now, mind you it might be just drugs now 'cos I mean he always comes to me 'cos I'm the one bringing the money in, he's with me the most. But like before we started drugs he were like home most of the time.

I want to sort me life out for a start, you know what I'm saying. I don't know what I want yet. Put it this way, I mean I'm not rich right, but when I've got a lot of money in my hand I'm changed. I think I'm the top, you know what I mean? I think I'm better than anyone else... 'cos I've got something and they haven't...

(female, 21)

Helplessness and power are closely linked. The power this young ofender has over other people is through money, through having what they want. The power she has over her boyfriend is also through money. He needs her for its sake. At the same time she is helpless. She feels 'second best'; she knows he normally puts his wife first, and she did not even know he was married. It is through him that she begins to be absorbed in drugs. She, like others, longs to meet 'the right person', who is anyone who contrasts with her previous experience. The likelihood of suddenly coming across a quite different group of people depends entirely on changing neighbourhoods, so there is little chance of that. Again she will be back with the same acquaintances and same influences.

'Normality' and security and finding the right man are significant because these wishes are juxtaposed against actual experiences. The longing for stability, for good friends, for a nice house and for a man is driven by the alternative.

This big seven-litre Mercedes, and parked outside my mum's home and my mum was like 'Oh my god, who's that' and then he came and he said don't leave me and all that. So I went back and stayed with him and then he just started battering me and that and he wouldn't let me leave. He used to lock me in the house and all sorts. I mean he's just a total bastard and he loves the way he is. He's just horrible, he's evil… I was scared of him. I was terrified. I was on the run from him…

(female, 18)

The attraction of brutal power quickly turns sour, but by that time he has a hold over her, mental as well as physical. He 'batters' his wife and he finds out where people are when they try to escape from him. Underneath the ambivalent and personal side of criminality the young offenders also glimpse the next level, the next stage of total brutality, astonished by the use of drugs and guns. And what they see is the lack of any self-doubt or conscience. 'He loves the way he is' is a telling phrase. For these witnesses still are shrouded in self-doubt, in the awareness of alternatives. They might be weak and prone to temptation but they have not yet determined to go down the path of unequivocal villainy. That some might end up like that is clear enough; but it is not inevitable.

The sometimes literal stranglehold of the man committed to violence and brutality is a forceful reminder of an alternative way of living, if that is possible. It is possible in the imagination, certainly, but it is held the more precious because the young criminals bring with them many experiences of violence, sometimes gratuitous and sometimes directed against them. It is not as if they were merely perpetuators, the ones that inflicted harm on others. They are also themselves victims, just as they were in school, combining bullying with being teased, subversion and humiliation. Surrounding them is the culture of incipient violence. It does not have to be physical, but there is always the potential for it to be expressed in that way. The ideal of normality and stability is placed in a volatile setting.

'Cos I was a young girl living on my own they could just take liberties with me… because I was saying no, I put me foot down I said listen I'm not doing it, get somebody else to do it and then they smashed up my flat took everything that, I mean them things I had in there. I mean I know that I'd been robbing for the money to buy them but I'd actually bought them and it weren't like they were stolen or anything. Like they took everything. They even like ripped up my photos of my little sister and things like that, just petty things and I couldn't even go in there again.

(female, 19)

There are many temptations embedded in the milieu in which young offenders live, but there are also threats. To say no is difficult for more than one reason. What is 'petty' is also the most hurtful. And what also hurts is the sense of ambiguous shock that technically those things that were smashed were not actually stolen, but paid for, even if the money was stolen. It made the goods almost sacrosanct. But more importantly the furniture and the possessions gave her a sense of ownership. They were a symbol of stability, something that belonged to her, like her integrity, and to which she belonged. And then they were all taken apart.

The realities of everyday experience

Such a life with its vignettes of threat, its flashes of violence, reminds them and us of all the contrasts in different circumstances of living. On the one hand there are those who have adapted to the steady and the certain. And on the other there is an almost pervasive sense of habitual and routine threat.

> But when you're young you just don't think; it's just when you get older and you know what you've missed when you look at other people when they're signing papers and you're thinking 'I can't sign them' it gets to you.
> Like everyday like you see people getting beat… 'cos in bang they're all selfish, they all want their selves…
>
> (male, 18)

The power of those who have enough self-absorption or self-confidence to wish to dominate others through force is in direct juxtaposition to what appears so mild and so successful by comparison. What really 'gets to him' is the sense of inadequacy in the face of those who are able to do the gentler, more cerebral, things in life. Again we see the regret at lost opportunities. At the time, being 'hard' and overcoming the status quo seemed such an attraction. On reflection, all that really counts are the wrong choices of opportunities. By that time he is deeply ensconced in the subtle distinctions of criminal behaviour, between the softer and harder prisons, between those where violence prevails and those in which violence is contained. But violence is still the theme. The assumption of violence as a spreading contamination involves everyone.

> I would have just picked up the nearest plank of wood. Them gypsies, they'll do anything, they don't care, been brought up rough. They'll just kill you, they're not bothered.
>
> (male, 16)

Apart from the deep-seated prejudice, this gives an insight once again into two key phrases: 'been brought up rough', 'they're not bothered'.[6] The upbringing, those forces that mould character, and their consequences are instinctively recognized. Whilst there are shared and common views about criminality – 'some people are born hard, some people aren't' – the young offenders' own experience suggests that it is circumstances that mould them. What is certain is that those who are 'born hard' are always other people, never themselves. They are prey to all kinds of influences. They acknowledge it. What they cannot explain is the *results* of circumstances, with certain people seemingly unleashed with terrifying fierceness. The explanation of behaviour as being genetically based is significantly applied only to other people. They know that their own reality is different. They might not be 'bothered', but they do care. Judging by the experience of the young offenders, the number of criminals who are truly 'hardened' is very small. And yet, for one reason or another, that 1 per cent seems to attract all the attention and the fascination of the Home Office and the media.

To some extent those really 'hard' cases, like those who dominate women and who exercise seemingly unlimited power, also fascinate the young offenders. They exhibit all kinds of dislocated and misconstrued charisma.[7] They inhabit a dangerous world of their own and those who come near them are always in danger of attracting anger or enmity. These people can be dangerous. When they unbend, and show humour, when the threat is lifted even momentarily, then the would-be victim is grateful, and subservient. The charisma of power, of unpredictability, of the contrast between authority and friendliness, distance and openness, is here transferred from the teacher to the gang leader. A similar fascination prevails. There are certain figures who appear to absorb the attention of others, who seem like heroes, not because they are to be admired but because they are dangerous. In that particular kind of 'community' it is difficult not to be absorbed.[8]

> Everyone knows who I am. 'Cos they know what I'm like, plus I know too many people you know all the criminals round my way know me, so they don't want to... Like most criminals live in council houses anyway.
>
> (male, 19)

He might want to change but he is a target as well as a victim of repeat crime, of the fact that too many people are locked together in the same outlook. Underneath the macho-type assertion of 'everyone knows who I am' is the still, small voice of realization that that very reputation that is forced upon him is, even if willingly received, damaging and ultimately destructive. On one level the immediate approval of peers – like politicians and academics 'networking' – is all that matters. That is how the corruption and the poison spread. For being in the 'right' circle is also to be subservient to it. For those who have little esteem, the need for approval, so universally necessary for all individuals, is not just paramount but immediate.

I'm always uptight when I'm on me own. Well, I have to be really 'cos no one else is looking out for me. I don't know. I think it's when I'm not with all these criminals I feel secure 'cos I feel settled then 'cos I'm not going to get into trouble, well, I say that but I do get into trouble now and then on me own, but apart from that I don't being on me own and with me family.

(female, 19)

The muddle of intention and reality, personal responsibility and weakness, and sur-face and deep insight is summed up here. Being looked after is juxtaposed against having someone being responsible. The family is a bulwark against 'these crimi-nals'. The important matter is the way these separate and distinct realities coincide into a coherent and incoherent whole. This young offender both needs other peo-ple and is threatened by them. Time and again the general state of affairs, the steady state, is undermined until the feeling of 'security' and being 'settled' becomes itself a temporary one, far from any ontological security that is supposed to emanate from the home. On the one hand she is not going to get into trouble; but at the same time she does get into trouble, 'now and again'. She is 'uptight' when by her-self, but easily led by others... This is an expression of longing for security.

What is clear in these accounts is not just the fragility of the circumstances, the sense of deep insecurity, and temporality, but desire for someone *else* to provide stability, someone who contrasts with those the young offenders are intimately associated with. The world they live in is full of excitement, but the excitement does not last, since it feeds on the need for ever new excitements, and distractions. The contrast between dull security and the temporality and danger of alternative lifestyles is always in the back of their minds. The essential ambiguity of their out-look rests on this. There are different compensations and different dangers associ-ated with both ways of life, the 'normal' and the antisocial. And between these contrasts are all the middle stages, the realization that they can choose which way to go. The irony is that this realization that they have made choices, and are responsible for their actions, is compensated for by their understanding of the strength of the pressure of relationships. They know the importance of 'neigh-bourhood' and the arbitrariness of their circumstances. Had they not seen a certain action, had they not met a particular person, life could have been very different. They understand the arbitrariness of chance. At the same time they appear to sense, but certainly reveal, that tension between a rather broader coalition of fac-tors. Certain events and certain people stand out. But the crucial circumstances are a mixture of their own peer groups, the community generally, and their own atti-tudes. It is the way these intermingle that, given other chances, forms their pat-terns of behaviour. The neighbourhood is one factor.

'Cos I know people who I used to hang... older than me, they still living in C. and they're doing exactly the same thing today as they were doing six or seven years ago, just sitting around and not doing anything with their lives... yeah, boredom. It's like some people, like some lads I know have been doing it for years and, erm, never had a girlfriend in their life, their teeth are rotten, still just stay in bed, 'till two o'clock in the afternoon and that; erm, their flat's dirty and that and they wind up in here. I won't end up like that.

The main reason for crime is drugs, that's one of the main reasons, boredom and money.

(male, 19)

Boredom, drugs and greed. The people this young offender knows and by whom he has been nurtured might be despised, but they are a sign of his own essential rootlessness of a kind. He can see the meaninglessness of their lives, and yet from their point of view the existential fact of their existence would seem to have roots in a different kind of reality, admired by Genet and writers of that kind.[9] They seem to demonstrate both an atavistic essence of life, and a peculiarly modern sense of displacement.

In fact there is no real literary sense of self-consciousness. The everyday reality is rather more superficial and more self-deceiving. He says that he wouldn't end up like that, winding up in 'here'. But it is from prison that he makes these judgements. He can see the weakness and the existential absurdity of that kind of life. And yet that is exactly what he has achieved. The question remains, given the community influences, what makes the individual respond to them? What has happened to them that makes them so vulnerable?

References

1. Garnetski, N and Dickstva, R (1995) Youth under threat, in *Childhood and Youth in Germany and The Netherlands: Transitions and Coping Strategies of Adolescents*, eds M. du Bois Reymond *et al*, pp 257–86, Walter de Gruyter, Berlin
2. Ibid. Eleven per cent admitted being involved in vandalism.
3. eg White, R with Brockington, D (1993) *Tales out of School*, Routledge and Kegan Paul, London
4. Cullingford, C (1991) *The Inner World of the School*, Cassell, London
5. Whitcutt, D (ed) (1996) *Towards Employability*, Industry in Education, London
6. Toivonen, K and Cullingford, C (in press) *Politics, Groups and the Individual*
7. cf Weber, M (1947) *The Theory of Social and Economic Organization*, Oxford University Press, New York
8. Pease, K (1993) Individual and community influences on victimisation and their implications for crime prevention, in *Integrating Individual and Ecological Aspects of Crime*, eds D Farrington *et al*, BRA report
Sherman, L *et al* (1997) *Preventing Crime: What works, what doesn't, what's promising*, US Congress
9. eg *Waiting for Godot* and *Happy Days*

9

The self and the social world: relationships with parents

Introduction

Young children's social abilities and their acute analysis of other people's behaviour are already well established even before they can articulate them. The earliest relationships are therefore of the greatest importance. Long before the difficulties with school arise, the dichotomy between the sense of personality and emotional needs on the one hand and the anonymous and external demands of order and discipline on the other is made manifest. It has long been acknowledged that the genesis of delinquency lies in the home.[1] The reasons for this are not the crude matters of poverty or status, single parents or dysfunctional families but in the relationships that are made or broken. Parental mishandling is one of the main factors in predicting offending.[2] What these young criminals make clear is how this takes place and why it matters. That parents are a crucial influence is clear, although the analyses of the effects of parenting tend to be generalized.[3] The insights that the young offenders offer into their own early lives reveal just how crucial are the effects of parental relationships; not just that they matter but why and how.

In the literature on parenting, whether it is of advice or is based on research, the focus of attention is on the balance between kindness and discipline.[4] The authoritative, seemingly successful parent manages to be both firm and concerned. Against that kind of adjustment to the needs of relationships are set up the two extremes of failing parents: those who are over-controlling, harsh and dominating, the 'authoritarians', and those who seem indifferent to what their children do, the 'laissez-faire'. Being a good parent, even a good enough parent, is hard work. The constant attention to detail, of following up instructions to make sure they are carried out, and the interest in the activities of children all demand energy and time. It is easy to see why some find it too much of a challenge, either by remaining casual and indifferent to behaviour or by having such strict and inflexible rules of behaviour that there is no room for negotiation or dialogue.

The relationships with parents are, of course, complicated and do not depend on simple patterns of behaviour. The laissez-faire parents can suddenly become authoritarian, lose their tempers and make extreme demands. The disciplinarians can become tired, or fed up, and give up all insistence. The truth is that there is not a simple typology of parents, one way of being bad and one way of being successful, not a simple matter of patterns of behaviour, but a dysfunction, a dichotomy between two styles of approach. We have already noted the difficulties of young people in school. When there is a clash between personality and the anonymity of roles, between personal desire and discipline, tensions are set up that can spill over into extreme feelings of rejection and bad behaviour. What the estranged pupils bring with them to school is an inability to 'play' with the roles of teachers and the rules of school. They mix up orders with personal animosities. They see indifference to them when they should be detecting generalized commands applicable to everyone. Or they assume that the projection of a role is something very personalized. There is a dichotomy for them in the demands of personality; close relationships, either with friends or enemies, and the anonymous requirements of the social order; discipline and expectations; impersonal demands and general rules.

This inability to strike the right balance between the habits of individual relationships and the rules of society is learned in the early days at home. All relationships are governed by rules, by subtle understandings about behaviour. But if the earliest ones are unstable or insecure then it will always be difficult for children to come to terms with the complex demands of a wider society.[5] There have been many observations made of the extremes of behaviour by parents, when they swing from one mood to another, shouting at their children hysterically at one moment and smothering them with ice-creams the next. In these conditions the children do not really know where they are or what to make of the relationship. It affects their subsequent relationships with their peers and others.[6]

Extreme changes of behaviour, like swings of mood, are easy to detect and observe. But we should make a clear distinction between behaviours and relationships. Under the patina of parental discipline, of giving commands or not, is a far more complex and subtle matter of interpersonal relationships. When childhood is recollected the first images are of extremes of behaviour. They are symbolic of the more everyday strain of dealing with parents. It is soon clear that they are but signs of something more troubling. That some of the traditional rules that defined relationships between parents and children are breaking down seems clear.[7] The simple forms of control no longer apply. But children still rely on their parents to remind them of the principles of reality.[8] They need the framework of rules as much as ever, if not more so, since the collective assumptions of behaviour are replaced by the impositions of individual will.

When the earliest of relationships are reflected upon, two strands of evidence emerge. One is to do with actual physical behaviour, of being hit or being ignored. The other is concerned with the sense of the relationship; the extent to which there is reciprocal understanding. All the young people in this study regret not being disciplined. But this is not a simple matter of learning rule-bound behaviour. It goes deeper than that. At one level we might think that they regret not learning how to adapt themselves to other people's demands. They might think they could have coped with school were they not so accustomed to behaving in ways in which they wanted to and which were self-absorbed. But at the deeper level what these young people regret is not discipline but what it symbolizes: an interest in them. It is only those who are concerned for their children who will pay attention to two kinds of detail: the insistence that certain acts are actually carried out, and the curiosity to share ideas. At one level the question 'did you wash your hands?' answered with a light 'yes' and followed up with 'did you *really* wash your hands? Let me see' symbolizes the avoidance of lies, of not allowing children to get away with laziness. It is harder work than accepting the first 'yes', or not even asking at all. But on another level such banal questioning is symbolic of personal interest. It is a sign that there is a real personal engagement, of the kind that can be followed up by a sharing of experience, and a proper personal dialogue.

The perils of indifference

Good personal relationships depend on negotiation and on mutual understanding. They demand some degree of insight, into other people's needs and moods. They are fuelled by an unselfconscious interest and concern for the other, a genuine curiosity in their being. It does not need insisting upon but it is always there. When such a disinterested concern is missing there are all kinds of consequences. The young people all say they regret the lack of discipline; but what they go on to reflect upon is the lack of interest. The most repeated and telling phrase is that their parents were 'not bothered'. Underlying the occasional outbreak of violence is the sense of indifference. The lack of any positive relationship in the real inner sense is what undermines the ways in which these young people subsequently behave. Their inability to deal with those in authority and their vulnerability to their peers are rooted in the lack of relationships with adults, especially their parents, at an early age.[9]

There are then two consequences to laissez-faire attitudes. At one level there are opportunities to behave badly, to go out with 'mates' at any time and for any length of time. But at another level this ostensible freedom is really a matter of indifference. When they reflect on their own lives they realize that the core of a normal relationship is missing.

> My mum weren't bothered at all. I mean I went into care and when my mum came home from hospital I came back home and my mum wasn't bothered... She wasn't bothered. I was smoking when I was about 10 or 11. She knew I was smoking. I used to smoke in the house. She used to give me fags and that.
>
> (female, 18)

This is a cry not for greater social control, not a mere insistence on rules, but one of disappointment at the indifference being made manifest. For one reason or another the mother is absorbed in herself and in her own life. She is 'not bothered'. This creates a deep ontological insecurity in the child, an absence of something solid and dependable. This indifference is also taken personally, and therefore affects the personality. What at first seems a mere character trait – 'like me mum's easy going' (male, 20) – is in fact a void.

It is interesting to note how clear the young people are about their reactions to such indifference at the time and the subsequent reflections on it. At the time they acknowledge that having parents who were 'not bothered' had its attractions. They could do what they wanted. But they understand that they were really missing something far more important than instant gratification or indulgence. They were being denied a far more important connection than superficial pleasure. They were witnessing and suffering from a denial of a significant personal relationship. If there is no dialogue with the parent, how can there then be normal personal relationships with others? The lack of concern with their behaviour is just one sign of indifference. These people indicate that they were surprised at their parents' lack of energy in keeping an eye on them. It is easier not to be bothered than to try to exert some kind of control.

> She allowed me to smoke. 'Cos she knew she couldn't stop me and it were better to do it in front of her than behind her back... He says if I catch you, he says, you're getting a good hiding and he copped me when I were about 15 year old and like I was shocked 'cos he just walked round from nowhere and I'd got this fag going in me mouth and I thought 'shit'. He didn't say nowt though. He allowed me to smoke in front of him after that. 'Cos he said so many people had come up to him and told him I'd been smoking, they'd seen me.
>
> (female, 20)

Here we have a catalogue of excuses for not entering into any dialogue about smoking. The one threat is the physical one of a 'good hiding', not for smoking but for getting caught. This turns out to be an empty threat. The father had known about his daughter's smoking for a long time and failed to tackle her about it. The mother makes the lame excuse of not being able to stop her, and therefore not bothering, and the spurious assumption not that it is wrong to smoke but that it is better to do so overtly rather than covertly. The real point about expectations and standards is missed. It is really all symbolic of indifference.

It is clearly easy for parents to give up trying, and to suggest that there is nothing they can do. But this is the result not of a sudden assertion of will by their children but of years of inattention. The final consequence of such indifference is to put all the blame and responsibility on them.

> She knows I ain't gonna do what I'm told so she'll just leave me to it, let me do what I want. She's told me anyway do what you do, only your life you're messing up… dad's always in the pub…
>
> (male, 16)

This is not so much the counsel of despair as the final abrogation of responsibility. It is impossible for such assertions of personal autonomy to have grown out of years of anything but laissez-faire attitudes, of not being really interested, in the parents not feeling responsible for their own children, whether this is being away 'in the pub' or letting them do what they wish. These are all the signs of neglect, and subsequently recognized as such.

> I'd say I was neglected a bit, you know when I was younger. I was neglected. I wasn't bothered about, you know, I could do what I wanted and that. Maybe some kids would have thought that was great but after like a couple of years I just, I was used to it. Neglect; someone who's not worried about, not cared about, not given like love and stuff like that and support. You know you need your family when you're young. If like I come home and had trouble with homework and that, you'd like your parents to help you, but my mum never did, never bothered.
>
> (female, 21)

There is a recognition of the equivocal feelings of the time; the sense that the daughter could do what she wanted and that it was pleasurable, followed by the sense that such satiation in self-indulgence soon grew wearisome, and no longer the proud self-gratification that was once appreciated. There is also the clear connection with the inner meaning of such behaviour: neglect. This is all said without a sense of simple blame – 'I'm not blaming it on my mum or whatever' – but with a recognition of what was missing. Nor is it an excuse for subsequent behaviour, but an analysis of what she so palpably missed, not just support but some kind of personal interest and intellectual curiosity.

Actual absences – like fathers in the pub – are not as important as psychological absence. Whatever the circumstances or the behaviours, these young people have been deprived of those close personal relationships that shape the ability to cope with the social world. Actual separations from parents are known to have the potential to disrupt the security and self-belief of children.[10] But the emotional separation is of far greater significance and far more common. Providing physical needs is not nearly as important as the emotional and intellectual needs.

> I was bored and I was at that age… and me mum couldn't provide for me what I still wanted…
>
> (male, 19)

Being 'spoiled' is acknowledged as one of the most damaging occurrences of childhood. It is, in fact, a substitution of one form of concern and interest with another form of seemingly caring but actually indifferent behaviour. There are all kinds of ways of not 'bothering', including distractions from the real needs of everyday dialogue.

> It was me dad who used to blank me out and think, 'oh let him go'.
>
> (male, 20)

Being 'blanked out' has serious psychological consequences.[11]

The equivocation that the young people express are all to do with the attractions of self-indulgence which were felt at the time and the later realization that this was merely the outcome of an essential indifference. At the time they could not realize the consequences. They appeared to be luckier than their peers. Later, they understood what they had missed.

> My mum weren't bothered at all. 'Cos all their parents and stuff they'd be really strict and they'd think oh you're so lucky and that… your mum lets you do what you want but if I come back at four o'clock in the morning something my mum wouldn't say to me oh where have you been?… She weren't really bothered, whereas if me mates went home and came back at four in the morning their parents'd go mad and ground them for ages, but I suppose it was alright at the time. I thought it was alright you know. Do what I want and all that but then I just I realized she, the reason why she weren't doing anything about it, 'cos she wasn't bothered about it.
> She weren't bothered.
>
> (female, 18)

What appears at first as a benevolent 'laissez-faire' attitude is later recognized for what it, in fact, is: a genuine indifference to the well-being of the child. Other parents were not just 'really' strict and concerned enough to put sanctions into place, but revealed a relationship with their children, one that had expectations and the demands of trust, as well as mutual respect. What seemed like 'lucky' at the time is subsequently acknowledged as 'she weren't bothered'; indifferent, self-absorbed and emotionally neglectful.

Physical and psychological neglect

The literature on early childhood is full of case studies of children who are physically separated from their parents, or from relationships with adults. There is far less on emotional deprivation, or indifference within the home. But the literature on early childhood also detects the significance of the way in which an adult – any adult and not just the parent – interacts with the child. What children long for, and need, are constant and consistent interactions with others who have more understanding of the social world.[12] In the need to make sense of all the experiences of all the raw complexities of the physical and social world, children need people both to relate to and with whom they can share their own understandings. This is not just an emotional relationship but a joint dialogue about the experience of the world as a whole. Parenting is often associated purely with emotional warmth and physical care. The intellectual relationship that gives the child a strong sense of his or her own identity as a human being is far more significant. The crucial point of a child's growth, academic achievement and behavioural maturity is the relationship with an adult.[13] It does not have to be a parent, although this is the normal expectation. But if the parent does not take on this part, and no one else is there to do it, if the child finds that the social world in which he or she is placed is 'not bothered', all kinds of consequences follow.

What is being revealed is all kinds and forms of emotional neglect. Sometimes covered by a gloss of indulgence, occasionally shattered by an outbreak of uncontrolled anger, the perpetual door of indifference is the kind of barrier to relationships with anyone that affects these people's lives. At the time this insight is not open to them. But the effect is profound, as they stumblingly realize afterwards. They see how they have been essentially abandoned, left to their own devices. They understand the superficial attractions at the time, the potential for self-indulgence without reference to other people. Their lack of self-discipline has its later social consequences in this early arbitrary life.

> My dad used to give in to me you see... I didn't think very much of me mum at all... They took me back home and they asked me mum and dad if they wanted me back home and they told me mum and dad what I'd said and they just said yeah to agree with it...
>
> (female, 21)

Whatever is easiest seems to be the shrug of indifference, as if the parents felt themselves to be, or were perceived to be, helpless. 'I don't think they knew how to be strict' (male, 20), but this is put down to laziness.

> My dad, nothing. He sits on his arse all day. Like there was nothing she could do about it.
>
> (ibid)

Helplessness and indifference are close bedfellows.

The results of this essential lack of interest are clear (too late) to those who suffer from it.

> No, not strict. If they would've been more strict I don't think I would've been here. They never, when I used to do things they never used to keep me in like ground me and things like that, they never used to do that to me.
>
> (male, 18)

It is not as if the young offenders were laying blame to excuse themselves. If there had been any sense of trying to abrogate responsibility there could have been any number of other stories used as camouflage. There are many examples of physical abuse as well as emotional deprivation. But at the core is that mixture of indifference and self-indulgence, of being allowed to do what they please whatever the consequences. This makes them semi-independent but not autonomous human beings, going their arbitrary and self-indulgent ways without exploring or developing real social contacts with those with whom they should need to operate even if they do not want to. If the parents are not really in tune with them and do not foster negotiated understandings, how can anyone else construct a sense of reason? There is an essential sense of loneliness at the core of this neglect.

> When I used to wake up in the morning there only used to be me in the house… all at work, so there was just me and that was it.
>
> (male, 18)

Instead of the demands of relationships, the structures of social connection, there are the experiences of individuality let loose in an unconstrained, large and anonymous world.

Finding themselves without the parameters of social control, which are the foundations of self-control, the possibilities of an almost mindless and unknowing self-indulgence appear boundless. They are at home alone. They can do what they want.

> I thought I'd be getting away with anything. I were glad but I weren't glad if you know what I mean.
>
> (male, 17)

Always there is that note of equivocation. What appears at one moment as indulgence soon becomes a symbol of loneliness and of despair. The young people are not really glad to get away with anything. They see their parents locked into their own separate lives.

> I was able to stay out later when I was living with me dad 'cos he was always out with his girlfriend. I used to get the house to myself.
>
> (male, 19)

Whereas the memories of their mothers are mostly of a lack of discipline, a softness of indecision or a lack of firmness of mind, the recollections of the fathers are simply that they are rarely there. They are out in the pub, or with their girlfriends. They are away working, or at home watching the television. They are 'blanked out', not playing any major role.

> 'Cos he just goes in, that's it, well done son, has his dinner, goes back to work. Well, he comes home, has his dinner, puts his feet up, has a read, watches a bit of telly, goes back to work.
>
> (male, 16)

Both mothers and fathers are shadowy, if significant, figures in these accounts. There is a strong sense of absence, mostly emotional but also physical. The fathers are out, at work, or with their own independent interests. The mothers are more inwardly absent, backing away from control or confrontation. What is clear is that there are few emotional or intellectual bonds. They are not 'close'.

> I weren't even that close to my dad anyway, just like, he's alright and everything, got on with him but not really close. I never told him anything or anything like that, so… I can't really find him half the time.
>
> (male, 20)

The keynote is the absence of relationships, rather than difficult ones. The syndrome of not being close, of parents who are 'not bothered' and to whom one does not speak of anything of importance, is more significant than the more occasional, sporadic displays of temper and violence. The young people retain the sense that in a time when they are attempting to gain understanding about themselves as individuals and themselves as social beings in relation to others, there is little if any support. They want, as human beings do, to make connections with others. Of all things they most need, such relationships of mutual understanding, of shared perceptions of their environment, are the most crucial. But their closest relations appear locked in their own lives, clinging to their own emotional relationships, and never standing in a position where they can give support, either emotional or intellectual. The indifference of which these young people speak is not simply a matter of a lack of love, it is a lack of the intellectual energy on which the young depend. They are allowed to do what they want. And this is because the adults are essentially not 'bothered'.

The role of dialogue

The lack of a critical intensive dialogue between children and parents is recognized more by the former than the latter. The self-absorption of adults can be profound, the learned indifference to others the more severe for being so casual and habitual. The younger generations are not just influenced by that but have a sense of being abandoned that leads them, almost atavistically, to seek out alternative relationships. When they are young they think that they are indulged. Then they realize that they are being betrayed. When they are young they believe in the possibilities of intervention, that someone could help.[14] Then they become indifferent to such possibilities. They have learned that not being 'bothered' is catching, and they assume it is pervasive. If no one bothers about them, why should they bother about other people? If no one makes reasoned, caring demands, why should they put up with any demands at all? The young people do not know or define exactly what they long for. But it becomes more and more apparent. They long for dialogue, for discussion, for questioning, in fact for some form of reasoning that is moral in the broadest sense.[15] They acquire little of this in school; but even if they were to be confronted with it, they could not recognize it as such, given the absence of any groundwork in the home. It is not just a void they have acquired, some kind of absence, but a black hole, that sucks other matter into it, that is not just a deficit but a destructive force.

The importance of dialogue, and the effect of its absence, needs to be clearly recognized. These young people might not be articulate about the significance of relationships but their descriptions accurately suggest what is wanted and needed. They realize that they have never really had conversations with their parents. They have become accustomed to a *modus vivandi* in which people living in the same house ignore each other, or at best make verbal exchanges that are simple transactions to do with action rather than idea. Family dialogues and understandings are central in helping relationships not only with siblings but with friends.[16] The descent into a habit of nothing more than simple transactions, if there is any communication at all, means that the complex and necessary negotiations with other people become the more difficult. Atrophy spreads from one place to another. The habit of ignoring other people becomes strong.

... and just didn't speak to my dad in the end.

(male, 20)

Again and again we hear of family groups in which each person goes his or her own way, as if the only reason for being together is physical convenience.

I never used to talk to 'em. I never, don't think I've ever sat down and actually had a talk with 'em about anything... they just weren't part of my life, they were just there and like part of the furniture or something.

(male, 20)

On reflection it is to some extent a surprise to realize that there has never been any real conversation in the perception of a son. Parents are reduced, or have reduced themselves, to being little more than 'furniture'. Relationships can be made by the insistence of one person, and it takes one person to be good at creating and maintaining a relationship to make it happen. Relationships do not depend on the fine-tuning of two personalities to each other, but can be the result of the determination of just one person to forge an understanding.[17] There is, therefore, no reason why some kind of attempt to talk cannot be made. Whilst certain close relationships, like special friendships, do depend on a subtle mix of temperament and interests, normal dialogue with a variety of different people, from the exchanges in a shop to lengthy questions and answers, is always possible.

Here we see the absence of normal dialogue, a habit that has clearly grown during the years. Most of them do not talk; some of them, it appears, do not even know how to.

When I go home like, it's just like I don't talk to him. Well, I don't talk to him, it's like, it's like I want to talk to him but, like, we don't talk. It seems so natural to just sit down and pretend he's not there, he doesn't exist.

No conversation at all, you know what I mean, and if he wants to say something he'll find an excuse and start swearing or something you know what I mean but that's about it.

(male, 20)

We have noted the pain of inarticulacy in the school, and the frustration that comes with it. If the ability to explain, to reach agreements, to negotiate is not there, a great deal of emotional anger builds up. Those vulnerable to teasing are detected as having the frustration that can vent itself in outbursts of passion, like swearing. In some there is an almost deliberate avoidance of dialogue, as if a sustained relationship were too intellectually taxing to bother with. The result is to 'pretend' people do not exist, rather than face them and see them as they are. It seems at first easier to remain simply self-enclosed. But in the end, like a person who has suffered a stroke and cannot communicate in the way that was customary, the frustration builds up. Just as the superficial pleasures of laissez-faire seemed attractive at the time, so is the lack of conversational demands. But subsequently it is clear what they have missed.

Young children early on understand the meaning of responsibility and its every-day operational vocabulary.[18] They are aware of the subtleties of social interaction and can judge what is missing as well as what they observe. It would be a grave error to assume that the lack of articulacy, the difficulties of adapting to intellectual demands, are purely the transference of the culture of the home – a style of dialogue – to other situations. This would be to misunderstand the intelligence that is brought to bear on the circumstances; it would be a patronizing insult to suggest that the difficulties with negotiating formally are due to some innate deficiency. These young people not only reflect on the circumstances of their home lives with hindsight, but did so at the time. They were always making judgements.[19] With close observation they acknowledge and scrutinize different ways of parenting; and are critical of it. The typical dysfunctional family is not one of extreme violence but the more prosaic one of lack of dialogue, or connection between its members. Each person goes his or her own way, the father at work, the mother with her own concerns, and each sibling pursuing a separate path.

> He's always at work, you see... just me mum, but I'd do niggly things like and she can't handle it so... I weren't normally in the house all night... I'd take more notice of me mum 'cos I've been brought up with me mum all me life 'cos me dad's at work afternoons and nights.
>
> I'll walk in, say owt to me brother, he'll come running like and next minute I'll walk upstairs, switch music on, have a relaxing bath... I can't please me dad as much as me mum, 'cos he just goes 'is that it, well done son' has his dinner, puts his feet up, has a read, watches a bit of telly, goes back to work.
>
> (male, 16)

This is not a description of a pathological extreme, or anything exceptional. It is about indifference and self-absorption, of finding succour in alternative places since the lack of demands there is acceptable. It is as if there were higher expectations of the home. There should be 'more notice' taken of things, and the sharing of mutual interests. Even when the father is not at work he is set on his own interests and the occasional gesture of patronage is not felt by the son to be adequate.

In their observation of different families, children notice the great differences between those where the parents have a dialogue with each other as well as with the children, and those where each is a single entity, self-absorbed. In those homes where both parents remain together there is a sense of potential tension between them, a tension that can turn violent. But what children find difficult is that the same lack of conversation that affects them inhibits the relationship between their parents. Each is seen as separate. This can cause difficulties, especially when the children are divided in their loyalties by divorce. The importance in the eyes of children of a traditional family life, in which relationships as well as role models are central, cannot be underestimated.[20] They are pained by the strain of multiple, separate commitments. They wish to create a close and understanding relationship, and be part of a greater whole. Even one person will be enough; but the inadequacies or the difficulties are shown up when they find themselves divided by choice.

> I didn't think very much of me mum at all. I thought more of me dad than what I did me mum. I sort of went to me dad more than me mum. I still love me mum like a lot but I just used to go to me dad all the time. My dad used to give in to me you see. 'Cos there used to be a lot of arguments in our house.
>
> (female, 21)

What at first seems like a natural tendency to turn to one parent, with a strong daughter/father affinity, turns out to be the result of deeper undercurrents, of arguments and disagreements. But the battle is for ties. They want to 'belong', and still yearn to have that personal relationship that has been denied them over the years. There is a distinction made between 'love' and respect. Love is 'automatic' when it is recognized. Respect has to be earned.

The fact that there is a sense of rejection does not diminish the yearning for a relationship. This is brought out in the difficulties of choice and in the sense of personal guilt when domestic circumstances are going wrong.

> I didn't like to choose, 'cos I didn't, 'cos I felt guilty meself do you know what I mean? Say if I chose me mum I was feeling right guilty on me dad, and if I chose me dad feeling right guilty on me mum, so I just wanted really to go to me aunty's as well, to avoid that situation for a bit.
>
> (male, 19)

Again the confrontation with the difficult is too much. Avoidance is the easier option. Like so many, this is an example of someone not being brought up to deal with the difficulties of relationships. This is exacerbated by the real difficulty of choice and the sense of guilt. But this comes about not so much because these are close and intricate relationships but because these are not strong. Going to the aunt is not only neutral but probably as impersonal as being at 'home', whichever home that might be.

The sense of neutrality, of distance, of objective scrutiny pervades these accounts. The 'dads' are often seen as distant, remote figures who both temperamentally and for the sake of their job are never really there. Many have hardly any significance in the daily lives of their children – and this includes those still ostensibly at home.

> I don't really talk to me dad now… 'Cos he hasn't said nothing for about 10 years. Don't think he's been a father at all. Don't know what he has done or nothing, can't remember. 'Cos when I seen him like you know didn't even recognize him as me dad, 'cos I couldn't remember what he looked like.
>
> (male, 20)

Physical as well as emotional estrangement characterizes many of the fathers in these histories. In some cases the distance is a matter of divorce and new styles of living, of indifference and a lack of commitment to the responsibilities of the past. But in other cases the dad is looked at objectively as a real presence but one equally remote and meaningless.

> Me dad. Nothing. Sits on his arse all day… but he's just lazy. I don't think they know how to be strict.
>
> (male, 20)

Given the innate knowledge of what relationships with parents should be like, and given the objectivity of the intelligence brought to bear as well as the emotional needs, it is not surprising that it is easy to characterize these parents as failures, with problems of their own, either of self-indulgence or inadequacy. It all ends in a sense of the parents' crucial indifference. They become remote figures, essentially absent in one way or another.

> She's weird, I mean she's weird now, I mean, I love her and that but she doesn't seem to make sense to me, the things she says and stuff, it's just weird. She's a bit dopey and that. I'm not being horrible or anything but it's like it's affected her.
>
> (female, 18)

The distinction between the assumption of personal ties and the objective judgement is clearly made. The mother 'doesn't make sense'. She is 'weird' and 'dopey'. It follows that it is impossible to make a relationship. The absence is inward. But it is just as affective as any other.

> When me dad left she got well into it, it's hard to explain. She just kept staying out most of the days and that, go all day and come in about 10 at night. When me dad left her she started getting it real bad. He just hated her when she was on the tablets.
>
> (male, 16)

There is a groundswell of helplessness, of not knowing what can be done, other than escape. Being unused to normal dialogue, how can a child engage with the difficult, let alone the intractable?

Violent emotions and violent acts

One result of the lack of normal dialogue with parents goes beyond hatred or indifference. The emotions involved, like the disappointments, are never simple. There are many ties, desired as well as denied. There are so many wishes unful-filled. And one of the ways of coming to terms, one result of the disconnection, is reaction against the parents. We have seen how many are despised; 'loved' and yet despised. But parents are treated in turn in the way in which they treat their chil-dren. The two-way process reinforces the difficulty.

> She can't really say anything. She just says she's gob-smacked and that. She just says she can't help me because I'm too wild and that... No, treat her like shit. I always used to do that. I used to run off from home all the time as well... Didn't really used to care, now I do. I know what she feels like now. Wish I never did it.
>
> (female, 16)

The volatility of the relationship, the mixture of tenderness, regret and hatred are all encapsulated in the 'wildness'. In place of any sense of reason or reasonableness we see the constant testing. How much can the mother actually 'help'? What kind of strength is there that can be relied upon? In the end she 'can't really do any-thing'. At the same moment there is the self-assertion of greater strength and the sad regret that such an assertion was both a mistake and a sign of inner weakness. The breakdown in the relationship has nothing to do with a simple matter of defi-cits, in the one or the other. On the contrary, the daughter shows insight, with all those layers of realization, including remorse, that shows that understanding is not just a matter of knowing or acknowledging but is a deeply affecting process. What has gone wrong is the style of parenting, the lack of a central platform of awareness on which everything else rests. The socio-economically neglected children can have just as good an academic profile as anyone else – ostensibly. But they have to overcome those kinds of parenting habits that end in neglect, in deficiencies of one kind or another. The neglect is emotional and intellectual rather than purely economic.

This is not to suggest that physical circumstances do not, in themselves, make a difference. It is rather to reiterate that relationships are so important that the sense of being neglected can arise as often from jealousy, from the usurpation of emotional place. The guilt felt about the choices between parents is paralleled by the feeling of being abandoned by one or the other. The sense of the lack of personal relationship is made the stronger by the intrusion of another who seems to take up all the interest of the parent. Where the relationship is weak and the real centre of attention is elsewhere, the displacement can be sudden and brutal. There is no undercurrent of individual attention. One distraction is replaced by another. Neglect is central and built in. It can also be made the more significant by circumstances. Neglect is not circumstantial but it is reinforced by all kinds of events that cause the sense of isolation to be felt the more deeply.

> When my mum met Dave, me step-dad, I mean he was brilliant, he made her happy and everything so I was happy for that, but then I felt lonely 'cos me mum didn't need me so much.
> I still feel as though I'm on me own because I'm the oldest and I can look after myself, or thought I could, things like that.
>
> (female, 19)

The new figure in the mother's life is good, but seeing that relationship and recognizing its meaning still throws the daughter back on herself; the responsible one, the one most relied upon and then no longer needed in the same way. Many children try to make up for neglect by trying harder, by attempting to compensate in one way or another. Their sense of guilt derives from their understanding of how relationships should work, and how responsible they are for their own. But such a burden of personal responsibility can easily be shaken by the entrance of other people, and new connections.

> I hated her. I mean I'll be civil to her for me dad's sake and me little sister's sake 'cos he's got a new baby with her, but apart from that I ain't got the time of day for her. She thinks that like she's got some hold over me dad. That's how I see it. She thinks she's got some hold over him and that there's no room in his life for us lot anymore.
> I used to hate lads. I think it was because with me dad always hitting me and things like that I hated men. I wish I still did.
>
> (female, 19)

Contradictions abound. The daughter's dad is special, and yet he has taught her to be suspicious of men. The equivocation that she has about her attitudes generally is deeply rooted in her experience. The fragility, the sense of loss, are compounded by the spurious responsibilities placed upon her. What she experiences of the parent's differential treatment – girlfriend first, the siblings in some kind of order – then relates to the way in which she reacts to others. Differential treatment, of whatever kind, does not just cause instant pain, but long-lasting resentment.[21] This resentment is highlighted by the experience of extreme behaviour, including violence against the mother or the child. It should be stressed that whilst there is no excuse for violence and that any kind of abuse has a damaging effect, it is the fact of violence as a symbol of dysfunctional relationships that is most significant.[22] Whilst domestic violence is linked to children's subsequent psychopathology, this is because it is the ultimate manifestation of not being able to make normal relationships.

This distinction between maladjusted relationships and physical abuse is an important one. Whilst the most extreme and most moving as well as shocking demonstrations of negative relationships are physical ones, the damage done by other forms of violence can be just as severe. There is something physical about any non-verbal dialogue, about sharing the functions of a house without talking. The absence of interest, the withdrawal of personal curiosity, have as much of an effect as outbreaks of unreasoned temper. But there are also times when there is a confusion between interest or even manifested affection and physical abuse.

> I was confused 'cos like he always made me feel like I was the only one special in his life and things like that and then when I see him hurting me mum I couldn't take it... I can't exactly remember but I've been told by me family and that he used to put pillows over me head to stop me from crying. He used to, I mean he has broke every bone in me body. He used to hit me a lot, but I used to forgive him because he was me dad and that.
>
> (female, 19)

Even physical violence cannot altogether diminish that sense of a personal relationship. This demonstrates in its own way the distinction between the intellectual, interpersonal understanding and the alternative pathological forms of relationship. There is a pattern to the father's behaviour, an extreme that is marked by violence in affection or hate, in the inability to deal with any kind of psychological threat to an everyday equilibrium. Even crying elicits an extreme reaction. And the physical abuse of the wife as well as the daughter is typical.[23] Violence is not only a deliberate attempt to direct attention to an individual, defended as punishment or threat. It is a lack of self-control, an inability to deal in any reasoned or reasonable dialogue.

The violent outbreaks of inarticulacy and frustration do not have any reasoning behind them. There might be subsequent excuses but that is all they are, like the self-pity of lame apologies.

> My dad used to have the excuse saying 'oh you're all bad', blaming it on me mum and beating her up right and then that made me run away more, and that used to give him more excuses.
> My dad, he's still the same. I don't think he's ever going to change.
>
> (male, 20)

Here the imposition of a father's will, the over-autocratic rule in which children are to be 'good little boys' or 'sitting at home', is again the sign of no real personal negotiation or understanding. It is the child who can find excuses, to get away from that atmosphere of heavy-handed threat, violence and blame. The result is that any sign of anger is taken almost more personally; the children long for the conflict to be resolved, but try to hide from it at the same time.[24]

One of the underlying causes for the withdrawal from normal family life, either through extreme inhibition or the reversion to the alternative succour of the peer group, is the sense of threat from parents. It is well known that harsh discipline has the opposite effect to that intended. This is true of schools as well as homes, of the legal system as well as personal relationships. In all the studies of parental behaviour, there is a standard pattern depicted of the two extremes of over-authoritarianism or laissez-faire, in the middle of which comes that correct balance of the authoritative – firmness tempered with understanding.[25] Authoritative parents understand the distinctions between moral, conventional and personal issues in their judgements.[26] They are both responsive and demanding. Authoritarian parents are depicted as demanding, not responsive, and *laissez-faire* parents as responding but not demanding. Looking at the evidence accumulated here, it should be argued that the two extremes of pathological parenting are just different manifestations of the same thing. Both harshness and neglect are signs of indifference, of the breakdown of the normal interactive, iterative relationship that children need. The permissive parents are not 'responsive'. They find it easier to ignore than to understand and engage in the real dialogues that teach the standards of behaviour. The harsh parents are equally distant. They assume that the setting of rules, and the sense of threat, relieves them of any more complicated responsibility.

The consistent concern in the experience of the socially excluded is the absence of a real relationship, of their parents' indifference or self-absorption. The lack of reason leads to outbreaks of unreasoned behaviour. The affect of harsh treatment is to make children in turn more aggressive.[27] It is not just harsh parenting – the sign of essential indifference – that has its effects. Inconsistency and negativity, another form of neglect, also encourage subsequent antisocial behaviour.[28] The link between poor parenting and anti-social behaviour has been made again and again, in study after study, from a variety of disciplines. The level of consensus is so high that it is surprising how little has been done to act on the findings. All the analyses of family factors show how much anti-social behaviour can be predicted.[29] The effects of indifference, of threats and of criticism are strong on the sense of inhibition and a lack of self-esteem, that base on which aggression is so often built.[30]

The connection between the breakdown of relationships with parents, and the subsequent difficulties in making normal relationships with others, is clear. The vulnerability to being teased and the inability to cope with anything less than violence are all based on the early experiences of home. All that has been learned is to react to aggression with more aggression. This can feed on itself, can grow from small incidents to large ones. When parents are told of their child's aggressive behaviour, for example, they often respond with greater threats of punishment.[31] The more assertive the parents, the less controlled the child. Parents present models of aggressive behaviour, an aggression based on a lack of real interest. There are many examples of the parents not only being indifferent, but taking out their indifference on their children.

> She was bad tempered. She only has to slap you and you've got a bruise. We were wagging it and she didn't know about it at the time but mainly she knew about it and she slapped me.
>
> (female, 21)

One of the most undermining aspects of violence is the uncertainty of it. The children never know when they might be attacked. It is unpredictable and inexplicable. There can be excuses – like coming home late at night – but the hatred that is felt by the children is based on the perception that the violence is a kind of terrible self-indulgence, an outbreak of temper rather than a punishment. They never know when they will witness it or suffer it. This is why they find themselves cutting off their relationships even more dramatically – 'I hated them, then... we was just arguing all the time... and in the end I just had enough and left home' (female, 19).

Indifference and inconsistency are very close to each other. The need to strive for a sense of order, and the energy to keep to it, is ignored. Just as the need for consistent dependency is what young children strive for, so is the later desire for the equilibrium of a steady and certain relationship. Inconsistent behaviour causes uncertainty.[32] Those parents that provide the reliability and security that children strive for do not merely impose an impersonal discipline. They give children a greater sense of their own self-control. They coach them rather than coerce. They reason and explain rather than force and control.[33]

Once the desired stability of family life, with its dialogue and its sustaining interest, is taken away, children try to find some alternative kind of security. They want to play truant from their own homes, and often do. They are sometimes excluded. The same difficulties that are experienced in school of being picked on, or ignored, or being harshly dealt with, or suddenly finding themselves confronted when they least expected it, are also experienced in the home. This is true of all kinds of homes, of parents who have stayed together, of single parents, or parents with new partners. The one factor that makes single parenting difficult is the supervision of the children.[34] Having more than one parent makes the simple physical tasks, let alone the intellectual tasks, five times easier.

The effects of inadequate parenting

If the home lives of these young people are unstable and uncertain, so is their subsequent behaviour. One of the means of avoiding the traumas of home is, quite simply, getting out if they can find a place to stay. In one case the difficulties of choosing between the mother and the father led to living with an aunt. Even if they are still at home they tend to be there by themselves whilst the parents are out, working or in the pub. The sense of rootlessness is strong. They lead peripatetic existences, physically as well as mentally.

> I travel all around I do. Sleep at one sister's one night and one brother's the next.
>
> (male, 16)

This is not so much a choice as an avoidance: the father at the pub and the house therefore empty, or the mother both strict and bad tempered. There is always the sense of threat in adolescence, to run away. These young people make it a way of life.

> I went back to live with me dad in A. with this woman called Julie and then he got in a bit more trouble again and he got sent down again and we was all living with her and there was five of us and she had a child of her own and she was only young, only one, two, when he was inside she had another child and it died you know and I felt a bit bad about that and then we all got put in foster homes...
>
> (male, 17)

The constant disruption and insecurity are highlighted by many things. The young find themselves in this ultimate diaspora, sent to anonymous people willing to put up with them. They have arrived at someone who is not related to them and who cannot really cope. The one reason for their being there has been removed. And, as the final symbol of mutability, the next child died. This is a sign of circumstances that are the outcome of all kinds of deep inner disruption and insecurity. The tragedy is that the young become accustomed to such a sense of rootlessness, to the lack of stability. It becomes not just a problem but a way of life.

> I got so used to living on me own that there was no way I was gonna think you know of coming back home and stay with my family. I've tried it you know a couple of times, that was then, and nothin' changed you know what I mean, and I thought hack it.
>
> (male, 20)

The son gets 'used' to being on his own, separated essentially from his family, inwardly as well as outwardly, so that any attempt to reopen the dialogue is bound to fail. Nothing seems to change. So he concludes that he has nothing to lose by 'hacking' it.

All these are signs of the failure of home life. The connection between that and antisocial behaviour is well established. But there is a tendency simply to blame parents, as if there were some kind of automatic defect that could not be helped. The difference between good and bad parenting is profound. It all hinges on the interest shown in the child, the simple concern and curiosity, that treats the other as a significant individual. There are all kinds of different types of parenting. Baumrind, for example, summarizes them in seven different ways, from the well-established 'authoritative' parent who is warm, firm, consistent and support-ive, to the different ways of being either adequate or a disaster.[35] But at the heart of all these distinctions is the profound importance of the relationship that is ener-getic enough to be able to respond to need. What is successful in parenting is not dependent on socio-economic variables, although we should not underestimate the strains of poverty. Nor is it dependent on the status of the family in terms of the avoidance of separation and divorce, although we should not underestimate the demands of being a single parent. At the heart is the ability of one side or the other to make the kind of relationship in which that close scrutiny of the community and the environment can be shared and communicated. Children spend their time at different ages and in different ways trying to make sense of the world they live in. Often what they observe is traumatic. They seek help and support for their under-standing. If this is denied they are in difficulties.

Parenting can be done well or badly. It can therefore also be learned.[36] It depends on the ability to create a relationship through dialogue. It includes the sharing or intellectual curiosity about the environment. Children seek out a per-son to help them come to understand the circumstances in which they find them-selves. Usually, and properly, this is a parent. But it does not have to be. This leads to the conclusion that children need anyone who can proffer that attention to them as thinking beings. Much has been made of parental love. This is not simply a mat-ter of emotional instinct, dependent on mood. It is as much a disinterested concern for the other, most close, relationship. Stability with parents is crucial. The 'neigh-bourhood' factor is clearly important.[37] But this is because there are no *other* people to intervene, to provide that essential factor of parenting, the glimpse into shared curiosity. The most vulnerable will seek each other out and reinforce their own antisocial tendencies.[38] The conclusion therefore is both sad and optimistic. The socially estranged have had all the experiences that explain why they have ended up where they are. But it need not have been like that. What looks with hindsight as inevitable is also clearly preventable.

References

1. Utting, D, Bright, J and Henricson, C (1993) *Crime and the Family*, Family Policy Studies Centre, London
2. West, D and Farrington, D (1973) *Who Becomes Delinquent*, Heinemann, London
Farrington, D and West, D (1990) The Cambridge study in delinquent development, in *Criminality, Personality, Behaviour, Life History*, eds G Kaiser and H Kerners, Springer-Verlag, Berlin
3. Hollin, C (1992) *Criminal Behaviour: A Psychological Approach to Explanation and Prevention*, Falmer Press, London
Quinton, D and Rutter, M (1985) Family pathology and child psychiatric disorder, in *Longitudinal Studies in Child Psychology and Psychiatry*, ed A Nicol, Wiley, Chichester
4. eg The works of Bettleheim.
5. Wells, G (1985) *Language Development in the Pre-School Years*, Cambridge University Press, Cambridge
Richman, N, Stevenson, J and Graham, P (1982) *Pre-School to School: A Behavioural Study*, Academic Press, London
6. Dunn, J (1988) *The Beginnings of Social Understanding*, Basil Blackwell, Oxford
7. Du Bois Reymond, M (1998) 'I don't want to commit myself yet': young people's real life concepts, *Journal of Youth Studies*, 1 (1), pp 63–79
8. eg 'Allmacht des Gedankens'.
9. qv Cullingford, C (1990) *The Nature of Learning*, Cassell, London
10. Barglow, P, Vaughn, B and Molitor, N (1987) Effects of maternal absence due to employment in the quality of infant–mother attachment in a low-risk sample, *Child Development*, 58 (4), pp 945–54
It is an oft-repeated anecdote that the most stressful experience for a baboon is being yawned at by a peer; supposedly worse than being chased by a lion.
11. Gunnar, M, Larson, M, Hertsgaard, L, Harris, M and Brodersen, L (1992) The stressfulness of separation among nine-month-old infants: effects of social context variables and infant temperament, *Child Development*, 63 (2), pp 290–303
12. Vygotsky's 'Zone of Proximal Development' is simply this.
13. Richman *et al*, op cit
14. Covell, K and Miles, B (1992) Children's beliefs about strategies to reduce parental anger, *Child Development*, 63 (2), pp 381–90
15. Walker, L and Taylor, J (1991) Family interactions and the development of moral reasoning, *Child Development*, 63 (2), pp 264–83
16. Brody, G, Stoneman, J, McCoy, K and Forehand, R (1992) Contemporaneous and longitudinal associations of sibling conflict with family relationship assessments and family discussions about sibling problems, *Child Development*, 63 (2), pp 391–40
Herzberher, S and Hall, J (1993) Consequences of retaliatory aggression against siblings and peers: urban minority children's expectations, *Child Development*, 64 (6), pp 1773–85
17. Richman *et al*, op cit
18. Graham, S and Hoehn, S (1995) Children's understanding of aggression and withdrawal as social stigmas: an attributional analysis, *Child Development*, 66 (4), pp 1143–61
19. Weiner (1992) *Psycological Disturbance in Adolescence*, Wiley, New York

20. Moore, M, Sixsmith, J, Knowles, K, with Kagan, C, Lewis, S, Beazley, S and Rout, U (1996) *Children's Reflections of Family Life*, Falmer Press, London

21. Kowal, A and Kramer, L (1997) Children's understanding of parental differential treatment, *Child Development*, **68** (5), pp 113–26

22. McClosky, L, Figueredo, A and Koss, M (1995) The effects of systemic family violence on children's mental health, *Child Development*, **66** (5), pp 1239–61

23. Ibid

24. Hennessy, K, Rabidean, G, Cicchelti, D and Cummings, E (1994) Responses of physically abused and non-abused children to different forms of inter-adult anger, *Child Development*, **65** (3), pp 815–28

25. Smetana, J (1995) Parenting styles and conceptions of parental authority during adolescence, *Child Development*, **66** (2), pp 299–316

26. Ibid, p 313

27. Weiss, B, Dodge, K, Bates, J and Pettit, G (1992) Some consequences of early harsh discipline: child aggression and a maladaptive social information processing style, *Child Development*, **63** (6), pp 1321–35

28. Dishion, T, Andrews, D and Crosby, L (1995) Anti-social boys and their friends in early adolescence: relationships, characteristics, quality and interactional process, *Child Development*, **66** (1), pp 139–51

29. Patterson, G (1982) *A Social Learning Approach: Vol. 3, Coercive Family Processes*, Castalia Publishing, Eugene, Oregon
Loeber, J and Loeber, S (1986) Family factors as correlates and predictors of juvenile conduct problems and delinquency, in *Crime and Justice: an annual review of research*, Vol. 7, eds M Toury and N. Morris, Chicago University Press, Chicago
Hagell, A and Newburn T (1994) *Persistent Young Offenders*, Policy Studies Institute, London

30. Kochanska, G and Radke-Yarrow, M (1992) Inhibition in toddlerhood and the dynamics of the child's interaction with an unfamiliar peer at age five, *Child Development*, **63** (2), pp 325–35
Heyman, G, Dweck, C and Cain, K (1992) Young children's vulnerability to self-blame and helplessness: relationships to beliefs about goodness, *Child Development*, **63** (2), pp 401–15

31. Randall, P (1996) *A Community Approach to Bullying*, Trentham Books, Stoke-on-Trent

32. Cassidy, J and Berlin, L (1994) The insecure/ambivalent pattern of attachment: theory and research, *Child Development*, **63** (4), pp 971–91

33. Hart, C, De Wolf, M, Wozniak, P and Burts, D (1992) Maternal and paternal disciplinary styles: relations with pre-schoolers playground behavioural orientations and peer status, *Child Development*, **63** (4), pp 879–92

34. Reiss, A (1988) Co-offending and criminal careers, in *Crime and Justice*, Vol. 10, eds M Toury and N Morris, University of Chicago Press, Chicago

35. Baumrind, D (1991) The influence of parenting styles on adolescent competence and substance use, *Journal of Early Adolescence*, **11**, pp 56–95

36. Pugh, G, De'Ath, E and Smith, C (1994) *Confident Parents, Confident Children. Policy and Practice in Parent Education and Support*, National Children's Bureau, London

37. Kupersmidt, J, Griesler, P, De Rosier, M, Patterson, C and Davis, P (1995) Childhood aggression and peer relations in the context of family and neighbourhood factors, *Child Development*, **66** (2), pp 360–75

38. Dishion *et al*, op cit

10

Anger and despair: the causes of behaviour

Introduction

Early personal experiences create characters. The 'character', rather than the 'culture', depends on personal disposition, not only the circumstances and their effect, but the way in which they are absorbed or rejected. The influence of significant relationships on subsequent behaviour lies not in imitation but in temperament. Young people do not simply copy what they see but react against it. They either learn how to deal with intractable problems, negotiating new territory, or they learn to react in a more violent, inarticulate way. Relating in a real way with other people is something that needs to be learned. If people are to succeed in programmes such as High/Scope they depend on the learning of social skills first, from which intellectual development then follows.[1] Young children not only long for relationships but understand them, understanding not only their heavy influence but their limitations, their negative effects. At pre-school level, for instance, they are perfectly aware of the distinctions between behaviours that are explained by external reasons, and those that are driven by internal psychological causes.[2] They have a clear insight into the psychology of emotion and behaviour.

The fact that people understand the causes of behaviour does not mean that they are less vulnerable to outbreaks of temper or reactions to provocation. What it means is that they are articulate about their own characters, their weakness and frustration. They are aware of what it is that drives them to behave as they do, and even they can make the connection between the patterns of their early relationships with inconsistency and indifference, and their subsequent difficulties with coping with other people. They do not make any excuses, for they reflect on the stupidity of many of their actions, and regret their repeated patterns of behaviour. They do not simply dismiss their actions as inevitable in the circumstances. They do not fall into that tempting trap of false innocence, blaming through a form of 'psycho-babble' everything on their upbringing. Whilst the realization of what has gone wrong is recognized, the responsibility for their own actions is accepted firmly as their own.

The loss of self-control

One of the main insights that these angry and frustrated young people have is into the emotional instability that makes them react so violently. Suddenly they find themselves losing their temper, going 'off me head'. They might, with hindsight, feel 'pathetic', but that is what they acknowledge as a defect, difficult to control. They know that this is unlikely to change.

> 'Cos I'm too wild... Yeah, probably like it when I get out as well, probably end up back in here knowing me.
>
> (female, 16)

'Knowing me'. The insight that young people have into the distinctions between intentionality and the *effects* of hurting, and between moral concepts and social concepts, never leave them and start early.[3] But this does not necessarily become translated into or applied to the actual events where judgements must be made at a time of raw emotions. The theoretical knowledge is there, but maturity derives from being able to turn all the understandings of motivation and behaviour into immediate action and precise moral judgement. The 'wildness' has consequences but, 'knowing me', it remains in place.

> I used to go off me head and just hit 'em. It's pathetic when I think about it, it's pathetic.
>
> (female, 19)

On reflection it might be 'pathetic' but it is a sign of a lack of self-control, and vulnerability to provocation. The relationship between emotional reactivity, negative emotionality and social and behaviour problems is clear.[4]

The question is whether it is possible to change a certain style of reactive behaviour. Was it inevitable that these young people would clash violently with teachers at some stage? Was it to be foreseen that they would be caught up in fighting?

> But now if people said it to me now I'd just blank it, wouldn't be bothered. I just couldn't stop what I was doing. It was just like a habit. You can't stop it when you're young.
>
> (male, 18)

It is the case that most criminal acts are committed by young men, some of whom do not return to crime – those who have 'calmed down'. There are social as well as emotional reasons for this. But the reaction to what is seen as provocation or opposition is not something that can be 'blanked out'. The sense of helplessness of young offenders in the face of their own temperament is clear. But it is also soon a 'habit', a way of behaving that is ritualistic rather than occasional and exceptional. Several of them feel that in their adolescence they went through a phase where violent emotions overruled their powers of reasoning.

> I don't know. I just click. I've quietened down now. When I was younger it was just like for a buzz, just something to do to pass the time.
>
> (male, 20)

There is always a balance to be struck between emotional intensity and the various kinds of regulation and self-control.[5] These people never had the chance to learn to control their responses, or to channel them, given the crudeness of their early relationships, the lack of demand as well as the lack of real interest.

The result of a deficiency in the ability to develop dialogue is a bad temper. The only response is through emotion rather than through reasoning. The response to emotional challenges is fierce and uncontrolled. They have seen the same reactions in their parents and it comes out in them.

> If I'd got one of me paddies on. Erm, kicking off, do you know them terms? If I were in that kind of temperamental mood I just used to sit there and rip me books up, throw it at 'em and just walk out of the classroom. We argued, and like a lot of 'em backed down because they knew what I were like, getting bad tempered and like I could just go off it. That's how me temper came out. He thought I were jealous.
>
> (female, 20)

Bad temper is not an inevitability. It is something that is allowed to grow, even if there is a sense that it is inexplicable. The aggressive reactions are developed in certain circumstances. The only really unexplained side of it is the timing. The young offenders do not know what exactly will provoke their anger. That a more general bad temper is born in frustrated anger is clear; tearing up books and threatening others are both signs of protest and disturbance. The lack of any kind of self-control is also clear; 'one of me paddies', 'kicking off', and 'just going off it' makes her someone potentially and actually dangerous, and she knows it. She is another one who finds herself going 'off me head'.

There are also some whose aggression is driven by their need for drugs.

I haven't talked about it, that's why I'm upset, 'cos it's all built up inside and I need to get it out and it won't come out… It's just having the will-power to stop it when I'm out. Depends what company I'm with. I've just too bad nerves, me. I need a cigarette, something to do. And I if I were cracked in the head I'd go out and I'd be back in for murder, man. I'm not being funny. I mean if I were on drugs. I'm not that easy, because a lot of people on drugs aren't easy, 'cos you get aggressive if you can't get your drugs, it's like food, know what I mean 'cos you're poorly and you're run down and that.

(female, 21)

Drugs provide an ostensible motivation but also produce a certain type of behaviour. They are both an escape and a deeper trap. She knows her weakness in the face of certain kinds of company and certain kinds of opportunity. She knows that she has failed her own child since, with drugs or when withdrawing, she 'couldn't handle it'. Again, the emotional pressure, the inability to cope, is clear. Every parent knows the strain of a baby that keeps on screaming, helplessly, and the helpless despair that makes one feel tempted to do almost anything to stop the sound. With these young people we see what their parents actually did to them, and what they are doing to their own offspring. Every parent understands the feelings; but these are people who are out of control. Aggression and a lack of 'will-power' go together, whether they are drug induced or not. For the aggression that is depicted here is not directed deliberately at any target, but is reactive and uncontrolled.

Reactions to provocation

This kind of aggression is also easily provoked. The incidents of fighting, interpreted often as 'fighting back', are many. The young offenders have won for themselves a reputation for being not only aggressive but easily teased. It is partly a matter of temperament.

Then you'd get all hyped up over nothing and start fighting with them. 'Cos it's not right is it? Tripping a girl up so I went off me head and I got done for it. 'Cos I didn't care. Some of 'em thought they was well hard.

(female, 16)

The justification of 'it's not right is it?' is balanced by the acknowledgement of extreme reactions – 'went off me head'. This young offender is someone who gets all 'hyped up' and no doubt shares the reputation with others of being 'well hard'. But this is again based on weakness, of being so easily provoked rather than on the real hardness of self-control.

I did retaliate to a few but I just tried to keep me head down, 'cos I didn't want no trouble. Fighting, 'cos I had like an aggression problem. 'Cos of what happened through me life. I can get worked up really easy. I got a name as being like the clown of the class so everyone expected me to be stupid in school, so I just lived up to me reputation. I just get worked up with little things. I just started fighting again and being stupid.

Like I just start fighting with him and then just went over the top and smashed the place up. I even cut me wrists. When I get out I must just go like I were...

(male, 17)

The subtle contradictions of temperament, the recognition of the dangers of retaliation and the unsuccessful desire to avoid it are displayed. He knows he has an aggression problem and that even little things will get him 'worked up'. He knows he has a weakness for living up to his reputation and also enough weakness or lack of self-control to go back to his old ways. The recognition of the problem is just that, not an excuse for it. He might know that there are reasons for his being as he is because of things that 'happened in his life'. But he remains as he is. The 'problem' is not just a matter of character inflicted on him at birth, but circumstances and his inability to cope with them. Whereas socially competent and popular children can cope with anger and minimize conflict, he typically cannot.[6]

It is always the 'little things' that provoke extreme reactions.

And then when I was at school anybody, they only had to say to me that me hair was a mess, or just one little thing and I'd be fighting with them.

(female, 19)

Those who are easily provoked are those who are essentially inhibited and unsociable.[7] The disposition to react against strangers as if every comment or remark were personal marks out these people's vulnerability. Again and again we recognize the phrases like 'done me head in'. Their bad temper and frustration is just waiting to emerge.

I tried but I just couldn't help it. I just lost me temper all the time. I still lose me temper but not as much as I used to. I've calmed down a lot now. I just take it as a joke, only through learning through me mistakes.

It was just dead hard people saying things to me. Instead of just let it go in one ear and out the other it were just sticking in the middle, sticking in me head and I was just flipping all the time, just fighting all the time.

(male, 21)

The irony is that after years of being ignored, of not having a real relationship, every remark and every gesture is taken personally. It is clear that the peer group cannot resist goading this young offender into a violent reaction. He is learning the hard way to discriminate between those remarks he should ignore and those that should be taken seriously.

The feelings of aggression are held at times by all children and young people, but not all of them react to their feelings by acting on them in such an extreme manner. The depressed children assume that aggressive behaviour will lead to unfortunate results.[8] But others do not even think of suppressing their actions or their feelings.

> Depends on how me temper goes. If somebody's hitting you, you hit them back and that's about it. Don't stand there. Normally, instead of asking questions they'll just hit you and then ask questions after. I try asking them what's up. If that don't work and they come to hit me I just hit 'em back.
>
> I threatened to stab manager 'cos I was sick and tired of cutting elastic... it were doing me head in.
>
> (female, 20)

Whilst the assumption is that it is always other people, in school, that start the fight, it is actually clear that the sense of threat and violence is pervasive. She is the one who threatens the manager. She is the one equally willing to hit back rather than 'standing there'. And she is the one with the temper and who finds the circumstances that 'do me head in'.

Again we find that phrase redolent of the anger and frustration, the sense of helplessness in the face of their own weakness.

> I just went over... it were my fault like... It's just this lad, done me head in, so I just got him in the toilets and just gave him a pounding.
>
> I've cut it down a bit since I had that fight in the toilets, cut it down, but if anybody says I want that, I'll just tell 'em to take their hook. If they start I'll just start back. If I tell 'em to shit off, I just have to paste 'em. Just do me head in. Yeah. I try to ignore them but if they just keep doing it I'll just double back and just paste 'em, give 'em a booting.
>
> If I could change it I'd stop me fighting... that's what I'd do.
>
> (male, 16)

'If'. The desire to change, the recognition of fault is again divorced from reality. The young offender knows that he is constantly fighting. He knows it is his fault. The phrases – 'pounding, pasting and booting' – all are redolent of a satisfying aggression. Cutting it 'down' is not the same as cutting it 'out'. So many little things can 'do his head in'. It is a term that suggests the pent-up anger, the sense that all is too much and that they are no longer in control of themselves. The link between frustration and aggression is constantly seen.

> I just flipped in that second. They used to wind me up. It sort of builds me temper up inside do you know what I mean but I hold it back. But I know one of these days I'm gonna say something that I'm gonna regret... I don't think it's fair I don't.
>   It used to get to me a lot. I didn't like it and I used to start crying and getting all frustrated and then I'd start smashing things up and things like that 'cos I couldn't stand me mum and dad arguing.
>
> (female, 21)

The link between the frustration of home life and the inability to deal with it, transferred to other circumstances, is also clearly made. This young offender finds herself accustomed not only to her temper 'building up inside' but to being 'wound up'. The vulnerability to provocation almost invites such treatment. She exhibits a wounded willingness to wound. The frustration, the attempts to suppress the explosive feelings and a deep sense of unfairness are all apparent. Aggression derives not from a show of strength but from the reactions to fear.

Knowing their limitations

The self-awareness of the springs of their own characters and their inability to cope are apparent in all the interviews. The same reflections and even the same phrases recur.

> I don't like making enemies. I don't like being an enemy. I don't like people hating me to tell you the truth. Someone says a bad word about me I want to know why.
>   I was mad. It were driving my brain mad. I couldn't take it.
>
> (male, 20)

What starts as self-assertion and a semblance of feigned innocence is unpeeled into the various levels. The young offender wishes to avoid making enemies, but he is aware that he *is* an enemy. He realizes that he is hated and he resents this. The response to that pain, however, is an aggressive 'I want to know why'. The aggression is derived from pain. The 'madness' comes about because he cannot 'take' it.

Knowing that it is easy to lose one's temper does not mitigate the fact. The weakness is acknowledged, like the temptation of the peer group.

So I'd lose me temper easily, so like, if someone says something like I'd just start getting angry, anyway so I was having a lot of fights over that. It depends how they said it, and things like that, but the slightest like I could ignore something when someone's really getting at me, but I'd snap at little things. So it was hard to like judge it. I just wouldn't know if I was going to go off or not until it happened. 'Cos I probably will come back [to prison] eventually. But I might get nicked the first week I'm out or might go for a few months or years...

(male, 20)

The most telling phrase is 'it was hard to... judge it'. It is this lack of the ability to know how to negotiate reasonably that is most significant. The young offender might know himself but he does not know *when* his bad temper will be triggered. It does not depend on logic or reason or the steady accumulation of pressure. Something large can be ignored, and then something trivial elicits an inappropriately violent response. He would only afterwards think about the way that 'it happened'. He would 'go off' with all the emotions ripped apart from reasoning. The result is that he is essentially out of his own self-control. This augurs badly for the future. It seems almost inevitable that he will return to prison, and it could even be immediately. For he has no way of telling how he will react.

There are no indications that the violence depicted here, or in school, is approved of. Whilst there is something about being 'macho', being one of the 'hard ones', this is not sorted out through aggression. Instead it is more the aftermath of constant provocation. The young offenders sense that a reputation is forced upon them. They might play up to it after a time but it is not the result of a deliberate policy or campaign. Violence is the outcome of their own weakness, their lack of self-control. It is not approved of. There should be no assumptions made about the celebration of aggression, even if they have won the reputation of being 'well hard'. Whilst these people are caught up in violent acts, they see it as a result of their own temperaments – which they also despise. Like very young children they concentrate more on the effects of being hurt, the consequences, than on any thought-out intention.[9] They do not necessarily 'mean' to do what they do, whilst being responsible for their own actions. All children, from an early age, condemn unprovoked violence, but they see the distinction between that and 'hitting back'.[10] In the circumstances of their experience at both home and school there are all kinds of ambiguities, of intention and effect, of provocation and defence. Whilst the act in itself is never justified – like taking a saucepan to hit a father in defence of the mother – it is often explained. And in the constant bickering and teasing of school, those who are easily provoked become irresistible for 'picking on'. Who then bears the greatest blame?

At the heart of the problem is a lack of self-esteem. The very tone with which they talk about themselves – 'it's pathetic' – reveals this. The experiences they have had, of being ignored at home, or finding themselves up against indifference in school, all lead to the loss of self-belief. Any attempt to gain attention then is liable to meet not with indifference but downright hostility. Many children experience difficult and indeed traumatic events, but even in the same family deal with them very differently.[11] Some translate their experiences into lower perceived self-competence. They take the events out on themselves, as if they were somehow obscurely responsible. But the resulting lack of self-confidence leads to a sense of lesser personal responsibility. They cannot 'face up' to the demands of social groups. This is the point at which they realize that they do not like 'rules' or being told what to do.

The easiest way to deal with problems is to escape, to hide from them. It is easier to 'drop out' rather than be determined to face the demands of life.[12]

> And that really upset me yesterday and I thought, well, there's no point in it no more, I may as well when I get out just start back on the drugs and things like that. Whenever I'm down or I've got bad problems I always turn to 'em, but I've got to learn that I can't do that anymore.
>
> I used to put them to the back of me head and ignore them... When I'm on drugs I don't think about it. 'Cos if you think about it when you're on drugs it just makes you even worse and you feel like killing yourself...
>
> (female, 19)

There is plenty of evidence, and every reason, for avoiding drugs. But the weakness remains. Just as reactions to provocations will always be a source of trouble, so will reactions to the temptations. Whilst the long-term ill-effects of drugs are acknowledged, the smallest incident can overcome the logic of desisting. This young offender becomes 'really upset', concludes 'there is no point in it anymore', and immediately thinks of her habitual escape route. On the one hand she's 'got to learn'. On the other her despair and desire for escape might get the better of her. Young offenders are often on the limits of their self-belief, and often lose all trace.

> Just couldn't learn anything so that's when I gave up hope on every-thing... If I get bored I know where I'm coming, back here, well I won't go here this time I'll go to Coventry.
>
> (male, 21)

Giving up hope is the essential lack of self-belief. There are all kinds of responses to that, but all are fuelled by the desire to escape, to turn away from the circumstances. The sense of being rejected by others leads to all kinds of conduct problems, from aggression to passivity.[13] There are different kinds of responses to a sense of failure and a feeling of rejection. Some children try to overcome the problems. Others believe they have the ability to overcome the difficulties but do not want to risk even the possibility of failing if they try.[14] These young people, however, give every indication of seeing failure as inevitable. They wish to give up or hide. To confront their difficulties would be a way of exposing themselves to ever more humiliation. What they really want is to be away, to be alone, physically or mentally. There is a sense of 'noli me tangere': a fear of closeness to other people.

> I'm doing them on me own and I've got nobody touching me or anything like that. I think I've always liked to do things on me own. I like to be in me own little space in me own little world. 'Cos then people can't get in your way and get you into trouble then.
>
> (female, 21)

Other people offer trouble. There is a fear of the social world as a whole with its demanding relationships for which this young offender does not feel herself to be equipped. So she not only wishes to 'do' things on her own but to be in her own 'little' world. It is both a physical space and a symbolically complete 'world' in itself.

> Nobody bugging me head. Me own time, me own little world, do me own little things. If I'm with a lot of people I get confused. I can get angry easier, I can lose me temper and end up hurting myself instead of them.
>
> (female, 20)

The desire for a 'little' space is the desire to escape from other people. Other people 'confuse' as well as hurt, they provoke as well as demand. All these are signs of the failure to be able to make relationships. The lack of self-esteem that comes from a sense of being rejected derives from this.

The answer for young offenders is to reject relationships in their turn. They try to ignore those, like teachers, who make demands on them. Their immediate reactions to other people's attention is to treat them as if they were hostile. Having been accustomed to being ignored, they assume the potential of malicious intent in the mere approach of someone else.

> Because I can't really learn things with people about, because if anybody talks, that's it. Then if they start me off that's it, I don't stop.
>
> (male, 18)

Avoiding others, 'keeping meself to meself' (female, 21) seems to be the preferred solution to the difficulties of relationships. It is, after all, the easiest for those who have never learned to make them.

The loss of self-esteem

In all the evidence there are many signs of failure. Some of these are to do with the sense of rejection, failure in the sight of others. Some are to do with the inability to cope with social demands, failure in the sight of institutions. But the most severe sense of failure comes about from young offenders' own lack of faith in themselves. They did not have connections with normal demanding relationships. They seek escape in a variety of ways. The lack of self-esteem could be manifested both in aggression, in violent reaction, and in passive avoidance of any real challenge. There are often supposed to be two types of rejected children, those who are deemed unpopular for one reason or another.[15] One type is aggressive; the other tries to remain as anonymous, as disconnected, as possible. But the rejection is not a result of what other people think of them as much as what they think of themselves. Some turn their sense of rejection into aggression and some submit themselves to it meekly. Certainly it is easier to cope with the academic demands of school by being submissive. Those who retaliate to rejection by aggression soon become formally rejected by the system. But in fact the two types of reaction overlap. There are periods of response to provocation and at the same time the desire to be alone. Both the seemingly passive and the overtly reactionary are found in the same person. Both are based not only on low self-esteem but on a strong sense of weakness. It is seen to be weak to strike out just as it is weak to want to run away.

All children have to cope with anger. Only those who are socially competent, and therefore popular – they can be related to on a steady basis – know how to cope with anger.[16] Those who, as here, have never learned essential social skills, and who are insensitive to the different social contexts in which they find themselves, find coping far more difficult.[17] They are the ones who mix up the private and the public, the personality and the role. They are the ones who find the rules which are paramount in order and authority personally intransigent and unnegotiable. It all derives not from a sense of alternative power and self-assertion but from an acute sense of weakness, against which they rail.

> I mean even when I was at school I had nothing, and I used to feel so inadequate. You know I had nothing so I used to lie and that and say I had this and I had that but really, I never had nothing. I suppose I was getting my own back or whatever.
>
> (female, 18)

The desire for 'attention' drives her into making false statements as well as being aggressive. It is not just a matter of 'having' nothing but feeling as if she had nothing to give. The lack of possessions is nothing compared to the sense of personal inadequacy. 'Getting me own back' is the expression of some vague enmity with the whole world, with that sense of anger and frustration which afflicts them all.

The sense of being trapped by their own weakness and the lack of understanding of how this has come about and why they should be so different, become pervasive. One feeling and one psychological urge overlaps with another. Anger is mixed with fear, sadness with inadequacy.

> I haven't talked about it, that's why I'm upset, 'cos it's all built up inside and I need to get it out and it won't come out.
>
> It's not having the will-power to stop it when I'm out. Depends what I'm coping with... I'm lazy at heart. I've got bad nerves me. I need a cigarette, something to do.
>
> (female, 21)

The jitteriness of the emotions, the longing for some quick 'fix' that will set her up, are all tumbled together with knowing that she cannot express herself, recognizing her laziness and acknowledging her weakness. She clearly cannot 'cope'; in her own words she talks of her lack of 'will-power'. It is this fundamental weakness which is at the heart of what has gone wrong, not some genetic streak of aggression or an innate desire to do wrong. Instead we witness inadequacy; loneliness and inadequacy.

The desire to be 'by myself', so often expressed, is paralleled by the perception of being rejected. The two go hand in hand. All children understand loneliness and feelings of loneliness from an early age.[18] It is at once a deep feeling and a social actuality. Negative self-perceptions, which have such adverse consequences, are not just the product of social circumstances; they are not imposed from a collective or shared perception.[19] Loneliness is produced by the mediation of self-perception and the acceptance of distance from the peer group. Again, it is a complicated balance of the individual and the environment, a matter of relationships. Some rejected children respond to the sense of rejection with aggression and find difficulties. Others are submissive to it, and survive.[20] The result is, once again, a jumble of different (and by now familiar) feelings.

> I don't think I'll be doing it again. I don't know yet. When I get out I might just go like I were. I used to say to myself when I were doing it, I'll, I'll stop soon. I'll get a car and settle down, and you can't, you just can't. As soon as you wake up you want drugs... it's just greed really.
>
> I've heard people say it before and they've come back. I don't know, it's just being told what to do really just can't stand it.
>
> I've been thinking in bed 'I've been stupid' and I think 'no I'm not gonna smoke no more' and I cover up me fags and as soon as I wake up 'where's me fags...'

[job] Just does me head in.

I thought I were just shy at first and then I were that paranoiac some-times I couldn't talk. You know every time I had to say something I had to think about what I say in case I said it wrong and I think I'm just paranoid...

(male, 17)

All the elements of the lack of relationships are here. The seeming shyness turns out to be a fear of rejection, the personal desire to give utterance driven back on itself by the barrier of being wrong. The sense of personal inadequacy in the face of temptation is matched by the contrast between desire and reality. What people say is not what they do; but they understand the difference. Self-loathing is made the deeper by the recognition that it will make no difference to subsequent styles of behaviour.

It is apparent that these people present a significant type of insight into their own deficiencies. It is also apparent that they recognize that one central weakness is the fact that insight is not turned into action. There is a failure in dealing with external demands as well as internal desires. There is a chasm between themselves and others. The place where they learned certain behaviours and approaches to other people was, in the first instance, their own home.[21] The contrast between emotional intensity leading to uncontrolled anger and the ability to regulate and cope with feelings is already sharp by the age of four.[22] Those who have learned to cope with themselves through relationships with their parents and others can deal with anger, and negotiate with others using considerable social skills.[23] Those who have not learned are both aggressive and escapist. At the heart of the matter is the human power to understand social circumstances through others. When this is denied they turn their own self-contempt into a pathological form of personal dia-logue and make enemies through it. And once the whole of society is perceived as a perpetual enemy, they reach the ultimate loneliness.

References

1. Schwienhart, L and Weikart, D (1993) *A Summary of Significant Benefits: The High/Scope Perry Pre-School Study through age 27*, High/Scope, Washington, DC
2. Miller, P and Aloise, P (1989) Young children's understanding of the psychological causes of behaviour: a review. *Child Development*, **60** (2), pp 257–85
3. Helwig, C, Hildebrandt, C and Turiel, E (1995) Children's judgements about psycholog-ical harm in social context, *Child Development*, **66** (6), pp 1680–93
4. Eisenberg, N, Fabes, R, Murphy, B, Maszk, P, Smith, P and Karbon, M (1995) The role of emotionality and regulation in children's social functioning: a longitudinal study, *Child Development*, **66** (5), pp 1360–84

5. Ibid
6. Fabes, R and Eisenberg, N (1992) Young children's coping with interpersonal anger, *Child Development*, **63** (1), pp 116–28
7. Asendorpf, J (1991) Development of inhibited children's coping with unfamiliarity, *Child Development*, **62** (6), pp 1460–74
8. Quiggle, N, Garber, J, Panak, W and Dodge, A (1992) Social information processing in aggressive and depressed children, *Child Development*, **63** (6), pp 1305–20
9. Helwig *et al*, op cit
10. Astor, R (1994) Children's moral reasoning about family and peer violence: the role of provocation and retribution, *Child Development*, **65** (4), pp 1054–67
11. Beardall, L and Dunn, J (1992) Adversities in childhood: sibling's experiences and their relations to self-esteem, *Journal of Child Psychology and Psychiatry*, **33** (2), pp 349–74
12. Cullingford, C (1999) *The Human Experience: The Early Years*, Ashgate, Aldershot
13. Bierman, K, Smoot, D and Anmuller, K (1993) Characteristics of aggressive-rejected, aggressive (non-rejected) and rejected (non-aggressive) boys, *Child Development*, **64** (1), pp 139–51
14. Galloway, D, Rogers, L and Armstrong, D (1996) Maladaptive motivational style: the role of domain specific task demands in English and Mathematics, *British Journal of Educational Psychology*, **66**, pp 197–207
15. Wentzel, K and Asher, S (1995) The academic lives of neglected, rejected, popular and controversial children, *Child Development*, **66** (3), pp 754–63
16. Fabes and Eisenberg, op cit
17. Underwood, M, Coie, J and Herbsman, C (1992) Display rules for anger and aggression in school-age children, *Child Development*, **63** (2), pp 366–80
18. Cassidy, J and Asher, S (1992) Loneliness and peer relations in young children, *Child Development*, **63** (2), pp 350–65
19. Sletta, O, Valås, H, Skaalvik, E and Søbstad, F (1996) Peer relations, loneliness and self-perceptions in school-aged children, *British Journal of Educational Psychology*, **66** (4), pp 431–45
20. Rabiner, D and Gordon, L (1992) The coordination of conflicting social goals: differences between rejected and non-rejected boys, *Child Development*, **63** (6), pp 1344–50
21. Feldman, S and Weinberger, D (1994) Self-restraint as a mediator of family influences on boys' delinquent behaviour: a longitudinal study, *Child Development*, **65** (1), pp 195–211
22. Eisenberg, N, Febes, R, Nyman, M, Bernsweig, J and Pinuelas, A (1994) The relations of emotionality and regulation to children's anger-related reactions, *Child Development*, **65** (1), pp 109–28
23. Dunn, J (1988) *The Beginnings of Social Understanding*, Basil Blackwell, Oxford

11

Perpetuation: the following generation

Introduction

There is a popular, if misrepresented, poem by Philip Larkin that is based on the premise that parents hand over all their faults to their children, and some extra ones.[1] It is as if the human condition could only get worse. That mankind hands on misery to 'man' is one of the abiding themes of literature. It is also corroborated by research. The sense of the sins of the fathers benighting their sons is very strong. Many studies, like that of Farrington and his colleagues, show how often the conditions, the circumstances and the relationships in one generation are repeated in the next.[2] This could be the most depressing of the findings, but needs careful scrutiny. We have noted that it is not simply circumstances that count. This means that it is not a matter of changing living conditions or socio-economic factors, as if simple social and economic control could make significant differences. It suggests that intervention is possible, but at a far more subtle level.

That parents, including the experience of the earliest years as a whole, are crucial is without doubt. Those earliest of formative influences create the potential for what will happen to children in the rest of their lives. The young mind is alert and intelligent. It interprets what it witnesses. On the interpretation rests the way in which it will subsequently act. What is seen and observed is therefore very important. The question remains how deep these formative experiences go. We know the connection between parents and their offspring. We understand the correlation. But few have yet really explained *why* and how this influence is so pervasive and so long lasting.

In the reflections of the young offenders there is no real question about the influence of parents. They have astringent views on the responsibilities of parenting, even if, as we will see, they once again do not necessarily follow their own best advice. The gap between insight and action remains. But the sense that parents are responsible is crucial.

I don't blame them. I blame the parents.

(female, 20)

This statement is both a result of general observation, watching the way in which children are treated, and a precise reflection of the young offender's own experience. Young people instinctively understand the nature of the earliest of experiences, an insight that is constantly reiterated in research, if from a more distant point of view. The theoretical is never so rich as when it is borne out from the inside.

Well, it's the way they've been brought up, isn't it. They don't care, shoplifting in town, y'know what I mean? I think a lot of it is down to the way they're brought up. Don't know. Parents don't care about them so they don't care about anyone else, dunno, that's it really.

(male, 19)

This is not a statement that is grafted out of an excuse. It is not an attempt to alleviate personal responsibility. What is observed is a lack of 'caring'. But at the same time the lack of caring is widespread. The impoverishment of relationships and the absence of accountability have their inevitable consequences. One generation is seen to hand on the same attitudes to the next. This is not an abrogation of guilt, of shoplifting or anything else young offenders might do. But the 'way they have been brought up' is confirmed as crucial.

Children's analysis of parental limitations

These young people are attempting to come to terms with their own experiences and their effects. They are found guilty as individuals. But there are circumstances that suggest that what they have done has some kind of explanation far more complex than either a simple genetic fault or a simplistic environmental generalization. There are some clear correlations. Nearly all these young people, however young they might be to have reached the minimum age for prison, have children of their own. Young parenthood is itself a problem, a sign of personal irresponsibility and the lack of maturity in the bringing up of the next generation. Separations abound. The crude circumstances of upbringing are themselves a factor. Disruptive homes, absent parents and arguments are clearly a breeding ground for problems. But they are also the results, the symbols, of dislocated relationships, of irresponsibility, of selfishness and of escape. If there cannot be a solid and rational relationship entered into with that mixture of personal passion and moral certainty, then there is almost bound to be trouble. The *fact* of single parenthood is not in itself the problem. It is

the result of the problem, of not seeing relationships as a concentration of commitment as well as feeling. The really long-lasting or permanent relationships are public as well as private, a matter of determination as well as desire.

These young people, dislocated from the experience of permanence, and from
the rectitude of determination, strike up with the ephemeral, the easily available.
The consequences seem to them inconsequential. The irony is that they have to
live with the unforeseen consequences. The question of whose 'fault' it is remains
an open one between one generation and the next. When they try to work out for
themselves, from their own points of view, the meaning of their own and other
lives, they detect very clearly what they have missed.

> But I wouldn't be too protective and I wouldn't you know, I wouldn't let
> them out 'till all hours of the morning. I dunno. I wouldn't have kids. I'd
> just... I wouldn't be really really strict. I'd be strict about smoking and
> drinking and stuff like that.
>
> (female, 21)

The tension between the over-authoritarian and the indifferent is clearly detected,
and the instinct that there is another way, a delicate balance, tentatively stated. Not
to be too 'protective', not to be too 'strict', these are significant issues. But the difficulties of responsibility are also clearly faced. This young offender understands the
issues. At what point should the will be asserted? What are the really significant
actions on which parental authority needs to be asserted?

At the same time she understands the temptations, the emotional ties and
ambiguities.

> And going round with the wrong crowd... I, me, I'd dress me children
> really smart. I dunno, 'cos they'd feel better about themselves and that and
> wouldn't worry about the way they look. I'd just give them loads of love
> and stuff but I'd never... I'd always worry about them and that and never
> let them out. I would let them out but I'd never let them out 'till all hours
> of the morning.
>
> (ibid)

The actual tensions of decision are recognized. The sense of personal responsibility and enjoyment are understood. How do parents save their own children from
embarrassment at a superficial as well as a more profound level? Would the parent
over-indulge her children? Would she be able to bear being really strict? All these
innocent remarks are squeezed out of experience. 'Loads of love' is tempered by
worry. Never letting them out is mitigated by more complex rules and sanctions.
And what would parents be able to do about the 'wrong crowd', those moments
when they feel helpless, with the children beyond immediate control?

These instinctive judgements are founded in experience. They are unaffected by any summaries of literature or theory. They are intelligent and give deep, if academically unformed, accounts of the issues.

> A lot of people say you know it's not the parents' fault, you know if people are in prison and that, it's nothing to do with them but it is you know, it's the way they've been brought up and stuff. I'm not blaming it on my mum or whatever because what I've done I chose to do you know but like I said before say I was brought up by the Queen or whatever, I wouldn't have turned out like this would I?

> (ibid)

This commentary contains a number of contradictions, but that makes it probably truer to any summary of findings than any bland statement could be. There is firstly the desire to find a simple link between cause and effect. If there is someone in prison it is their own responsibility. In the eyes of the law punishment means guilt. It also means that any collective responsibility can be eschewed. Up to a point one can accept the simple case of personal blame. Given a single act, the legal system cannot then pore over the many causes and circumstances that gave the enfolding conditions for that act. And yet 'the way they have been brought up' has clearly a great deal to do with what happens next. She makes a fair point not just about circumstances – and whilst the contrast is exaggerated it remains true – but about the particular role of parents. At the same time she does not 'blame her mum'. That would be simplistic, as if the finger of the law were merely to be pointed elsewhere. She knows that she has at once 'chosen' to do what she did but is also aware of all the influences that have made her what she is. Of course she is, like the Queen, a cultural artefact as well as an individual human being.

Children learn from their parents, subconsciously and consciously. Even before they develop their own *modus vivendi* they are aware of certain characteristics they would wish to avoid. They are determined to behave differently from their own experience, even if the determination is difficult to put into practice.

> I'd never let that happen. If I did fall out or something with me girlfriend there'd be no argument. I'd just, I'd have to do something serious and I'd just stop it there and then. 'Cos, obviously it upsets children you know, shouting. Crying, all that, fighting, 'cos I used to worry more about me mum but I was worried about both of them… I've got a girlfriend and when I go away she's like, don't go and that you know? Like crying and that so that puts me off going as well…

> (male, 19)

Even in the course of the argument there are subtle shifts of emphasis that suggest the complexity of influence and example. Parents help form behaviour and attitude not only by how they behave, as something to be imitated, but by what ought to be avoided. This young offender has a desire not to take the same argumentative line as his parents, for all the psychological damage that they have done. The shouting, the crying and the fighting have all left deep scars. At the same time, whilst the idea of merely stepping away from the problem seems at once sensible and attractive, we witness the beginnings of the same claustrophobic conditions, with his girlfriend holding him back. The 'crying' is repeated.

The perpetuation of parental limitation

Insidiously, and subtly, the influence of the parents lingers on, and there is a recognition of the repeated patterns of behaviour. Explaining their own behaviour makes young offenders want to blame their parents the more. Seeing how they behave makes them realize more about their parents and their own motivations.

> I've got to be careful here 'cos I've got a child myself and like the girl I was with she like dumped me. Erm and for me to say no, he's not a good father because he was never hardly there I can't say the same, 'cos I know like I'm never gonna be all the time there 'cos like this girl I went out with she doesn't want me anyway. So I see my son and that but I'm never always gonna be there. If I say to you now my father's a bad dad 'cos he was never there I'm saying to myself that I'm gonna be a bad dad 'cos I'm never there.
>
> (male, 20)

How can this young offender truly blame his absent father when he is an absent father himself? But it is not a question of blame, as such. The equivocal nature of his response is the realization that he has suffered from not having a father and how he is going to perpetuate the same suffering, even if it is no explicit 'fault' of his own. 'Like father, like son' includes the circumstances. He wants to be able to say that he suffered from absence: but that is not the same as blame. The pity of it lies in the fact that there are some traumatic and terrible consequences as a result of parental behaviour. But this is not assuaged by suggestions of punishment. The blame might lie there but such blame is not the same as legal guilt. All this is the background and the root cause of the action. But most if not all of the attention given to crime and criminality is driven towards the final action and its punishment.

Getting away from circumstances, escaping from responsibility, is always a strong temptation. Whilst it sometimes seems to be the choice of the girlfriend, it can also be an instinctive reaction to events. The girl is pregnant and the boy is not 'ready' for it.

> I didn't want to see her for some reason, just didn't want to... I didn't wanna be having a family and that and with Jade because I might start acting stupid or something under the influence of drugs. I thought no, I can't do that no more so I just stopped going round... Her mum come round and she said 'you know she's pregnant'. It just didn't bother me. I don't know why... I just wanna find out what it's gonna be like when I get out. Am I gonna be the same or have I really changed?
>
> (male, 17)

Having realized, despite rumours to the contrary, that the child is his own, this young offender feels some paternal responsibility. But this is rather an old-fashioned paternalism. The set of attitudes that are brought to bear are those of the clear distinctions between the behaviour of the sexes, the predatory male and the domestic female. The views of young offenders sometimes seem to be somewhat more up to date but essentially the same role differences are in place.

> She could go out to work as long as she gets someone to mind the kids... Not much I could do is there?
>
> (male, 20)

> Nothing, just nothing. She looks after the baby.
>
> (male, 18)

In many ways it is a sign of how little in their parents' relationships has been really examined or understood that these simple attitudes are struck. Rather than perceiving the subtleties of relationships they witness the separate roles. Instead of entering into the world of dialogue, of mutual respect and support, they have merely observed the functioning of separate lives when the only real dialogues are domestic decisions or clashes of personality. No wonder the ancient traditions and unfocused assumptions prevail.

> Forget them. I'd rather be on me own, 'cos men, like, think they own you, some of 'em do anyway, not all, never found the right one yet, but they think they own you. You've always got to cook and clean for them, you're just like a slave, like if you're on your own you just do your own thing and look after yourself and your child, don't you?
>
> (female, 20)

The prevailing assumption is that people will not change. But the underlying revelation is that people are perceived as bundles of habits and roles. There might be
'the right one', but this is at the level of patterns of behaviour. The routines of
domestic life become stronger than the intricacies of relationships.

This suggests a view of parenting and of marital or cohabiting relationships that
is a matter of superficial attraction or convenience. How could it be otherwise if
there has been no learning of a deeper sense of dialogue? The routines of every day
are no substitute for understanding. The rough and tumble of role playing is no
proper alternative to the attempts to see into the mind and the needs of others.
Deprived of those essential relationships, even the outlook of young offenders on
their own future is blighted. This means that if things do not work out simply and
automatically there could be trouble, either the clash of wills, or the escape from
the problem. The essence of the 'laissez-faire' attitude is that it suggests that *nothing*
can be done. There is no personal engagement.

> Say like… I've done something wrong, like me mum must have felt like
> she did something wrong, but it's not, you can't watch them every five
> minutes, can't do. As they get older you just can't stop them. You have to
> start when they're young, really young.
>
> (male, 18)

Whilst the Jesuitical truth of insisting on the importance of the early years must be
acknowledged, the prevailing assumption is that 'you can't stop them'. There is a
sense of helplessness in the face of a problem as if you 'cannot' do what is needed.
At the same time there is a percipience of responsibility; the mother *must* have felt
she had done something 'wrong', but the comfort is not just how hard it is to be a
'good enough' parent but how there is nothing that can be done about it. 'You
can't…', 'can't do'. Thus not only the habits and circumstances of single parenthood and dysfunctional families are perpetuated but the prevailing attitudes that
underlie them as well.[3]

The relationships that these people have observed from an early age have been
at best superficial and separate, each parent playing their own role, and at worst
violent and unforgiving. The unspoken hope is that life could be different for
them, and that they will have learned how to avoid the same difficulties. The question remains whether they can ever really become uncontaminated from their own
early experiences. The terror of perpetuation hangs over them, but do they inevitably suffer from the same circumstances?

That most subtle of distinctions between the socio-economic conditions, the
cultural conditioning and the personal relationships are here, once more, at their
most apparent. The most crucial level is the interplay between one person and
another. If there are no other learned forms of dialogue, there is no real surprise
that emotions should be expressed in the harshest of ways. What is most clearly

perpetuated are actions and the ways in which they are presented. But what is also perpetuated is at once a cultural artefact, a way of expression that is rooted only in some conditions, and a prevailing ethos. These young people have suffered from seeing their parents behave in the way they did. Does this then strengthen them or protect them from similar forms of behaviour?

> And like Toby he used to beat me up all the time. I left him and since then like all the lads I've been going out with or tried to make a go of it with they've just done me head in really. If they try and tell me that I can't do something then because they've said that I go out and do it.
>
> (female, 19)

The attitudes that have been so strongly learned fester in new relationships. The connection between circumstance ('beat me up'), frustration ('done me head in') and anger ('I go out and do it') are clear. Circumstances and relationships become one.

No close relationships, and there are many, mostly including children, are talked about with any pleasure. Here the word relationship is used in the neutral sense. It does not include the real goal of understanding, which is personal dialogue. The relationships young offenders talk about are circumstantial – the person 'I live with' rather than the person 'I love'. There are girlfriends and boyfriends, sometimes significant ones. But they are just as likely to 'do my head in' as anyone else.

> She just sits at home worrying about me, like. When I were first going out with her it was just like, you know, always arguing like, but now I'm in here, she's gone all soppy like. Well it's alright but some of the things what she says makes me go red like. When you get out you think 'oh no, what's she on about?'
>
> (male, 16)

Even without having to note the age it is possible to see all kinds of incipient problems, of misunderstandings both at an emotional and intellectual level. Indeed, the misapprehensions involve both. This young offender cannot enter into the feelings that produce the 'worrying' or the 'soppiness' and no doubt his girlfriend cannot perceive what makes him go either 'red' or 'oh no'. The misunderstandings and the arguments are bound to continue. The lack of real communication is clear.

There are strong indications that the personal experience of home is to be repeated in their own lives. They often remind us of this fact. Sometimes it is the lack of dialogue or misunderstanding; at other times it is physical abuse that is repeated.

> I don't think [violent dads] deserve to live, sorry, you know what I
> mean… I'm like a prostitute know what I mean and I've been raped four
> times in just over one and a half years… And my boyfriend beats me up so
> it all like comes together and I'm thinking me step-dad did as well, see
> what I mean?… So he like beats me up all the time but when he does it just
> brings a lot of memories back.
>
> (female, 21)

'It all comes together'. 'It just brings a lot of memories back'. That sense of déjà-vu is
pervasive. But why should experiences of that kind be repeated? To suggest there is
the possibility of an attraction to that very same violence would be both insulting and
missing the point. No one would seek out what is happening to this young offender.
Whilst it might be to some extent associated with her style of life, that does not either
condone or explain it. The boyfriend is the 'first guy I've ever been out with, properly' and is married. The root of the problem, however, goes deeper. That anger and
frustration from which the violence derives are, in the case of her step-father and the
boyfriend, a characteristic of the lack of a normal stable relationship resting on dialogue and understanding. It is too easy to associate physical violence merely with a
certain *modus vivendi*, as if in certain socio-economic conditions it were inevitable. It
is never as simple as that. The problem is that such violence is often a product of dysfunctional families, in the sense of either physical separation or a verbal and physical
enmity. In this case she has been brought up intermittently 'in care and that in children's homes'. There has been no true stability in her life.

The early experiences of this girl were of separation from her family and when
not separated of being 'beaten up'. What then is either likely to happen, or might
happen to her own offspring?

> And I've got a kid to him as well… but she got took off me… I were on
> drugs, I were withdrawing, right. I'd cleaned her, fed her, played with her
> and every time I put her down she kept screaming and I couldn't handle it,
> and like there were nobody there to help. Me boyfriend were never there,
> man, never helped me at all, never bought her nowt, never did owt for her,
> never did owt for me; all he were worried about were his drugs, do you
> know what I mean and that just cracked me head up and I took it out on
> the poor little baby, man.
>
> (ibid)

That scenario that is recognized by all parents, of desperation with helplessness in
the face of a baby's incessant crying, is here turned into the violence that was
inflicted on her in her turn. The lack of support or interest and the absorption with
drugs have their consequences. Whilst she says that her baby 'be better off where
she is at the moment' one cannot help but fear for the future; the lack of stability

and whatever the feelings the mother might have, the lack of will-power to put those feelings into supportive action.

> It's just having the will-power to stop it…

(ibid)

This is at the heart of what is missing.

The result is that the baby is seen almost in isolation, as a human being *against* whom actions are taken. In a sense this baby has been discarded. She might be missed and she might be better off isolated from the mother with her drug problem, but she is discarded nevertheless. Young children are, after all, a problem. They are hard work. They demand attention. For these people, with their own early experiences, they are not so much infants who have a relationship with their parents as creatures who are going their own way. Their characteristics are seen as the result of how they are, as if nothing can be done about it. The way this mother talks about her child is not untypical.

> I've got a kid. She's two and a half. She's a rebel. Definitely. I'll hate to see her at school. She's a rebel. I think she's gonna be one of the bullies. Because if she sees any kids with toys she'll just snatch it out their hands and like we're trying to get it out of her. She won't have it. She'll just throw the toy at us. I'm just gonna start getting her mixing with kids now and hopefully she'll grow out of it…

(female, 20)

Is this a sign of laissez-faire, or abrogation of responsibility or the genetic make-up passed on by the father? It is clear that from the mother's point of view the will-power of the infant is stronger than hers: 'She won't have it'. All we are left with is 'hopefully she'll grow out of it'.

Apart from the desire to get the child 'mixing' with other children, the conditions are of a one-parent family. Her future is predicted, as one of the 'rebels' and a 'bully'; the two characteristics are again linked tellingly. But the conditions of the home strike an all too familiar chord.

> We did split up, er, just after she were born and he hasn't seen her since… 'Cos he were doing me head in and he raped his sister. Yeah, he hit me and just generally being a twat. I just couldn't take it being smacked 'cos like I didn't want to hit him back 'cos like I was pregnant at the time when he hit me but he were drunk so I thought, well, he might end up going further. He only hit me like twice and it were my fault 'cos I were mouthing at him. I were giving a lot of backchat, accusing him of this, that and t'other… like pregnant women normally do, 'cos like he were out all hours and so I were like jealous.

> It were over his sister. Erm, she wanted to come and live with us and he
> wanted her to come and live with us and I said 'no way, she's a slag' and it
> all started from that; 'she's not a slag'. So like he started pushing me
> around and I just like head-butted him.
>
> (ibid)

What is strikingly called 'normal' – jealousy and accusations – rapidly becomes a
different sort of 'normality', of arguments and violence, of conversation turned
into abuse, as if an argument could be won by assertion. The strong antipathy and
rejection of someone else, either because of some fault of their own – 'she's a slag' –
or because of a personal reaction – 'he were doing me head in' – are clearly seen.
Before physical violence comes emotional violence, the extremes of passion and
hate. It is therefore less of a surprise to find such feelings also being taken out on
the child. All the mother could imagine from a future with him would be further
and more extreme violence.

The breakdown of relationships and their consequences

Again and again we see a familiar pattern of behaviour repeated and perpetuated.
This seems to happen even when every effort is made to change. These young people are clear about the negative aspects of their own upbringing. They do 'blame
the parents'. They would wish to be different. But they also know that the effects
of their own upbringing go deep. They are aware of their own weakness and limitations. We can therefore see clearly the incipient problems even for those who
intend to lead a normal life. The final example of this is from a man who says he
has 'learned from it this time' and intends to sort out his life with his girlfriend and
his 'little lad'.

> Well, while I'm in here me girlfriend's not very happy about him going up
> every weekend 'cos she's bored. She's got nothing to do and they're start-
> ing to get a cob on, writing letters to me saying they won't let the baby
> come up for a weekend and all this, that and the other and there's nothing
> I can do about it is there really?
>
> (male, 21)

Even at a distance there is a sense of trouble and of disappointment. His girlfriend
is not only 'bored' but 'gets a cob on' and keeps her distance. But what he also
learns is for him too familiar territory.

> Sometimes me girlfriend's started doing it and I'm gonna end up… 'cos
> I've been brought up to see me dad hitting me mum and that and seeing
> me dad hitting other people. I'm gonna end up hitting her because my lit-
> tle lad, he's got away with too much, he's been spoilt by me mum and
> [step] dad because with them not being able to have any themselves
> they've spoiled him rotten and he gets away with murder, gets away with
> everything and I didn't want that. I wanted him to be brought up proper,
> not the way I was brought up.
>
> (ibid)

We have at once and at the same time both sides of learning from the past: the
determination to act differently and in contrast, and the recognition of repeating
the same mistakes. He sees the limitations of the way he was brought up, with all
the signs of laissez-faire, being 'spoiled rotten'. At the same time he has deeply
embedded in his own consciousness the symbol of how his father dealt with his
mother. His determination to do what he sees as right for his child could well be
expressed forcibly, as strongly as his language.

He is not the only one for whom it is natural to express control or punishment
in physical terms.

> But when he's at home he doesn't get 'em and she ends up smacking him
> 'cos he's crying for them really hard and many a time, before I came in
> here, many a time I've been ready for banging her and I've thought no. I've
> been through enough of that in my life. I just accept it like.
>
> (ibid)

Again, there is a tension between perpetuating the violence and wishing to control
it. The example of the past should constrain. Up to a point it does but how many
more times will he be tempted to, or think of, 'banging her'? How else can he
assert his will-power? How else can he communicate his wishes? How long can he
hold his feelings in check?

> I said to her the other week when I was on me home leave, I said 'look if
> you keep hitting him the way you are' 'cos I was sat there watching the TV,
> he was falling asleep and you know what kids are like, they always cry,
> moan for something… he was crying, crying his eyes out and she walked
> over to him like that 'mum, mum' like that she just pushed him on the
> floor like that and I jumped up and grabbed her by her throat and said
> 'look if you do that again I'm gonna kill you'.
>
> (ibid)

The child is not only a victim but a witness. Not only does it receive a mixture of over-indulgence and harsh physical abuse, but it sees the parents arguing, or intent on their own lives, or physically assaulting each other.

The problem is that they cannot cope, or will not cope, with the child.

> She goes 'oh I can't cope with him no more. He's getting too much for me'. She said 'it's alright for you, you're stuck in there relaxing', she goes 'while I'm 'ere at home I've gotta look after that little brat'. And turned round and said 'right but when I come out if I find out you've hit him any more I'm gonna grab that baby, grab his stuff, grab my stuff and I'm going. I'm going to live at me mum's and you'll never see him again', and I would.
>
> (ibid)

This is a man who can easily get a 'cob on'. Mostly he avoids his girlfriend's moaning by not dealing with it but going out. But when he does say what he thinks it is done with the most extreme of threats. There is no hint of moderation. 'I'm gonna kill you', 'you'll never see him again' is the language of extremes, as if there were no negotiating position except threat. The 'little lad' therefore faces a bleak future. He is going to suffer from all the main conditions of the pathological family. He could be 'spoiled rotten' by one family. He could be physically abused. And he will witness not only the violent side of his parents' behaviour against each other but their two separate ways of dealing with him. The one, apart from hitting him, is continually 'moaning' at 'the little brat'. The other does not stay to help but 'I just get off and go again'.

> I've been brought up to see me dad hittin' me mum.
>
> (ibid)

That action is likely to be repeated. It is certainly threatened, and even if he has not yet started 'banging' he has grabbed her by the throat. The sad fact is that the most crucial aspects of behaviour are learned not from mere imitation but from the absence of positive dialogue. If the parents cannot communicate in the full sense with each other, how can they really communicate with their offspring? The importance of the relationship between the early years and subsequent behaviour is continually acknowledged. It is seen in the connection of bullying and crime.[4] It is possible to predict from an early age which children may fall into crime, as if the whole process were self-perpetuating. In his longitudinal study, Farrington points to several factors that are significant. He cites poverty, low intelligence, failure, truancy, lack of qualifications and low pay.[5] All these hang together. One thing leads to another. But at the heart of the matter is, as the young offenders themselves subliminally acknowledge, the relationships, at an early age, with their parents. In demonstrating that they themselves would and do behave in a similar way to their own offspring, they show how deep the influence goes. If young people cannot create a dialogue with others they are bound to communicate through other means. They are bound not to be able to cope with school. And from these early conditions – not of poverty as such, not of the community as such, not of the issues of single parents as such, but in the nature of the relationships, are all the subsequent difficulties born.

References

1. Larkin, P (1986) *This be the way*, High Windows, Faber, London
2. Farrington, D and West, D (1990) *The Cambridge Study in Delinquent Behaviour*, Springer-Verlag, London
3. Kiernan, K (1997) Becoming a young parent: a longitudinal study of associated factors, *British Journal of Sociology*, **48** (3), pp 406–28
4. Lane, D (1989) Violent histories: bullying and criminality, in *Bullying in Schools*, eds D. Tattum and D. Lane, pp 95–104, Trentham Books, Stoke-on-Trent
5. Farrington, op cit

Conclusion

All the factors that come together and cause such an estrangement from ordered society give a sense that there is something inevitable about the process that leads to such outcomes. Difficult lives at home and a lack of positive and personal dialogue cause an inability to deal with relationships, and a difficulty in discriminating between the way that people play a role and the ways in which they remain individual personalities. Such a vulnerability of temperament and tact makes these young people targets for bullying and for being 'picked on' by the system. Clashes between formal orders and private passions cause the kinds of disjunctions that make social order and social behaviour rejected. With hindsight, the narrative drives of these young offenders' lives suggest the inevitable. What happens to them can be predicted; and it seems likely that their experiences will be perpetuated in the next generation. Whatever happens to them next, whether they repeat crime or manage to change, the environmental and personal factors that combined to explain where they ended up are consistent and clear.

But the real message of this research is that although on the face of it there is an inevitability in their turning to crime, it is in fact unnecessary. At every stage experiences could have been so different. At any time there could have been the possibility of preventative measures. The inevitable conclusion of the book is both obvious and widely ignored. Crime is not some immutable fact of life. Just as anyone reading this, from whatever background, has had the privilege or the fortune not even to think about undertaking a criminal act, and who has not felt fundamentally alienated from society, so it could be the same for all. Criminality is not genetic.

After looking at the evidence, that is the only conclusion that can be drawn. But in the world of social exclusion and psychological truancy, as well as that of criminology let alone of politics, to draw a conclusion after looking at the evidence is rare. It even has the hint of the eccentric. Most measures to do with exclusion, from truancy onwards, start with a conclusion, or hypothesis, and then test it. Many approaches are tested. Whilst it would be considered unethical to experiment with people's bodies, there appears to be no such inhibition in experimenting on people's minds. There are many social experiments carried out to see how people behave in certain conditions. As a result we have accumulated a great deal of knowledge, expensively acquired, about what does *not* work. The Sherman report spends much of its time pointing to all the failed attempts to make changes through social experiments.[1] All the money spent on the problems of truancy has merely demonstrated how many different measures have failed.

It says something about the pathology of the human mind that there is so little attention paid to the evidence on which policy should be based. For the evidence is clear. Whilst this book seeks to explain *why* people behave as they do, the broad principles of social exclusion and of crime prevention are clear. The irony is that even those who are responsible for crime reduction are aware of what is needed, but continue to ignore their own evidence. Let us take the report *Reducing Offending*, produced by the Home Office, as an example.[2] Like the Sherman report it repudiates many of the anti-crime strategies that receive political support. It lists all the experiments that do not work. They include:

- Random police patrolling; 'bobbies on the beat'
- Arresting more people
- Neighbourhood Watch
- 'Community Policing'
- Restorative justice
- Zero tolerance

and most significant of all,

- Imprisonment

All of these do not lead to reductions in crime. This is not to suggest that they have no effects at all; imprisonment protects the public from criminals. Restorative justice does produce greater respect for the police. Police patrols reduce the fear of crime.

What does not work points up the more clearly what does. At one level focusing attention on repeat crime, on particular places and people, does have an effect.[3] But the real way of dealing with crime is through the reduction in criminality. And the reduction of criminality depends upon the prevention of social exclusion. And this depends on the home and the school.

Schooling is, in itself, an intervention into the lives of private citizens. It is meant to provide not just knowledge and skills, but social understanding, the implementation of rules and standards of behaviour. Those who do not comply with the requirements of the school cause disruption to themselves and to others. We have seen that even the most 'hardened' of antisocial cases find certain aspects of school attractive, and appreciate at least some teachers and some lessons. There are all kinds of measures that schools could take that would prevent exclusions. These depend upon an understanding of the reasons for disaffection. The measures are both subtle and time-consuming but they are all dependent on psychological shifts in emphasis. The purpose of this book is to present the evidence and the implications rather than expand all the policy implications, which are many and profound. The primary task is to have insight into the reasons for these sudden outbursts of temper, against what are seen as petty rules or insistence of authority, or the deliberate provocation of others.

By the time disaffection with school reveals itself in truancy or exclusion, the mind-set of those involved is clearly drawn up. Schools are crucial in the development of their pupils but they are dealing with a whole range of children, many of whom bring their problems and their attitudes straight from home. The most powerful of possible interventions are the earliest ones. If parents are so crucial, especially in their relationships, why cannot anything be done to help them? There is plenty of blame. But all parents, not just the disadvantaged, deserve help, and there is no stigma in that. If the educational process as a whole were taken seriously much more could be done.

All the examples of early intervention programmes reveal the potential of success. Sometimes the evidence is inadvertent. Simple statistics demonstrate that with targeted support, effective intervention is possible and significantly reduces subsequent crime.[4] The widespread realization that the home makes a difference deserves both the explanation of why this should be so, as in this book, and some kind of policy initiative as a response.

All we need to do here is to point out the weight of evidence that suggests a change of focus, from the 'fight' against crime, to the prevention of criminality. It is possible to predict from an early age which children are likely to feel socially excluded and therefore fall into crime.[5] The whole process seems so self-perpetuating, from poverty, to failure, to truancy, to low pay, and back to failure, that it seems like a cycle, but it is one that can be broken. There are certain symbolic acts that draw attention to those who are likely to turn to crime. Bullying is an obvious one, those acts of wilful desperation that spring out of anger and alienation. But much earlier than that, the longitudinal Cambridge study of delinquent development drew attention to parenting styles.

Interventions can work. Parent training with pre-adolescents is effective in reducing disruptive behaviour.[6] As Sherman notes, 'programs intended to improve parents' child-rearing skills, children's academic skills, or children's mental health... have often resulted – almost coincidentally – in reduced crime'.[7] The phrase 'almost coincidentally' is telling. It is as if such evidence were not sought out, as if there were no deliberate attempt to help the disaffection because of the motive of crime prevention. Certain kinds of intervention work. Home visits which are linked to pre-school children, undertaken for educational reasons, rather than motivated by fear of child-abuse, make a difference.[8] Visits by clinical or education staff work much better than those by the police. Uniforms of any kind create an adverse reaction.[9] The more sympathetic and the less confrontational the approach, the more successful it is. This is true of whatever stage the intervention takes place.[10] Whilst 'restorative justice', the meeting of the criminal with the victim, does not at once seem to make a difference, the principles of understanding that can be invoked in the meeting of bullies and victims (insofar as they can be clearly distinguished) does.[11]

The changing of patterns of behaviour, as exemplified in incidents of bullying, is a subtle and complex matter. Too often the desire to take action swiftly and decisively – the crude hypothesis of the simplistic target – makes little difference.[12] The desire to find simple measures to change social behaviour is understandable, but unless it is based on a deeper concern with social attitudes, it comes to nothing.[13] And of course, the earlier the attempts are made to help, the better. One significant reason for this is that it is axiomatic that early intervention deals with attitudes, ideas and feelings, with the inner world of individuals, rather than their obvious manifestations in action. Too often control is associated with restraint, as if tying up a child in a garb designed to prevent movement, or 'pinning down', were itself an answer. It is an atavistic instinct to react only when there is clear threat and to react violently. The alternative is to make no assumptions of innocence, but to deal in understanding.

This understanding of the reasons for certain kinds of behaviour is driven not by sympathy for whatever action an individual takes. On the contrary. It is the result of the desire to see moral behaviour, to enhance kindness and support to other people. The real prevention of bullying is more than a simple matter of waiting for it to happen and then either 'dealing' with it or ignoring it. It is the result of a belief in the highest standards of behaviour and in the human capacity to understand what these are. The most emphatic need is the positive support for all, since all need it, rather than the 'fight' 'against' the bad.

The distinction, which must be reiterated, is between simple models of intervention and the more subtle concern with human development. This is as true of the experience of school, with psychological exclusion, as it is of criminality. All kinds of events, especially stressful ones, have an effect on school performance.[14] Many of these are either ignored or not even noticed. There are, for example, many children who are 'invisible' in school who are having all kinds of difficulties.[15] They are so quiet that there is a certain advantage in ignoring them as they cause few ostensible difficulties.[16] This is a symptom both of paying exclusive attention to difficulties, to methods of control and reaction, and to the lack of thought given to the inner purposes, moral and social, of school.

The shift of emphasis from reaction to an event to the anticipation of it is crucial. Instead of wasting resources in counteracting the preventable, it is far more sensible to intervene early and decisively. This is also a matter of practicality. It should not be supposed that a sympathetic understanding of the causes of exclusion is somehow 'soft'. It might lack that appeal of the Hollywood thriller, of the hero's ability to gun down the bad, but it is both pragmatic and cost effective. Many of the programmes to combat bad behaviour, within schools and outside, are not only expensive but have the opposite effect to that intended. The truant-catching industry, for example, contributes to the problems it purports to solve.[17] This is partly because of inter-agency rivalry, between schools, education welfare, social services, the police and juvenile courts. The invocation of the law against parents who are held responsible for their children's absence from school can cause permanent truancy.[18]

The general political truism, or motivation, is that general behaviour can be affected by legal will, that there are simple, if crude, measures that can be taken to change the way that people behave. Put like this, one might think this sounds absurd, but if the political actions are analysed, they are all those that combine a certain approach, or change of approach, with a lot of money. They are like a fascination with CCTV systems, hoping both to record crime and to warn individuals off it, without understanding how or why they work, let alone understanding why the person would want to take part in crime in the first place. Discipline in the school is necessary, but is it there to hold down the otherwise uncontainable anguish of the pupils, or as an initiation into individual and social responsibility?

With a singular irony, even that most instrumental and mechanistic of institutions, the Office for Standards in Education, in its discovery that children in care have low standards, concludes that it is not the people who are at fault but the system.[19] This is due to the lack of coordination between schools and social service departments, or between social workers, carers and teachers. The instinctive assumption might be that this is a structural matter, which reorganization can put right with a modicum of political will. But it is, in fact, an insight into the lack of attention paid to the individual realities of people's lives, of the need for far greater concern for the influences of the environment as a whole – the personal circumstances, the personal relationships and the personal responses. The irony is that if the system is 'rotten' and the individuals within it mean well, then it is the people to whom one should pay attention and support, and find the means of doing so.

This tension between 'structure and agency', the systems and the people in them, is actually a false one, in that the two are so closely interdependent they are almost the same thing, or in fact exactly the same thing. It is just that there are temptations to think that it is possible to change systems without having recourse to understand people, that targets or outcomes, easily and speedily measured, are all that count. There has always been a debate about the relationship between the autonomy of families and state intervention, as if the two were alien to each other.[20] What we are now questioning is whether the two are in fact separable. Certainly, the political assumption has been that to deal with one, all one can do is to deal with the other, that instruments are what guide people, as they guide laws. That is the assumption questioned by all the evidence of research. Social intervention is possible. It is inevitable. It is essential. But it involves the understanding of the individual, from the earliest years.

'Intervention' sounds like interference or like patronage. Perhaps there should be another term both for the anticipation of problems and for their inevitability. Those who have any wisdom at all are aware of the complexities, the difficulties of parenting, with the inadvertent as significant as the obvious.[21] The awareness of the importance of the early years is so ancient and so widespread that one wonders about the human capacity to ignore it.[22] Every study reveals not only the importance of the major factors of parenting, like time, attention and dialogue, but the possibilities of helping to develop the social skills of young children through support from other people.[23] Early home–school-based interventions make an essential difference.[24] The wonder is that these findings appear to be confined to one-off experiments, and are never acted upon as wholescale policy measures.

There is a consistency to the evidence that makes it compelling. We know the crucial influences and the points at which they make an impact. We are aware of all the temperamental factors that aid and abet the lack of consistent relationships with other people and with social systems. But this research is not about the general factors as much as about why they have the impact they do. We see that subtle effect of other people, and not just 'communities'. We reveal the types of interaction that are so important as well as the circumstances in which they take place.

This is all about people, in all their individuality. It is about their relationships, their reaction to others, their ways of dealing with circumstances. To say that people are the results of their cultural environment is a truism, as exhibited in the language they acquire, even if the proportion of 'nurture' as opposed to 'nature' is disputed. If the circumstances in which they are learning and to which they are responding are so important, they can be helped. To wait for signs of failure is too late. Relationships, like dialogue, can be learned. Conversation, the rational exchange of information, is an acquired skill. Intellectual dialogue is as much a right and a desire as food, warmth and affection.

The problem for the excluded is not just that they are deprived of emotional support. What makes them ill-equipped for the formal demands of school and sensible, ordered, social interaction is the clash between their experience of home and their experience of large groups. This reveals itself in three ways. The first is the difference in the uses of language, between language used for personal comment and transactions, and that used for definition and analysis. The dialogues of the home and school are often fundamentally different. The second clash is between the idea of the person as being an individual whose every act is motivated by feeling and desire, and the idea of the private person also fulfilling a role, with self-control, a sense of duty, and a disinterested concern for others. The third is between the idea of a micro-society being a number of individuals with their own personal agendas, sometimes clashing against each other, and the macro-society of people who are trying to develop a collective idea, a sense of common purpose.

All these matters can be, and need to be, dealt with sensitively and patiently. There is no good reason why this cannot be done. Throughout all the statements made by the witnesses and representatives there are signs of how they might have, or could have, responded. There are many clues about what kind of intervention could be effective:

- Parenting is an issue, as they struggle to deal with the same mistakes that were perpetuated on them.
- The sense of being listened to seriously, as an individual who is capable of self-awareness and thoughtfulness, is clearly a great relief. But it is also a sign of the possibilities that have only rarely been taken seriously.
- The purpose of school could clearly have been explained. Instead of the instrumental delivery of a curriculum with a series of given facts and teachers fearful for their accountability, there could be a greater sense of the exploration of what schools are for, far beyond the skills of employability.
- Those flash points that provide a final psychological break with the 'system' could be avoided.
- Parents could be far more sympathetically involved in the school, despite the time it takes. Early intervention is far less expensive than the later attempts to involve the whole paraphernalia of the judicial system.
- Bullying should be dealt with not as a phenomenon to be controlled but as something utterly abhorrent to the social system of the school.

There are many points that could be elaborated. But the purpose of the book is to reveal, to give the evidence. It is to enable reflection on what could be done, in a variety of circumstances, given the results. This book reiterates and reinforces what we know about the causes of exclusion. It also adds that most important of dimensions: *why* individuals become what they are. The underlying hope is that one day people will listen, both to the evidence, and to the needs of young people.

References

1. Sherman, L, Gottfredson, D, MacKenzie, D, Eck, J, Reuter, P and Burkway, S (1997) *Preventing Crime: What works, what doesn't, what's promising*, National Institute of Justice, Washington, DC

2. Home Office (1998) *Reducing Offending*, HMSO, London

3. Pease, K (1993) Individual and community influence on victimization and their implications for crime prevention, in *Integrating Individual and Ecological Aspects of Crime*, eds D Farrington, R Sampson and P Wikström, BRA Report

4. (1999) The Criminality of Former 'Excluded from School' Adolescents as Young Adults [16–23 yrs]: Cost and Practice Implications, *Journal of Adolescence*

5. Farrington, D and West, D (1990) *The Cambridge Study in Delinquent Development*, Springer-Verlag, London

6. Kazdin, A (1987) Treatment of anti-social behaviour in children: current status and future directions, *Psychological Bulletin*, No. 102, pp 187–203

Dumas, J (1989) Treating anti-social behaviour in children: child and family approaches, *Clinical Psychology Review*, 9, pp 197–212

7. See Sherman *et al*, op cit, p 2

8. Ibid

9. eg The Drug Abuse Resistance Education (DARE), a drugs awareness programme in the US, made no difference when carried out by the police.

10. Lowenstein, L (1995) Bullying: an intensive and multi-dimensional treatment approach in a therapeutic community, *Education Today*, 45 (1), pp 19–24

11. Duncan, A (1996) The shared concern method of resolving group bullying in schools, *Educational Psychology in Practice*, 12 (2), pp 94–98

12. Arora, C (1994) Is there any point in trying to reduce bullying in secondary schools? *Educational Psychology in Practice*, 10 (3), pp 155–62

13. Smith, P and Sharp, S (eds) (1994) *The Problem of School Bullying: Insights and Perspectives*, Routledge, London

14. du Bois, Reymond, M and Oechsle, M (eds) (1990) *Neue Ingend Biographie? Zum Strukturwandel des Jugenphase*, Leske & Budrich, Opladen

15. Pye, J (1989) *Invisible Children: who are the real losers at school?*, Oxford University Press, Oxford

16. Collins, J (1996) *The Quiet Child*, Cassell, London

17. Carless, P, Gleeson, D and Wardhaugh, J (1992) *Truancy: The Politics of Compulsory Schooling*, Open University Press, Buckingham

18. Blyth, E and Milner, J (1999) *A Good Enough Parent: The guide to bringing up your child*, Thames and Hudson, London

19. Ofsted (1995) *The Education of Children who are looked after by Local Authorities*, HMSO, London

20. Foucault, J (1979) *Discipline and Punish: Birth of the Prison*, Allen and Unwin, London

21. Blyth, E and McIner, J (1999) *Improving School Attendance*, Routledge, London

22. As exemplified by the series of Royal (and other) Commissions.

23. Walker, D, Greenwood, B and Carta, J (1994) Prediction of school outcomes based on early language production and socioeconomic factors, *Child Development*, 65 (2), pp 606–21

24. Hart, B and Risley, T (1992) American parenting of language-learning children: persisting difficulties in family–child interactions observed in natural home environments, *Developmental Psychology*, 28, pp 1096–105

INDEX

Visit Kogan Page on-line

Comprehensive information on
Kogan Page titles

Features include

- complete catalogue listings,
  including book reviews and
  descriptions

- on-line discounts on a variety
  of titles

- special monthly promotions

- information and discounts on
  NEW titles and BESTSELLING titles

- a secure shopping basket facility
  for on-line ordering

- infoZones, with links and
  information on specific areas of
  interest

PLUS everything you need to know
about KOGAN PAGE

http://www.kogan-page.co.uk